CORNELL STUDIES IN CLASSICAL PHILOLOGY

EDITED BY

JAMES HUTTON * G. M. KIRKWOOD
GORDON M. MESSING * PIERO PUCCI

VOLUME XXXVII

Early Greek Monody

The History of a Poetic Type

by G. M. KIRKWOOD

The Attalids of Pergamon

by Esther V. Hansen

Sophrosyne

by Helen North

St. Jerome as a Satirist

by David S. Wiesen

OTHER WORKS BY G. M. KIRKWOOD

A Study of Sophoclean Drama
A Short Guide to Classical Mythology

EARLY GREEK MONODY

The History of a Poetic Type

G. M. KIRKWOOD

CORNELL UNIVERSITY PRESS
ITHACA AND LONDON

This book has been published with the aid of a grant from
The Hull Memorial Publication Fund of Cornell University.

First published 1974 by Cornell University Press.
Published in the United Kingdom by Cornell University Press Ltd.,
2-4 Brook Street, London W1Y 1AA.

International Standard Book Number 0-8014-0795-8
Library of Congress Catalog Card Number 73-8411

Composed in Belgium by the Saint-Catherine Press, Ltd.
Printed in the United States of America.

To the memory of my mother

Preface

The monodists, with Archilochus as their precursor or initiating genius, provide in themselves a reasonably clear and complete picture of a type of poetry, from its beginnings to the point at which it is transformed into and replaced by other kinds of poetry. The purpose of this book is to present an account of monodic poetry and its stages of development.

I have approached the undertaking primarily in two ways. It seemed to me advisable to provide whatever introductory information and interpretative aid may be necessary for those who wish to read the extant fragments, even though much of this guidance is available elsewhere. To this end I give a conservative, moderately restored text, following standard modern editions, for all major fragments, and a translation, my own, intended to provide a key and an illustration for the Greek text. Verse form is often used, to indicate the exact order and divisions of the Greek poems. Had it been realistic to depend entirely on the reader's command of the original I should have preferred to do so, but while most of those who use this book will have some knowledge of Greek, few are likely to have a close knowledge of the lyric poets and their dialects, and without such knowledge many of these fragmentary texts are difficult. The footnotes provide a rather full commentary on the philological problems, with discussions of textual and interpretative proposals of editors and critics. I have deliberately relegated most of such discussion to the notes.

The reader who wants only the restored texts and a consideration of them need not be constantly led into philological and bibliographical detours.

My second method of procedure is to emphasize the various stages of formal development of monody. This is not an easy task. The fact that the texts are fragmentary creates severe enough problems, but at least as great difficulty in the study of the poems is due to our having no earlier poetry of a comparable type against which to measure the poets' development of styles and forms, their borrowings and imitations, their assertions of independence, their reinterpretations of traditional themes. It is hard to imagine a study of Horace's lyric poetry without some attention to his Greek predecessors, or of *Paradise Lost* or the *Divine Comedy* without the *Aeneid*. There is no such guide and authority for the early Greek lyric poets, and their poetry is therefore isolated and distant. We cannot be sure that we really understand their approach, the degree of self-consciousness or detachment they may have from their themes, what sense of separation they feel from the *persona* which they assume when they write in the first person, as they nearly always do. The lyric poets are as pristine as Homer, and unlike Homer they are slight and fragmentary.

As a result of this twofold bar to understanding, early lyric poetry has usually been approached more as a source of historical information and of evidence of developing concepts and outlooks than as poetry that achieves intrinsic life and meaning through the form it takes and the organization and emphasis of its material. In the past few years criticism of some intrinsic poetic values in early Greek lyric has appeared, in a number of essays concerned with imagery. But while Pindar's poetry lends itself very well to such study, monodic poetry, with the partial exception of Sappho's and Anacreon's, does not, because it is relatively direct and often depends less on metaphor than on descriptions of the poet's circumstances and on the ornamental epithets that are an inheritance from epic. Moreover, since the remaining poetry is very fragmentary and the dialect and culture remote and unfamilar, analysis of the meanings implicit in a poet's choice of images is limited; the emotional and psychological context can often only be guessed at very imperfectly. Therefore the analysis of imagery is undertaken here only tentatively and with restraint.

Two procedures have been followed more—perhaps too—confidently. I have emphasized the Homeric heritage, especially in the chapter on Archilochus. I have tried not to exaggerate the affiliations, but a basic thesis of that chapter is that Archilochus is, uniquely, the pivot in the change from Homeric tradition to lyric style and outlook, and even, to some degree, lyric form. It is this belief that justifies a substantial chapter, in a book on lyric poetry, devoted to Archilochus, who is not formally a lyric poet.

Secondly, I have said as much as seems allowable about the structure of monodic lyric, especially in the chapters on Sappho and Anacreon. In what remains of these two poets the evidence of the papyrus discoveries of the past seventy-five years provides enough indications of formal organization to permit a discussion of what kinds of poetry—not just what outlooks or what subjects—are typical of the work of these two poets. Because I think that such observations are possible and can add something to our understanding of the poetry, I have gone with some thoroughness into such questions as whether we have the whole of a given poem, and what portion of a poem a fragment represents.

The material of this study is inevitably scattered, involving as it does a number of poets whose remaining fragments raise diverse questions of text, interpretation, meter, and so on. Consequently my debts to modern criticism of the material are likewise scattered, as well as voluminous. Specific debts are acknowledged in the notes. It would not be possible for me to acknowledge all the more general assistance I have had, both from written works and personal discussion. There are, however, editions and books of criticism of the poetry that I have relied on constantly for enlightenment and authority. For the Lesbian poets I have followed the text of *Poetarum Lesbiorum Fragmenta*, edited by Edgar Lobel and Denys Page, and have depended constantly on the learning and exegetical skill of Denys Page in his *Sappho and Alcaeus*; my disagreements with this book in questions of interpretation have not hidden from me, and should not hide from the reader, my dependence on it. I did not have Eva-Maria Voigt's magnificent text edition of Sappho and Alcaeus until my work was finished, and I have consequently referred to it in my notes less often than its intrinsic merits would justify; it will be of enormous value, as a text and as a reference source, for future studies of these poets. Max Treu's compact and judiciously annotated texts of Alcaeus, Archilochus, and Sappho have been very useful. For Archilochus I have regularly consulted also the Budé edition by Lasserre and Bonnard, though I have normally followed the text of the third edition of Diehl's *Anthologia Lyrica Graeca*. For Anacreon and the minor poets I have generally followed Page's *Poetae Melici Graeci*, but I have found Bruno Gentili's *Anacreon* also very valuable. Of books of interpretation, among those that have been most helpful for me are, in addition to Page's *Sappho and Alcaeus*, the relevant chapters of Bowra's *Greek Lyric Poetry* (second edition, 1961) and of Hermann Fränkel's *Dichtung und Philosophie des Frühen Griechentums*, B. A. van Groningen's *La Composition Littéraire Archaïque Grecque*, the opening chapters of Bruno Snell's *The Discovery of the Mind*, and Max Treu's *Von Homer zur Lyrik*. In bibliographical matters I am much indebted to Douglas Gerber both for his published work and private communications.

My work on Greek lyric poetry generally, including the material of this book, was assisted, during two sabbatic leaves granted by Cornell University, by the additional freedom from teaching responsibilities provided by fellowship grants. In 1956–57 I held a John Simon Guggenheim Memorial Fellowship and in 1962–63 a fellowship of the American Council of Learned Societies. My indebtedness to both awarding bodies is gratefully acknowledged. I wish to thank the Hull Memorial Publication Fund Committee for its generosity in providing a grant to aid the publication of this book. To my fellow editors of *Cornell Studies in Classical Philology*, to the anonymous reader for Cornell University Press, and to the editorial staff of the Press, in particular to David Rollow, I am much indebted for expert and sympathetic criticism. Three personal debts deserve special acknowledgment. James Hutton, Patricia Kirkwood, and Edward Spofford have each given the entire book a most thorough and valuable reading. Their careful and sensitive criticisms, both stylistic and substantive, have corrected, enlightened, and enlarged many aspects of my understanding of the poets.

G. M. K.

Ithaca, New York

Contents

Abbreviations

Note: Ancient authors and works are usually abbreviated in accordance with the practice of Liddell-Scott-Jones, *A Greek-English Lexicon;* see pp. xvi-xlvi of that work.

AFC: Anales de Filologia Clasica

AJA: American Journal of Archaeology

AJP: American Journal of Philology

ALG: See Diehl.

A & R: Atene e Roma

Barner, *Neuere Alkaios-Papyri:* Wilfried Barner, *Neuere Alkaios-Papyri aus Oxyrhynchos.* Spudasmata, Bd. 14. Hildesheim 1967.

BCH: Bulletin de Correspondance Hellénique

Bergk, *PLG* (or *PLG*⁴): *Poetae Lyrici Graeci,* edited by Theodor Bergk. 4th ed., Leipzig 1878–82. Unless another edition is specified, the fourth is cited.

Bowra, *GLP* (or *GLP*²): C. M. Bowra, *Greek Lyric Poetry from Alcman to Simonides.* 2d ed., Oxford 1961.

Campbell, *GLPS: Greek Lyric Poetry, a Selection,* edited by David A. Campbell. London and New York 1967.

CJ: Classical Journal

C & M: Classica et Mediaevalia

CP: Classical Philology

CQ: Classical Quarterly

CW: Classical World

Diehl (or D), *ALG: Anthologia Lyrica Graeca,* edited by Ernst Diehl. Leipzig 1924–52. Fascicles 1, *Poetae Elegiaci* (1949), 2, *Theognis et al.* (1950), and 3, *Iamborum Scriptores* (1952), are cited in the 3d edition, completed after Diehl's death by Rudolf Beutler.

Fascicle 4, *Poetae Melici: Monodi* (1935), is cited in the second edition, fascicle 5, *Poetae Melici: Chori* (1924), in the first.

Edmonds, *Elegy and Iambus: Elegy and Iambus, Greek Elegiac and Iambic Poets*, edited and translated by J. M. Edmonds. 2 vols. Loeb Classical Library. London and New York 1931.

Edmonds, *Lyra Graeca: Lyra Graeca, Greek Lyric Poets from Eumelus to Timotheus excepting Pindar*, edited and translated by J. M. Edmonds. 3 vols. Loeb Classical Library. London and New York 1922-27.

Färber: Hans Färber, *Die Lyrik in der Kunsttheorie der Antike*. Munich 1936.

Fränkel, *DuP:* Hermann Fränkel, *Dichtung und Philosophie des frühen Griechentums*. Philological Monographs, published by the American Philological Association, Vol. 13. New York 1951. 2d ed. revised, Munich 1962.

Fränkel, "Eine Stileigenheit": Hermann Fränkel, "Eine Stileigenheit der frühgriechischen Literatur," *Wege und Formen frühgriechischen Denkens* (2d ed., Munich 1960) 40-96.

Friedländer-Hoffleit: Paul Friedländer and Herbert B. Hoffleit, *Epigrammata*. Berkeley and Los Angeles 1948.

Gentili, *Anacreon: Anacreon*, edited by Bruno Gentili. Rome 1958.

Gerber, *Euterpe:* Douglas E. Gerber, *Euterpe: An Anthology of Early Greek Lyric, Elegiac, and Iambic Poetry*. Amsterdam 1970.

GRBS: Greek, Roman and Byzantine Studies

Hamm: Eva Maria Hamm, *Grammatik zu Sappho und Alkaios*. Berlin 1957.

HTR: Harvard Theological Review

IG: Inscriptiones Graecae. Berlin 1873-1939. Editio minor 1913-40.

Jaeger, *Paideia:* Werner Jaeger, *Paideia: The Ideals of Greek Culture*, translated by Gilbert Highet. 2d ed., New York 1945.

JHS: Journal of Hellenic Studies

Lasserre, *Les Épodes:* François Lasserre, *Les Épodes d'Archiloque*. Paris 1950.

Lasserre-Bonnard: *Archiloque, Fragments*, edited by François Lasserre, translated by André Bonnard. Collection Budé. Paris 1958.

Lobel, *Alkaiou Melê: Alkaiou Melê, the Fragments of the Lyrical Poems of Alcaeus*, edited by Edgar Lobel. Oxford 1927.

Lobel, *Sapphous Melê: Sapphous Melê, the Fragments of the Lyrical Poems of Sappho*, edited by Edgar Lobel. Oxford 1925.

LP or Lobel-Page: *Poetarum Lesbiorum Fragmenta*, edited by Edgar Lobel and Denys Page. Oxford 1955.

MH: Museum Helveticum

OCD: The Oxford Classical Dictionary. 2d ed., Oxford 1970.

Ox. Pap.: The Oxyrhynchus Papyri, edited by Bernard P. Grenfell and others. London 1898–1971.

Page, *LGS: Lyrica Graeca Selecta*, edited by D. L. Page. Oxford 1968.

Page, *PMG: Poetae Melici Graeci*, edited by D. L. Page. Oxford 1962.

Page, *SA:* Denys Page, *Sappho and Alcaeus.* Oxford 1955.

PCPS: Proceedings of the Cambridge Philological Society

Powell, *Collectanea Alexandrina: Collectanea Alexandrina, Reliquiae minores Poetarum Graecorum Aetatis Ptolemaicae*, edited by J. U. Powell. Oxford 1925.

POxy: Individual papyri in the volumes of *Ox. Pap.*, q.v.

PP: La Parola del Passato

PQ: Philological Quarterly

RA: Revue Archéologique

RBPH: Revue Belge de Philologie et d'Histoire

RE: Realencyclopädie der Classischen Altertumswissenschaft, edited by A. Pauly, G. Wissowa, W. Kroll, and Karl Mittelhaus. Stuttgart 1894–1968.

REA: Revue des Études Anciennes

REG: Revue des Études Grecques

RFIC: Rivista di Filologia e di Istruzione Classica

RhM: Rheinisches Museum

SCO: Studi Classici e Orientali

SIFC: Studi Italiana di Filologia Classica

SO: Symbolae Osloenses

TAPA: Transactions of the American Philological Association

Treu, *Alkaios: Alkaios, Griechisch und Deutsch*, edited and translated by Max Treu. Munich 1952.

Treu, *Archilochos: Archilochos, Griechisch und Deutsch*, edited and translated by Max Treu. Munich 1959.

Treu, *Sappho: Sappho, Griechisch und Deutsch*, edited and translated by Max Treu. 2d ed., Munich 1958.

Treu, *Von Homer zur Lyrik:* Max Treu, *Von Homer zur Lyrik. Zetemata,* Heft 12. Munich 1955.

Voigt, *SetA: Sappho et Alcaeus,* edited by Eva-Maria Voigt. Amsterdam 1971.

Wilamowitz, *SuS:* Ulrich von Wilamowitz-Moellendorff, *Sappho und Simonides.* Berlin 1913.

Wilamowitz, *Textgeschichte:* Ulrich von Wilamowitz-Moellendorff, *Die Textgeschichte der Griechischen Lyriker.* Berlin 1900.

WS: Wiener Studien

EARLY GREEK MONODY
The History of a Poetic Type

CHAPTER ONE

Introduction

What Is Greek Lyric Poetry?

Apart from such special types of composition as plays in verse and long narrative poems not much thought is usually given to the category of a modern poem. "Lyric" is used interchangeably with "poem" and "verse," and generally any relatively short poem expressing personal views and emotions can be called lyric, even if in fact it is a sonnet or a pastoral or is in ballad form. One poem may be more lyric, by which is usually meant more like a song, than another, but it is not a matter of exclusive or formal definition.[1] In the criticism of ancient Greek poetry, definition is more natural, because formal criteria, especially meters, are more frequently exact; elegiac couplet and iambic trimeter are precise and regular patterns, and by tradition they are not lyric patterns. As a consequence, different types and treatments of material tend to become associated with different metrical forms. Yet clear boundaries are hard to maintain, and any definition of ancient Greek lyric poetry runs the risk of being too inclusive to be very useful, or else too narrow.

If lyric is taken in its literal sense and lyric poetry is restricted to songs accompanied by the lyre, the definition leaves out the choruses of Greek tragedy and even some of Pindar's odes, which had a woodwind accompaniment instead of the lyre. If we say that lyric poetry is "sung poetry" or "poetry accompanied by music," we have to admit at least some elegy, perhaps some iambic poetry, possibly even epic recitations in

the earliest period, and hence "lyric poetry" would be little
different from "poetry." Traditionally, there are two conventional uses of the term, and one general understanding of
it that is identical with neither convention and cuts across
both. One tradition, which is exemplified by Bergk's *Poetae
Lyrici Graeci* and the *Anthologia Lyrica Graeca* that has sprung
from it, includes everything that is not epic (or formally in the
epic tradition, such as the Hesiodic poetry and the *Homeric
Hymns*) or dramatic.[2] A narrower use of the term describes
what was in Greek of the classical period called *melos*, "melic"
poetry.[3] The range of its meaning is approximately equivalent
to "song." It includes poetry *sung* to a musical accompaniment,
whether of strings or wind instruments; it is restricted to poetry
in which the element of music is of substantial importance; in
effect, it refers to Greek poetry until about 440 B.C., exclusive
of that written in dactylic hexameter, elegiac couplets, iambic
trimeter, and trochaic tetrameter. While this quasi-exact and
more or less exclusive definition is useful in outlining general
limits, it is not always adequate. There can be iambic or
hexameter or elegiac poems that are "melic" in tone and in
subject matter, and little is gained by disqualifying such poetry
from the designation lyric. Consequently it is practical, in discussing Greek lyric poetry, to take as its core the body of
poetry called melic but, while stopping far short of the inclusiveness of Bergk's collection, to recognize that lyric is to
some degree a matter of spirit and effect rather than purely of
form. Formal lines are useful but must sometimes be crossed.
Archilochus, who by formal classification is not a melic but an
iambic poet, is by virtue of some of his work the first Greek
lyric poet.

   If the formal limits of Greek lyric have been indefinite and
varied, the temporal limits that have been customarily observed
are surprisingly sharp. There was an Alexandrian canon of the
Nine Lyric Poets, as of the Ten Orators, the Seven Tragic
Poets of the Pleiades, and so forth.[4] The lyric nine were

Alcman, Stesichorus, Alcaeus, Sappho, Ibycus, Anacreon, Simonides, Pindar, and Bacchylides, all of them writers of melic poetry; other kinds of poetry such as elegy and iambic had their own canons. Some lists add Corinna as a tenth. The striking thing about the list is that all—with the possible exception of Corinna, a doubtful member—are from a relatively early period of Greek literature, roughly 650–450 B.C.[5] In general, the Alexandrian lists were selections, consisting of the writers of highest distinction in their fields, who were to be taken as standards of excellence and as authorities for matters of style and linguistic purity. It is not known whether the Nine Lyric Poets were such a selection or were, as Wilamowitz persuasively argued,[6] the only melic poets down to a certain point in time whose works were extant in sufficient quantity to justify an edition when the Alexandrian scholars began to edit the earlier literature. In any case, they came to be recognized as *the* lyric poets, and later poetry that formally has a claim to being regarded as melic was refused entry into the class.

The grounds for this exclusion are unknown. One point about the development of lyric poetry in the latter part of the fifth century, however, is both clear and relevant to the question: two kinds of lyric poetry, the nome and the dithyramb, began to dominate nondramatic poetic composition. Both were different from all the earlier melic types, including the earlier nome and dithyramb, in significant respects: they were nonstanzaic, the relative importance of music to words suddenly and greatly increased, and their affinity to drama was recognized; Aristotle groups them with tragedy and comedy in his classification of the mimetic arts at the beginning of the *Poetics*. It may be that the Alexandrian critics did not consider this new poetry, which continued dominant in the fourth century, to be of the same genre as melic poetry (nearly all of which was stanzaic), and for this reason excluded Timotheus, Philoxenus of Cythera, Cinesias, and the other writers of dithyrambs and nomes. But it is just as probable that reverence for the older poetry engendered hostility and contempt for these innovators, and that at least in this sense the canon of nine was a selection.[7] Of the contemporary hostility of critics to the poetry of the nomists and dithyrambists we have abundant evidence from Aristophanes, and this attitude may well have been taken up by the Alexandrian critics.[8]

Whatever we may think of the judgment of the Alexandrian critics and its effect on the criticism and preservation of lyric poetry, it is evident that the middle of the fifth century brought the beginning of profound changes in Greek poetry and in its relationship to the community. A decline in the prestige of some traditional public, religious, ceremonial occasions, such as the games, and a rise in that of other celebrations and hence of the art forms associated with them—such as the Dionysiac festivals of Athens and the dramatic poetry of those occasions —are the symptoms though not necessarily the causes of these changes, above all of the decline of personal poetry. Tragedy is of course much more impersonal than the solo and choral lyric poetry that was composed in the preceding two centuries; but merely to compare Bacchylides' dithyrambs with his epinicians is to see that the dithyramb too is moving in the same direction, away from the participation of the poet as a *persona* within his poems toward a narrative form that gains richness from the dramatic presentation of the narrative rather than from the traditional overt internal interaction of the poet and the events and persons that are the material of the poem. Probably the new and flourishing art form of drama hastened the process. The change was profound and lasting; never again, unless our evidence is strangely misleading, did personal lyric poetry regain a central place in ancient Greek literature. If Bacchylides' poetry exemplifies the transition, Timotheus's *Persians* shows its outcome. Even though there are personal statements by the poet about himself, they are not integral to the rest of the poem, which is essentially dramatic and largely in dialogue form; the poet's presence is appended as a highly formalized seal, and the morality or idea of the poem is no longer expressed, as in the Pindaric style, by direct observations of the poet's, but, as in drama, through the characterization of the participants in the story.

Later Greek poetry, after tragedy had worked its enormous changes in the form and spirit of all poetic expression, showed no tendency to return to a dominance by the old lyric forms and relationships. Personal poetry in the Hellenistic period and afterward largely takes the form of epigram, elegy, and idyll, and in Chapter Five attention will be drawn to signs of a trend toward epigram from formal lyric as early as the late sixth century. Formal Hellenistic lyric poetry is scanty in amount and generally sterile in content. Most of it consists either of, at best, mediocre poetry that uses the old forms for ritual occasions, or of minor and perhaps experimental or artificial pieces by major poets whose real interests lay elsewhere. The three poems of Theocritus in lyric meters (28, 29, and 30) are not among his best. The impression of intense personal participation made by the small remnant of the poetry of Erinna testifies that she was worthy of the older lyric tradition; but she is perhaps unique—we do not know Corinna's date—and the fact that what remains of her poetry is in hexameters and elegiacs is in keeping with the prevalent alienation from the old forms. Such attractive lyrics as the Grenfell papyrus, consisting of an anonymous love poem sung by a jilted girl, a very late poem (perhaps second century A.D.) on contentment with simplicity in life, in which each stanza begins with a successive letter of the alphabet, and the best of the *Anacreontics* are isolated remnants of what can never have been a broad tradition of late poetry more or less in the form and style of the old personal lyric.[9]

In such Hellenistic poetry as the idylls of Theocritus and the hymns of Callimachus there are important connections with the older tradition of lyric, and the degree and manner of this later continuation of the tradition are topics of moment for the general picture of ancient Greek lyric poetry. But the connections are indirect. The intervention of drama and of a succession of historical changes, from the assertion of individual personality in the archaic age to the public orientation of the classical period, and then to the universality, sophistication, and learning of the Hellenistic world—these were pervasive forces, creating a wide gap between the old and the new.

The transitions are not neatly marked off, and the line between archaic and classical must be drawn at a different point of time for each of the arts. In literature the overlap between melic and dramatic ascendancy is prolonged. Aeschylus's *Oresteia*, with its unrivalled combination of lyric and dramatic power, was produced just four years after one of the most celebrated of all specimens of choral lyric, Pindar's Fourth *Pythian*, and both Pindar and Bacchylides were still writing poetry, including some of their best poems (Pindar's Eighth *Pythian*, for example), when Sophocles was already in his maturity. The epinician odes of these two poets are no mere vestige of an essentially vanished period. The roots of the epinician ode are in the sixth century, the great period of the Greek games, but so far as our knowledge of Greek poetry goes, it is the fifth century which produced the best of this type of poetry, and we can hardly maintain that by midcentury the games had lost much of their hold on the minds of the Greeks, when Thucydides (6. 16. 2) can represent Alcibiades as boasting, in 415 B.C., that the unparalleled opulence he had displayed by entering seven chariots in the racing at Olympia was a benefit to Athens because of the impression of power it made on the Greeks. No more easily can we divide the Athenian period from the Hellenistic. Abstruseness, learnedness, and a search for novelty and for realism, features associated with Hellenistic literature, are already present in the lyrics of Timotheus, Philoxenus, and Philodamus of Scarpheia in the fifth and fourth centuries.

Types of Melic Poetry

Our concern is with all monody that is lyrical in the general sense of the word, not only with what can be formally designated as melic. But since it is convenient to regard the monodic melic forms as the central and normative material of our study, it is appropriate to glance briefly at some types of melic poetry and their history and to see, where we can, what relationships there are between the beginnings of these types and the extant monodic poems.[10]

The elaborate classification in the *Grammatical Chrestomathy* of Proclus, a work probably of the second century after Christ, need not detain us.[11] Its list of twenty-eight types in four categories applies mostly to choral poetry, and in any case its laborious dissections and tidy artificiality are much closer to library classification than to a description of poetry. It is not easy to recover from this evidence what conventions the poets actually recognized, but the names provided by Proclus and sometimes his descriptions help. Concerning the hymn, for example, though in Proclus's list it is just one of the forms of melic addressed to the gods, in an appended commentary he distinguishes two different uses of the term. In addition to the specific one implied by its place in the list it is used also, he tells us, for "all poems written for those achieving superiority."[12] Then he adds that "therefore the prosodion and the other types mentioned above appear to be in contrast to the hymn as species to genus. And in fact one hears in use the terms 'prosodiac hymn,' 'hymn of encomium,' 'hymn of paean' and the like." A hymn, then, can be either one type of lyric poem addressed to the gods, or it can indicate just about any kind of lyric poem, and the word requires the addition of a more exact

designation. It is clear, then, that hymn is not a neatly restricted technical term, even in Alexandrian scholarship.
Moreover, this informality accords with what can be determined about the way poets used the word. Pindar and
Bacchylides do not hesitate to call their epinicians hymns,
and Demodocus's song of the Wooden Horse, in *Odyssey* 8, is
(line 429) called a hymn. Even so specific a form as Aristonous's
paean to Apollo is called a hymn in the inscription in which
it is preserved.[13]

   In a passage in the *Laws* (700a-b), Plato insists that in
former times (the context shows that he means roughly until
the Persian wars) there were specific εἴδη καὶ σχήματα ("types
and forms") of poetry which it was not permissible to mix.
One kind of song consisted of prayers to the gods, and these
were called hymns. In contrast to this type was one called
dirge, and there were also paeans, dithyrambs (associated with
Dionysus), and nomes, further specified as citharoedic nomes
(nomes sung to lyre accompaniment). It is unlikely that Plato
meant to give a complete list, for the context is quite informal.
What is significant in the passage is that as early as Plato, and
if Plato is accurate, even a century earlier—certainly long
before the work of the Hellenistic scholars—there were recognized distinctions among poems that are similar in form,
substance, and apparent function. Plato's point in mentioning
them is to inveigh against the undisciplined way in which
later poets had combined and distorted the traditional forms.

   The passage gives us little specific knowledge about these
traditional forms. We do not need to be told that the dithyramb
is associated with Dionysus; there is no significance in the
omission of Apollo's name in connection with the paean, since
so little is said about any of the types. The one descriptive
phrase of some value is that hymns are "*prayers* to gods"; this
description suggests the traditional "cletic" hymn, invoking or
calling upon deity, songs such as Sappho's poems addressed to
Aphrodite (LP 1, 2) and Alcaeus's to the Dioscuri (LP 34a).

Whether this description really conforms with the most specific of Proclus's uses of the term hymn is open to doubt. Proclus contrasts "hymn proper" with the processional song, and says that it was sung by those *standing* (presumably at the altar of the god or gods concerned). This may mean a monostrophic form, since the more elaborate strophic divisions seem to correspond to dance movements, and presumably a song sung while standing had no dance movement.[14] Extant examples of cletic hymns do not conflict with this supposition.

Specific references to types in the poets themselves do not add much. A few names are to be found even in the *Iliad* and the *Odyssey*. In addition to the hymn, which we have noticed (p. 8), there is mention of the paean (*Iliad* 1. 472–74), marriage song (*Iliad* 18. 490), threnos (*Iliad* 24. 720–21), and the Linus song (*Iliad* 18. 570). There are also references to choral performances that may suggest such other lyric types as the hyporcheme (*Odyssey* 8. 256–65). The Linus song is clearly a harvest song, apparently one of a number of traditional song-types that did not achieve the dignity of frequent refinement at the hands of great poets and hence were not worthy of Alexandrian classification. The term dithyramb is used by Archilochus and Pindar; nome occurs in a fragment of Alcman and in two passages in Pindar. But none of these uses of terms or descriptions of songs tells much about the song-types to which they may refer.[15] What seems likely is that most of the identifiably precise terms, such as epinician, epithalamian, partheneion, specify the occasion or function rather than the form of the song, and though a traditional occasion is likely to engender some traditional features of form, there need not be, and indeed there is not, any great difference in form between a partheneion by Alcman, an epinician by Pindar, and a dithyramb by Bacchylides. There is more difference between a Pindaric and an Alcaic hymn than between a Pindaric hymn and a Pindaric epinician. That is, the difference is greater between choral and monodic poetry, whatever the particular occasion, than between types of choral or of monodic poetry. Yet nowhere in the ancient classifications is the distinction made between choral and monodic.[16]

The importance of this distinction has been variously evaluated by modern critics. To Bowra,[17] "The distinction between choral lyric and monody is fundamental." To Harvey, on the other hand, the division seems to be "of no particular value."[18] Bowra seems to me to be closer to the truth, though the poets are not completely divisible into those who wrote choral and those who wrote monodic poetry. Sappho wrote both, and there does not seem always to have been a substantial difference between her monodic and her choral poems; nobody really knows whether Corinna's poems are choral or monodic, and the two best fragments of Ibycus raise the same question.[19] On the other hand, the public nature of such poems as the epinicians and paeans written by Pindar, Bacchylides, and Simonides is conspicuous, and the whole tone of most such compositions is quite different from the personalness and intimacy of Sappho's hymns and songs of reminiscence and emotion and Alcaeus's songs of political hatred and comradeship.

While there are some ambiguities, and the distinction between solo and choral poetry can be purely functional—essentially the same kind of song may be sung by one person or by a group—there are significant general distinctions. The highest development of the two forms came in different areas of Greece, and, for the most part, at different periods, and they used different kinds of poetic language. Monody achieved its best form in the Aeolic and Ionian society of the eastern Aegean, in the period 650–500; choral poetry was especially associated with Dorian society, with its first beginnings in Sparta and its flowering in the epinicians of the later sixth and the fifth century, under the patronage, above all, of the Dorian princes of Sicily. In language monody was always close to the language of everyday life, strongly influenced by the poet's regional dialect; the choral poets, even though many of them were not Dorians nor residents of Dorian regions, used a highly artificial diction strongly influenced by the Dorian dialect.

The relationship between the nominal type of a poem and its content is, we have said, often hard to define. Monody especially eludes the standard types. Sappho's poems addressed to Aphrodite are, in form, hymns, but what category holds *Phaenetai moi* (LP 31), or the long fragment of a poem written in exile and about exile by Alcaeus (LP 130)? Furthermore, though the poems of Sappho that stand first and second in LP are both hymns, the second is more hymnal than the first. We shall consider these and similar problems in the examination of specific poems. Concerning lyric categories in general we may summarize as follows: traditional forms existed in both choral and solo poetry, but the poets were not much bound by formal tradition or religious restriction or requirement; we can be confident that the poets did not generally follow esoteric and precise patterns, lacking knowledge of which we cannot understand the structure and meaning of their poems.

Lyric Meters

In monody, category is less important than metrical form; Archilochus was more noted in antiquity as the inventor of various meters than as an early practitioner of the dithyramb, though he was this too, as we know from Fr. 77. Whereas the poetry of Pindar and Bacchylides was divided up by lyric categories in the Alexandrian editions, that of Sappho and Alcaeus was not. The edition of Sappho was based on metrical forms; the most conspicuous formal characteristic of Alcaeus's poetry is his use of the Alcaic stanza; of Pindar's it is the fact that he wrote epinician odes.[20]

Greek poetry is divided metrically into two main types, stichic poetry and poetry that consists of rhythmic parts called

periods. Stichic poetry is "line" poetry, poetry that consists of
a series of metrically identical verses, such as the dactylic
hexameter of epic and the iambic trimeter of drama; closely
related are the meters of elegy, consisting of series of couplets
in which the first line is a dactylic hexameter, the second an
elegiac pentameter. Most other Greek meters are divisible into
cola.[21] A colon is a series of short metrical units, such as
trochees and dactyls, in various combinations, forming something like a compound metrical foot or a line. But the colon is
unlike a line in that successive cola are often not identical or
closely similar units. While the cola of a series are metrically
related and compatible, they are combined, not just in pairs,
like elegiac couplets, but so that a larger metrical unit may be
composed of five or ten cola no two of which are identical.
Archilochus composed mostly in stichic verses (iambic or
trochaic) or in elegiac couplets; he uses also a rudimentary
stanza form, the epode, that lies between elegiac couplet and
the colonic structure of later lyric forms. Sappho, Alcaeus, and
Anacreon all use lyric cola, usually, if not always (the papyri
leave the matter in doubt), organized in stanza form.

While the metrical units and combinations of choral poetry
can be extremely complex, the monodic poems mostly consist
of short and simple stanzas, and the cola within the stanzas
tend to repeat. Each Sapphic stanza consists of a thrice-
repeated colon: $-\cup-\times-\cup\cup-\cup--$ followed by a different but
related colon, the adonic, as *clausula:* $-\cup\cup--$. Alcaeus frequently uses a four-line stanza, the Alcaic, consisting of two
identical lines, $\times-\cup-\times-\cup\cup-\cup-$, a third closely related,
$\times-\cup-\times-\cup--$, and a fourth with a changed rhythm,
$-\cup\cup-\cup\cup-\cup--$. Throughout this study standard metrical
terminology is used. The terms are succinct and therefore
useful; they are explained and illustrated in the Metrical
Appendix.

Music

Understanding of the rhythms of ancient Greek poetry is limited by our ignorance about the related components of music and choreography, although the latter is of no great consequence for monody, which, except for the nome, was not danced.[22] Various musical inventions are attached to various early names, but we are poorly informed as to what the music of Greek lyric poetry sounded like. Only a few general facts are clear. Ancient comments show that the music was subordinate to the words until the latter part of the fifth century, when musical experiment began to play an important part in the performance of the nome and the dithyramb. Greek music was throughout its history monophonic, melody without harmony or counterpoint; in choruses of men and women or men and boys, there was octave singing. The rhythms were dictated by the nature of the Greek language, which had, even in unsung verse and prose, a pattern of syllable length, a quantitative division into long and short syllables.

The most distinctive feature of Greek music, and the aspect of it to which most importance was attached, and to which ethical values were ascribed, was that of mode (*harmonia*). It is by its mode that a melody is regularly described, and it is the mode that gives a melody its character. Unfortunately we cannot tell exactly what ancient Greek mode was. That it was closely related to key is inescapable, but that it had some difference of meaning seems just as necessary, since it is difficult to see how mere key differentiation could have the character and ethical significance ascribed by ancient writers to mode. The word *harmonia* means a stringing of the lyre, and clearly each mode involved a different stringing of the lyre. But beyond this our authorities do not take us, and modern research has led to conflicting theories which need not concern us here.[23]

The Beginnings of Lyric Poetry

In melic and only in melic is there abundant metrical variety. Clearly meter is an area in which originality played an important part. Nevertheless, while we may reasonably assume that Sappho, Alcaeus, and Anacreon displayed metrical inventiveness, and that innovations of some kind constituted no small part of their contribution to the genre, we have surprisingly little information about their originality.

Ancient tradition, represented now principally by the records of late compilers, lexicographers, and biographers, assigns with great particularity specific metrical and generic inventions to one or another early figure: Archilochus "thought up" the iamb and "invented" the ithyphallic meter; Terpander was the "inventor" of the *skolion;* Amphion "invented" lyric poetry, and Alcman "invented" love poetry.[24] There is no reason for confidence in the historical accuracy of any of this information, but regarding the monodists whose works have survived in some quantity two general impressions emerge. First, Archilochus was greatly renowned as an innovator (the epode, the tetrameter, the cretic, and the prosodiac are ascribed to him, as well as the iamb and the ithyphallic). Second, the main forms and meters had probably taken shape before the other extant monodists. Alcman had already "invented love poems," and to Sappho only peripheral refinements are ascribed—the mixolydian *harmonia* and the *pêktis,* a kind of lyre.[25] In other words, apart from Archilochus, the monodists whose work we know are the inheritors and perfecters of techniques and forms rather than their originators. The origins of lyric poetry and some of its forms are older than they, but how much older and in what forms it is hard to say.[26] It is even possible that Sappho and Alcaeus were the first to use the Sapphic and Alcaic stanzas—we have no previous history of them—but the fact that both used both is against the assumption.

The record of lyric before the seventh century, the period of the earliest fragments, is an insubstantial and heterogeneous assortment of traditions. Singing to the lyre, like that of Achilles in *Iliad* 9 and Demodocus in *Odyssey* 8, and choral singing, especially on religious occasions, were probably as early in Greek culture as the Mycenaean age from which Homer's traditions came. Apparently a good deal of this poetry was in dactylic hexameter, and hence not essentially different from the epic itself, especially in its earlier and less monumental development. But some marriage hymns, laments, and other ritual songs were presumably in other meters, since from the beginning the element of dance was present in some poetry of this kind, and the dactylic hexameter is not associated with dance.[27] The earliest references to choral lyric poems, in the *Iliad*, call them *molpê*, which means dance as well as song. We know that choral lyric poetry, with dance and strophic form, had reached a high state of finish in the hands of Alcman in the seventh century. It is likely that many of its elements came from earlier times, but evidence, as distinct from inference, is very slight.

For the origins of monody there is even less evidence. It is reasonable to think that songs of personal emotion and experience long existed in some form. From later times examples of "popular" songs are preserved, songs of unknown authorship that were traditionally associated with formal or informal social or religious occasions or with work.[28] The Lesbian milling song (*PMG* 869), is an example:

"Άλει, μύλα, ἄλει ·
καὶ γὰρ Πιττακὸς ἄλει
μεγάλας Μυτιλήνας βασιλεύων.

Grind, mill, grind;
Pittacus grinds too,
He who is king of great Mytilene.

Most of these songs have metrical cola of the kind used in the
poetry of the monodists and there is evidence for the use of
stanza form.[29] It can be assumed that ancestors of these songs
influenced the development of more formal lyric poetry.

There is, for what it is worth, a long list of names antedating
the earliest fragments of authentic poetry.[30] It begins with a
series of writers of hymns, among them Olen the Lycian, who
wrote hexameter hymns, including one to the birth goddess
Eileithyia, and Pamphos, who wrote "the oldest hymns for the
Athenians" (Pausanias 9. 27. 2), also in hexameters, and on
such subjects as the daughters of Celeus, the rape of Kore, and
Artemis. The references to these two early hymnists have a
plausible particularity. Credence is strained when Pausanias
mentions Orpheus in the same breath with them, though he
shows a reassuring disinclination to accept everything under
Orpheus's name as having been written by him. He does,
however, ascribe hymns to him.

Of great antiquity are the early winners of hymn contests in
honor of Apollo at Delphi (Pausanias 10. 7. 2–4). Long before
the establishment of athletic contests at Delphi in 586, Pausanias
tells us, hymns were sung to the god, in a contest, with lyre
accompaniment. Chronology is inexplicit; Pausanias takes the
event back to the mists of mythology by informing us that
Orpheus and Musaeus could have competed, had they not
been too proud to submit to a contest. Pausanias gives the
names of winners: Chrysothemis of Crete, "whose father
Karmanor is said to have purified Apollo," Philammon, and
his son Thamyris, the Thracian bard of myth who defeated the
Muses themselves and was blinded for it. From other sources
we learn that Philammon established choruses at Delphi, wrote
hymns celebrating the births of Artemis, Apollo, and Leto,
and invented the nome, and that a certain Eleuther won the
contest at Delphi by singing a song composed by someone else.

Still in this dim, possibly pre-Homeric world are several
traditional figures of poetry connected with central Greece:

Amphion of Thebes, traditionally the first human lyrist;
Anthes of Anthedon in Boeotia, who composed hymns;
Eumolpus of Eleusis, a writer of hymns as well as founder of
the Mysteries; and, farther north, Pierus of Pieria, whose
daughters contested with the Muses.

From the conglomeration of lore a few facts emerge: there
was a very old tradition of compositions sung to the lyre; the
poetic type mentioned again and again is the hymn; the subject
matter is myth; the meter is dactylic hexameter;[31] the performance is both choral and solo; the milieu is that of religious
celebration. In these early traditions of the hymn no sharp
distinction is made between monody and choral poetry.

Forming a kind of bridge between these figures of the
mythological period and the Greek poets of history is Olympus
of Phrygia, who perhaps belongs to both.[32] There was, traditionally, an Olympus, pupil of the satyr Marsyas, from whom
he learned to play the flute. And there was an Olympus of the
eighth or seventh century who invented the "auletic nome,"
that is, the flute-played air. Perhaps he was a poet as well as
a musician, for Aristotle (*Pol.* 8. 5) speaks of *melê* of Olympus
as if they were extant in his day. The names of several nomes
(whether auletic, songs played on the flute, or aulodic, songs
accompanied by the flute) composed by Olympus are preserved: the "Many-Headed Nome," in honor of Apollo, the
Harmateian Nome to Athena; the Nome of Ares (in which the
Dorian mode was employed). He composed also, we are told,
an *epikedeion* ("lament") for the Python slain by Apollo at
Delphi. Various musical inventions are ascribed to Olympus,
and a number of meters, such as the prosodiac, the trochee,
and the bacchius. There are two new things here: the flute
replaces the lyre, and the meter is not only hexameter. The
mythological matter and the sacredness of the occasion remain.

This fragmentary and inexact information provides enough
evidence about hexameter hymns sung to the lyre that we can
hardly decline to believe that this form of poetry did in fact

exist before the seventh century. Of other meters, or of flute
accompaniment, there is a specific trace only in the half-
substantial person of Olympus, but the presence of a flute-
player in the Minoan Hagia Triada paintings makes it certain
that flute music was not a new import in the archaic age.[33]
There are flutes as well as lyres in the Homeric picture of
music too (*Iliad* 18. 495). The presence of dance means that
other meters were used early. Probably the extant poets too
were in fact metrical innovators to some extent, but it is only
in the poetry of Archilochus that this kind of originality is
certain. Tradition marks him as an innovator, and there seems
little doubt that his poetry constitutes a crucial point in the
development of lyric form.

A striking thing about the forms of the earliest extant poems
is the fact that they are used in ways that suggest that they had
already become familiar and could be turned to unconventional
use. Thus we have a poem by Archilochus, Fr. 79a, in which
bad wishes are offered, apparently, to an enemy about to
embark on a voyage. At a later period, there was a recognized
type of lyric poem, consisting of an expression of good wishes
on the occasion of an embarkation, and duly categorized as a
propemptikon. Was there already such a recognized type when
Archilochus composed his *dyspemptikon*, and was he thus deliberately parodying a conventional type of poem? It seems
likely, and the irony would add to the savageness of the poem's
attack. Thus, also, Sappho's most famous hymn to Aphrodite,
Fr. 1, is not a cult hymn but a personal poem which is put
quite largely in what we know from other poetry to have been
the regular form of the cletic hymn. Similarly, the short
Lesbian milling song, quoted above as an example of a work
song, is in all likelihood something else too. The reference to
the "grinding" performed by the great Pittacus, ruler of Lesbos,
is probably ambiguous, suggesting his "grinding" of his
subjects; it may also have a sexual connotation.

Thus we have departures from types before we have the

types. Surely the types existed earlier than the departures, but it would not be safe to assume that they had existed long. As we shall see in the following chapters, the evolution of monodic forms at the stages which we can perceive was a rapid process. So was the evolution of tragic form. Ancient Greek literary types seem to have wasted little time in "achieving their proper natures," and then, in effect, ceasing to be, by being superseded by other types. The same rapidity of formal evolution that we can see in fifth century drama appears to have attended the brief history of monodic lyric. Perhaps in fact there can only be memorable and really creative lyric poetry when an accepted form is turned to a use that has some element of irony or paradox in relation to its past use.

CHAPTER TWO

Archilochus and the Beginning
of Extant Lyric Poetry

The seventh century was a period of varied and substantial poetic creativity. Terpander is hardly more than a great name,[1] but there are other poets whose work we have something of: the elegists Callinus and Tyrtaeus, the iambic poet Semonides of Amorgos, and Alcman, composer of the earliest extant choral poetry. And there are still other, shadowy figures whose names and reputations help to show that there was a poetic movement of breadth and force: Thaletas of Crete, Clonas, Polymnastus of Colophon, all innovators in music and poetry. But Archilochus is by far the best representative of what is new and of lasting influence in the poetry of this period. Elegy is not very different from epic in form (though the flute accompaniment that probably was a part of the early elegy is an important departure),[2] and even Alcman, though in the fullest sense a lyric poet, shows neither such variety of form nor such originality in material as Archilochus.

Though the elegists, Alcman, and Archilochus share much that is new, there are large differences among them. They share a turn to new metrical forms and away from exclusive concentration on mythological subject matter; and along with this change in subject matter from myth toward contemporary experience, and underlying and necessitating the change, comes a new attitude to the place of the poet. He is no longer the vessel of the Muses, the recorder of other men's deeds and

thoughts. He is now a participant, and, to a greater or less
degree, speaks for himself; but an essential difference is to be
found in this respect between the elegists (and with them to
some degree Alcman) and Archilochus. The first word of the
first fragment in the standard collection (Bergk's *PLG*) of what
is left of Archilochus's poetry is *eimi*, "I am." The first phrase
of the first fragment of the earliest elegist, Callinus, is "How
long will *you* lie idle?" The specific location of these lines in
our texts is an accident of the organization of modern collections
of the poetry. Nevertheless, the difference which the two
fragments exemplify is basic, and symptomatic of a split in the
early history of archaic Greek poetry, between the poet who is
his own subject, and whose own emotions and activities
dominate his songs, and the poet who participates mostly as
an adviser, exhorter, and teacher. To the first group belong
Archilochus and the monodists; to the second the earliest
elegists and the choral poets, though the choral poet was from
the beginning to some degree the presenter of his own emotions
and experiences as well as an adviser.

The split is also geographical. Iambic and monodic melic
are the characteristic forms of the Ionian and Aeolian world
of the islands and Asia Minor. Elegy, though it begins with an
Ionian of Ephesus, has an early Dorian representative,
Tyrtaeus, while choral lyric, which we first find in Sparta,
throughout its history retains in its dialect evidence of its
Doric beginnings; furthermore, the two most substantial exponents of these two forms are Dorians, Theognis of Megara
for elegy and Pindar of Thebes for choral lyric, and the poetry
of Pindar has its chief connections with the Dorian areas of
Sicily and with the Dorian island state of Aegina. There is a
relationship, certainly not surprising, between the poetry and
the form and spirit of the society. Where the community
tended to encroach most upon the individual, and communal
life was most emphasized, the poet too blended with the life
of the group; hence the martial, rallying poetry of Tyrtaeus

and the communal celebration embodied in Alcman's par-
theneia and Pindar's epinicians. Where the exploits and the
fortunes of a person were more a matter of individual enter-
prise, the poet is the poet of "me" rather than the poet of "us"
or of "you," and this spirit of personal action and expression
typifies the poetry of Archilochus, Sappho, and Alcaeus. The
geographical distribution is not merely ethnic, Ionian as
distinct from Dorian. In Athens, as well as in Corinth and
Sparta, elegy and choral lyric flourished, followed, in Athens,
by drama. Only where communal discipline did not strongly
prevail, in the mobile and individualistic small states of the
eastern Aegean littoral and islands, did monody reach conspicuous heights.

The Aegean communities of the archaic age were founded
during the period of confusion, migration, and reformation
that followed the collapse of Bronze Age civilization. The
communities in Ionia and Lesbos developed as a result of
migration from mainland Greece to the Aegean islands and
Asia Minor. The aborigines were expelled or incorporated,
and the immigrants, of different communities, dialects, and
traditions, became welded into a new social group with a
considerable degree of cohesiveness. The aristocracy maintained the power it had won from the Mycenaean kings, but
there was much that was new, and a considerable degree of
equality and independence was available to most people in the
community. The states of the Dorian world were in mainland
Greece, at Sparta, Megara, Corinth, Thebes, and in Crete.
By an accident of history these communities found themselves
in the position of powerful minorities exercising control over
conquered populations whose lands they had invaded and
whom they held in submission by a rigorously maintained
military and organizational superiority.[3] Both kinds of community had much that was greatly changed from the kingdoms
of Mycenaean Greece, but the social atmospheres of the two
were of necessity radically different from each other.

It is to the Ionian and Aeolian world that the earliest extant poets belong: Archilochus of Paros and Thasos, Callinus of Ephesus, Alcman of Sardis (though he is most associated with Sparta),[4] Terpander of Lesbos, Semonides of Amorgos. In the case of Archilochus, Callinus, and the only slightly later Alcaeus, poetic activity seems associated with the restlessness, danger, and adventure in which these groups lived. On the Asia Minor coast there was constant danger of invasion from the hinterland. Archilochus engaged in warfare and died in battle; he joined in a migration, or an invasion, from Paros to Thasos. Alcaeus was an indefatigable partisan of a political faction on Lesbos and spent his life in civic tumult.

There is some temptation to suppose that these states were nascent and without a settled tradition, and to assume that their circumstances were a direct continuation of the age of migration. Motion and excitement were certainly present, but a long period of time intervened between the migratory age and the age in which archaic lyric poetry made its appearance. The migrations were largely over by about 1000.[5] That means that there was a period of three hundred years during which these east Greek communities developed traditions, stability, and prosperity. The literary bloom of the seventh and sixth centuries coincides in time with a widespread colonizing movement, but it was not only the sudden coruscation of the brilliance of adventurers and explorers; it was also the product of a long development of language, religious celebration, social growth, and probably literary tradition.

Archilochus is the first voice of the poetry of the individual man, and his closest kin in the family of poets are the melic monodists. It is not because he is an iambist that he plays this part. The iambist Semonides of Amorgos, almost as ancient as Archilochus, had no such reputation in antiquity, nor do the fragments of his poetry lead us to associate him with lyric. Furthermore, we have as many elegiac verses left from Archilochus as we have iambic, and more elegiacs of his than of

Callinus. The difference is not between one meter and another. Archilochus composed in many metrical forms.[6] There can be no doubt that this variety reflects metrical inventiveness on the part of the poet,[7] and this is an element in making his poetry lyric, but much more important than any specific aspect of form is the personalness of the poetry, its closeness to his own activities.[8]

It is the purpose of this chapter to discuss the poetry of Archilochus that belongs in the history of lyric monody, not to give an account of the life and works of Archilochus, but the boundary lines will be hard to maintain: since immediacy to personal experience is an essential quality of monodic lyric, some biography is necessary. And since the poet's combination of epic and non-epic is often the only available key to an understanding of his reaction to and contribution to the poetic tradition, it is necessary to take careful account of this element also, though it is not invariably and primarily identifiable as lyric. I shall try in the rest of this chapter to take these broad, contributory factors into consideration so as to illuminate Archilochus's place in the general picture of Greek poetry, but the main emphasis will be on those elements and examples of his work that are significantly lyrical or that contribute to the lyrical tradition. Among the things that will therefore merit close attention are: the combinations and conflicts between epic (above all Homeric) influences and the material drawn from immediate experience; the use and transformation of meaning of Homeric words, especially epithets; the ways in which Archilochus shows an outlook typical of post-epic archaic Greek thought; features of his poetry that seem to have had a lasting impact on Greek lyric poetry, such as the use of dramatic dialogue, the way he uses fable, and the metaphor of the Ship of State; above all, the poetry that most strikingly emphasizes the poet's expression of personal emotions, especially those of love and hate. To a considerable extent concentration on these features means a concentration on those poetic forms that are most akin to lyric.

What we know of Archilochus's life is from two kinds of sources: the fragments of his poems and the statements of ancient writers, who probably got most of their information from poems of Archilochus. The poet's father was an aristocrat of Paros, Telesicles by name, who led a colonizing expedition to Thasos near the end of the eighth century. Archilochus's mother is said to have been a slave named Enipo. We have no evidence of civil disability suffered by Archilochus because of his (presumably) bastard birth, nor of any sense of inferiority because of it.[9] At some point Archilochus, like his father before him, went to Thasos, driven from Paros, "by poverty and resourcelessness," as the poet himself is reputed to have said.[10] We know too that Archilochus spent time as a soldier; he calls himself the "squire of Enyalios" (1), and from other fragments we know that he fought against Thracian tribes and against Euboean warriors. He is said to have died in battle, killed by a Naxian. It may be that his fighting activities were largely or even entirely in the battles that occurred when Thasos was colonized, but there is in several of the fragments a warrior-like air that seems to be an essential part of the man's spirit. Finally, Archilochus was reputedly a suitor for the hand of a girl named Neobule, whose father Lycambes, after agreeing to the match, later changed his mind and rejected the poet as a son-in-law. In revenge, Archilochus attacked father and daughter (perhaps also another daughter) so bitterly in verse that both, or all three, hanged themselves. There are several fragments that may be parts of poems written in the savage reactive hatred of the scorned or tricked lover. We are not told why Lycambes spurned Archilochus.[11]

The evidence about the dates of Archilochus's life is more abundant than harmonious. Herodotus (1. 12) says he was coeval with Gyges, but there is some doubt about the date of Gyges. The Parian Marble probably says (though a good deal of restoration is necessary to make it do so) that Archilochus "made his appearance" in 681 B.C. There is much confused

information about the date at which Telesicles colonized
Thasos, none of it decisive for Archilochus. Finally, there is a
famous passage from the poet in which he speaks of an eclipse
(74):

> Now we must expect all, forswear nothing,
> Marvel at nothing, since Zeus the father Olympian
> Brought night from midday, hiding the light
> Of the shining sun. Pale fear came upon men.

There has been lively discussion as to which of two total
eclipses was meant by Archilochus, that of 711 or that of 648.
But another fragment (19a), referring to the "ills of the
Magnesians," is best taken to refer to the destruction of
Magnesia by the Trerians, in 652. Therefore the later eclipse
is more probable, and we may set the period 700–640 as
approximate limits for the poet's life, though the possibility
exists that Archilochus lived a generation or more earlier than
that.[12]

A good deal of further information, most of it mere legend
or too fragmentary to be of great value (and a disappointingly
slight addition to our knowledge of Archilochus's poetry), is
available from several inscriptions, discovered on Paros. These
originally stood in an Archilocheion, a monument of a religious
nature, presumably a kind of hero's shrine, erected in honor of
the poet long after his death. The first of these discoveries was
made about 1900 and the texts appear as Fr. 51. This inscription, on two marble slabs, was set up by one Sosthenes, or
Sostheus, about 100 B.C. Sosthenes gives an account of incidents from the life of Archilochus, to illustrate "his piety and
his patriotic zeal." Sosthenes' inscription contains a number
of tetrameter quotations from the poetry of Archilochus which,
though very fragmentary, add to the previous knowledge of
Archilochus's martial poetry. There is a story (given partly in
quotation, partly in Sosthenes' prose) of how one Koiranos
(perhaps simply "the leader," as the name implies) from

Miletus was saved by a dolphin; there are references, with quotations, to Archilochus's adventures on Thasos, which are presented as acts of Parian patriotism. There is apparently a reference to the event of Fr. 6, the poet's abandonment of his shield, about which more will be said below, and there is a reference to Archilochus's friend Glaucus. The fragment ends with an epigram by Sosthenes.

The more recent evidence, discovered in 1949, consists of two more slabs of marble, both of which originally had four columns of text. What remains legible is one nearly complete column of fifty-seven lines and the left half of most of two other columns. This inscription was set up by one Mnesiepes, and is from about the middle of the third century B.C. The most complete column contains three oracles, in which Apollo bids Mnesiepes to dedicate a shrine and altar, to worship various deities, and to honor Archilochus. Then follows a legend of how Archilochus, as a youth, encountered the Muses, who gave him a lyre in exchange for a cow which he was leading to market. The story is roughly parallel with Hesiod's encounter with the Muses (*Theogony* 22–34) and was probably inspired by it. One of the partially legible columns contains four or five line-beginnings of a hymn by Archilochus to Dionysus, and the accompanying prose commentary seems to say that the citizens were offended by the hymn, thinking it indecent, and in some way punished or dishonored the poet. As a result, sickness came upon them and on consulting Delphi they were bidden to honor Archilochus. The remaining fragmentary column refers to Archilochus's achievements and quotes thirty verses of his poetry. Since only the line-beginnings remain, the addition to our knowledge of his art is regrettably slight; the lines seem to contain a description of battle against the Naxians, and so again emphasis is on Archilochus's poetry of war. But the encounter with the Muses suggests a tradition of the poet's lyric poetry.[13]

There is no satisfactory way of categorizing the fragments;

metrical division, the traditional organization,[14] does not altogether correspond to differences of material or manner;[15]
iambic, elegiac, and trochaic forms are not reserved for different
themes, and we know too little about the range of the epodes
or of the other lyric or quasi-lyric forms such as the *asynarteta*
to say much.[16] But there is, as we shall see below, some cor-
relation between those metrical forms that are farthest from
epic meter and a style and material that are or seem to be
most original.

Papyrus discoveries, which have substantially enlarged the
scope of the extant poetry of Alcaeus and Sappho, and to a
more limited degree, of Anacreon, have not been fruitful for
Archilochus, especially for the illustration of his lyric qualities.
What is now the longest extant example of Archilochus's
poetry is, in fact, a papyrus fragment, POxy 2310, forty-one
iambic lines (preceded by traces of eight lines) all but fourteen
of which are in very fragmentary form. Lines 7–21, the part
best preserved, seem to contain a speech made by the poet to a
woman who, confusingly enough, appears to have taken a city
"by the spear," and thereby to have "won great glory." There
is a cryptic reference to an "ant" (*myrmêx*, line 15); the context
suggests that the poet is alluding to a fable. The preceding
sentence is to the effect, "I know how to love a friend and
how to hate and revile a foe."

The rest of the fragment has in it something about "with a
small ship," "you came from Gortynia," "I seize this," "cargo,"
"was destroyed," "a wave of the sea overwhelmed," "by the
hands of warriors." Line 35 has a striking phrase,

ἥβην ἀγλαὴν ἀπώλεσας

You lost your lovely youth,

which Anacreon imitated.[17] Unlike the passage in Anacreon,
Archilochus's phrase does not mean that the person addressed
died, since the next line has "deity saved you." The closing

lines seem to say that the person addressed found the poet deserted, that the poet was "lying in the dark," and "was restored to the light." The wreck of these final lines, with their suggestion of strong emotions, is especially deplorable.

Little more than chaos has issued from the study of this baffling fragment.[18] There seems to be no way of knowing at what point the words of the speaker (presumably Archilochus) to the woman end, though many have tried to determine a stopping point, since it is intrinsically unlikely that the words of 17–21, with their attribution of military exploits, are addressed to a woman. Attempts have been made to divide the lines into two or three separate poems, to interpret *myrmêx* as a man's name rather than as the lowly ant, to find an oracular response to the poet, to identify the woman as Neobule, and to argue that it is really a man who is addressed as "woman."[19] None of these carries much conviction, and in the absence of anything more persuasive it seems appropriate to take the lines at face value and presume that the woman continues to be addressed at least to line 21. We are thus left mystified as to who this remarkable but otherwise unknown Amazonian conqueror can have been, and equally in the dark as to the autobiographical (if it is in fact autobiographical rather than mythical or historical) material of these lines.

There are some important gains. The ethos of the poet is well illustrated by the stress on whole-heartedness in friendship and enmity. There is additional evidence for the poet as a soldier. The trenchant use of the ant as a parallel for human conduct—assuming that what is here meant is that the poet, like the ant, knows both loyalty and how to bite[20]—is similar to other animal references in Archilochus's poetry. It is just possible that some kind of artistic unity would arise from an analogy in the relationship between Archilochus and the woman in 8–21, as suggested by the reference to the ant, and in that between Archilochus and the friend referred to in the broken lines after 21.

Though the dearth of papyri suggests that Archilochus was not much read or studied in late antiquity, he was held in the kind of reverence usually reserved for Homer alone. In *On the Sublime* Archilochus is one of the authors judged most Homeric, and the two are several times coupled in ancient criticism.[21] There is some reason to believe that the comparison was a traditional *topos*. A papyrus fragment contains scraps of twelve lines of poetry alternating between Homer and Archilochus, apparently intended to point out similarities in their expression of general ideas.[22] There is not enough in these remains to add to our specific knowledge of the poetry of Archilochus, but its existence is important as an example of how far wrong a view of Archilochus as being essentially an anti-Homeric poet may be. It is of the most crucial importance for the understanding both of Archilochus and of the spirit of early lyric to clarify as much as possible the nature of the relationship of Archilochus to Homer and the epic tradition.

The first and perhaps the most basic distinction between Archilochus and the poet of the epic is exemplified by Fr. 1:[23]

εἰμὶ δ' ἐγὼ θεράπων μὲν 'Ενυαλίοιο ἄνακτος
καὶ Μουσέων ἐρατὸν δῶρον ἐπιστάμενος.

I am the squire of lord Enyalios,
And I know too the Muses' lovely gift.

Archilochus's words emphasize his debt to and his difference from Homer. The phrase *therapôn Enyalioio* in line 1 is a modification of a recurrent description of the Homeric warrior, not any one particular hero, but the Achaeans as warriors, θεράποντες "Αρηος ("squires of Ares," *Iliad* 2. 110 and elsewhere). The substitution of Enyalios for Ares may, in view of the unsavory character of Enyalios in later Greek literature, have a special point, stressing the harshness of warfare. In line 2, Archilochus sounds partly like the warrior of Homeric poetry who also sings κλέα ἀνδρῶν, as Achilles does, *Iliad* 9. 189. But no Homeric warrior would be characterized as Archilochus is characterized here; the words imply not only singing but the creation of poetry. There is a better analogy with Homer himself, perhaps an even closer one with Hesiod, whose references to the Muses reflect a strong sense of personal relationship. By pairing the two traditionally separate activities, Archilochus is asserting a new role in society, characteristic of the century that followed him, and played both by the elegist-politician Solon and by the lyricist-politician Alcaeus, a role that makes the man of the Muses no longer the onlooker.

Of Archilochus as a warrior there is substantial evidence elsewhere in the fragments, and his poetry of warfare gives evidence of fierce and full absorption. Some examples illustrate essential features of Archilochus's poetry. Fr. 2 is one such:

'Εν δορὶ μέν μοι μᾶζα μεμαγμένη, ἐν δορὶ δ' οἶνος
'Ισμαρικός, πίνω δ' ἐν δορὶ κεκλιμένος.

At the spear is my kneaded bread, at the spear my wine
Ismarican, and I drink as I recline at the spear.

The strong anaphora gives a sense of urgency and emphasis. The lines may suggest that the poet lives "by the spear," as a mercenary,[24] but the final word throws the emphasis on the first and more literal meaning of "at" the spear, and it would not be wise to press the other. All Archilochus's activities are "at the spear," that is, at his post of duty. The final word, κεκλιμένος, is ambiguous: we cannot distinguish between the meaning, "Even at rest (that is, reclining at leisure) I am still at the spear (on duty)" and the meaning, "I go only so far toward leisure as to lean on my spear while I drink."[25] The stressed ending of the couplet is an early example of a development in poetic form of crucial importance in the history of Greek poetry. Whether or not the two lines are a complete poem is unknown nor is it in this connection important. In any case the sense of completion that is inherent in the couplet

form is emphasized by placing at the end a particularly
arresting or sense-fulfilling word. This is a momentous departure from the stichic poetry of epic, with its frequent
enjambment; it is a move toward the stanza of lyric. In Chapter
Seven there will be occasion to look further at the relationship
between such "epigrammatic" style and lyric form.

Of Archilochus's extensive activity as a warrior, and of the
presence of Homeric color in his poetry of warfare, there can
be no doubt.[26] But just as Fr. 1 clearly announces a new double
role for Archilochus, other poems set forth, with startling
frankness and freshness of view, an outlook on warfare that is
fundamentally different from that of the Homeric warrior.
There is no more familiar fragment of Archilochus than Fr. 6:

> Ἀσπίδι μὲν Σαΐων τις ἀγάλλεται, ἣν παρὰ θάμνῳ
> ἔντος ἀμώμητον κάλλιπον οὐκ ἐθέλων,
> αὐτὸν δ' ἐξεσάωσα. τί μοι μέλει ἀσπὶς ἐκείνη;
> ἐρρέτω· ἐξαῦτις κτήσομαι οὐ κακίω.

> My shield brings joy to some Saian. Beside a bush
>   I left the blameless gear against my will.
> Myself I saved. What do I care for that shield?
>   To hell with it. I'll soon get another no worse.

The lines became the progenitor of a series of confessions made
by poets at war. But it is one thing for Horace or Anacreon,
neither of whom fancied himself at this kind of warfare, to
confess to such an act, another for Archilochus. Archilochus
does not say that he actually flung the "blameless gear" (the
epithet is epic, the word *entos* is found only here in the singular;
the combination of traditional and novel seems designedly odd)
away in battle. It is only centuries later that this charge is
made against him. On the contrary, he left his shield beside a
bush—hidden, perhaps, by the bush. There is no suggestion of
precipitate flight from open battle; that kind of flight leaves
no time to find a place to set a shield.[27]

But why does Archilochus report the event? Sometimes the poem is taken to be a declaration of independence from the Homeric tradition of dignity and decorum in battle.[28] Archilochus was clearly conscious of the Homeric picture of warfare and the warrior, and he felt himself to be different from the warrior of that ancient tradition. He was, and knew that he was, a mortal and a citizen, instead of a demigod of myth or a Homeric hero. But he does not portray himself as lacking in martial spirit, spurning epic traditions of chivalry at the expense of his own dignity. The implicit suggestion of blame in describing the shield as blameless is slight and ironical. If there is an anti-Homeric spirit in this poem it is incidental and oblique, not central.[29] Two other passages are of importance for the understanding of this poem and of a main component of Archilochus's spirit. In Fr. 60 Archilochus tells us what a military officer should be like:

Οὐ φιλέω μέγαν στρατηγὸν οὐδὲ διαπεπλιγμένον
οὐδὲ βοστρύχοισι γαῦρον οὐδ' ὑπεξυρημένον ·
ἀλλά μοι σμικρός τις εἴη καὶ περὶ κνήμας ἰδεῖν
ῥοικός, ἀσφαλέως βεβηκὼς ποσσί, καρδίης πλέως.

I have no love for a tall general, one who struts,
Proud of his curly hair, clean-shaven;
For my taste let him be short and obviously bow-legged,
Firmly set on his feet and full of heart.

This too is un-Homeric, but not anti-Homeric. It may owe something to the description of Odysseus in *Iliad* 3. 193–98.[30] Essentially it has the same outlook as Fr. 6, an outlook that puts effective action before appearance. In epic tradition there was almost no room for any such contrast: a great warrior looked the part and followed the code. Of course Archilochus exaggerates the contrast. There is nothing wrong with a man's keeping his shield if he can, nor with a handsome general, provided he is "full of heart." The poet is rejecting the sacredness of traditional appearances. Hardly less important as a symptom of the new insight that comes with lyric poetry is the closeness of observation; the generals of Fr. 60 are precisely conceived figures, and the incident of the shield is a vivid scene. Homeric poetry too is precise in description, but the particularity that is characteristic of lyric is different, because the events and persons belong to the poet's immediate experience. The element of narrative is incidental; the events are valuable not intrinsically but for what they tell us about the poet himself, his attitude, tastes, and emotions. The descriptions are not narrative, even when they tell "tales" ($αἶνοι$); they are scenes to convey Archilochus's judgments and outlook.[31]

Resignation, readiness to accept what deity brings, a sense of powerlessness in the hands of deity, a recognition of the ebb and flow of fortune, and resulting from all of these the thought that neither triumph nor defeat merits unreserved response—all these attitudes are typical of the moral, religious, and social milieu of archaic Greece; they are on the lips of Achilles in *Iliad* 24, of Solon in his elegies, and even on occasion, as we shall see, of Alcaeus, for all his partisan zeal. Archilochus is no exception; what is conspicuous in the fragments that reflect such views is their sense of personalness in reaction to the conditions of life and their originality of expression.

A number of elegiac fragments that may all be from a single poem occasioned by a shipwreck that brought death to his brother-in-law and other Parians exemplify both the archaic outlook and Archilochus's own style.[32] Fragments 10, 11, and 12 are too brief to provide more than phrases, but in doing so they reveal tenderness of expression and yet retain the hard energy and terseness that characterize the rest of Archilochus's poetry. In Fr. 12 the alliterative emphasis of one complete line, its ironic reflection of Homeric passages, and a striking combination of Homeric and non-Homeric wording produce both pathos and force:

πολλὰ δ᾽ εὐπλοκάμου πολιῆς ἁλὸς ἐν πελάγεσσι
θεσσάμενοι γλυκερὸν νόστον . . .

Praying much, in the swelling waves of the white sea with its
  beautiful hair,
For the sweetness of return home.

Euplokamos ("with beautiful hair") is familiar as a Homeric
epithet used of goddesses and women. The transfer to the sea,[33]
with its suggestion of the wind-blown spray from the wave-tips
in a storm, both recalls and contrasts with the rescue of
Odysseus from death at sea by Ino Leucothea, *Odyssey* 5; the
phrase *halos en pelagessi* ("in the swelling waves of the sea")
occurs in that scene (5. 334); the phrase *glukeron noston* ("the
sweetness of return") sharpens the Homeric, above all the
Odyssean, echo, and its combination with the non-Homeric
and rare word *thessamenoi* ("praying") continues the contrast,
as if the Odyssean *nostos* is denied by the interruption of the
Homeric phrases. Of like linguistic power is the mournful
oxymoron of "unlovely gifts of the lord Poseidon" in Fr. 11.

This tone of deep, strongly expressed grief is joined in Fr. 7,
the one substantial fragment in this group, with a call for
balance and moderation. After lines in which the grief of the
city for the lost men is expressed the poem continues (5–10):

ἀλλὰ θεοὶ γὰρ ἀνηκέστοισι κακοῖσιν,
ὦ φίλ᾽, ἐπὶ κρατερὴν τλημοσύνην ἔθεσαν
φάρμακον. ἄλλοτέ τ᾽ ἄλλος ἔχει τάδε · νῦν μὲν ἐς ἡμέας
ἐτράπεθ᾽, αἱματόεν δ᾽ ἕλκος ἀναστένομεν,
ἐξαῦτις δ᾽ ἑτέρους ἐπαμείψεται. ἀλλὰ τάχιστα
τλῆτε γυναικεῖον πένθος ἀπωσάμενοι.

Yet, for evils that cannot be healed, my friend,
The gods have appointed a remedy: the power to endure.
These woes visit every man in turn. Now they have come
To us, and we groan for a wound that takes our blood.
Soon it will be another man's turn. Quickly, then,
Thrust away womanly mourning, endure.

36 EARLY GREEK MONODY

Most striking of all such passages is 67a, in which the poet
addresses his *thumos*, urges it, even when "overwhelmed by
griefs beyond control," (ἀμηχάνοισι κήδεσιν κυκώμενε) to face
the enemy in battle, and continues thus (4–7):

καὶ μήτε νικῶν ἀμφάδην ἀγάλλεο
μηδὲ νικηθεὶς ἐν οἴκῳ καταπεσὼν ὀδύρεο.
ἀλλὰ χαρτοῖσίν τε χαῖρε καὶ κακοῖσιν ἀσχάλα
μὴ λίην · γίγνωσκε δ' οἷος ῥυσμὸς ἀνθρώπους ἔχει.

Neither exult openly in victory
Nor, defeated, lie moaning in your house.
Rejoice in joys, give way to sorrows,
Without excess. Realize what rhythm holds mankind.

The idea of the oscillation of fortune and the consequent
admonition of acceptance and endurance are related to the
concept of *tlemosyne*, "endurance," as embodied in Odysseus,
and the spirit of Archilochus shares also in the resourcefulness
and the belief in action that characterize Odysseus the *poly-
tropos*, the man of many ways. But there is nothing in epic that
so fully combines the mutability of human fortunes and the
helplessness of man. When Odysseus urges his *thumos* ("spirit")
to endure present misfortunes, even as it has endured worse in
the past, there is not the acceptance of mutability that marks
the poetry of Archilochus, because the endurance of Odysseus
has a goal, and can anticipate a permanent achievement. It is
striking and perhaps significant in this connection that although
Archilochus and the monodists continue, within their metrical
limits, to use epic epithets, the traditional combinations are
continued for such features of nature as land, sea, and moon,
and for deities, but scarcely at all for human beings. The per-
manency of status that is implied by a recurrent epithet is still
acceptable for the black earth and the boisterous sea, but not
for man. A fragment of Archilochus that trenchantly expresses
the impermanence of human fortunes imitates a passage in the
Odyssey (18. 130–37), in which Odysseus, disguised as a beggar

in his own palace, reflects on the impermanence of fortunes
and emphasizes that man's mind is dependent on the "day"
that the immortals bring upon him.[34] Archilochus's similar
reflection is in Fr. 68:

> Τοῖος ἀνθρώποισι θυμός, Γλαῦκε, Λεπτίνεω πάι,
> γίγνεται θνητοῖσ', ὁκοίην Ζεὺς ἐφ' ἡμέρην ἄγῃ,
> καὶ φρονεῦσι τοῖ', ὁκοίοισ' ἐγκυρέωσιν ἔργμασιν.

The spirit of mortal man, O Glaukos son of Leptines,
Becomes just such as the day Zeus brings upon him;
Just such his thoughts are as the events he meets.

The verbal similarity is great, but there is a crucial difference.
Odysseus the beggar is still Odysseus the king; there is no such
underlying security of status in the thought of Archilochus.

There is no contrast between this ascription of man's fortunes
to deity and the more impersonal concept of a "rhythm" of
fortune. What is beyond human control is called, in archaic
Greek literature, fate, or *tyche, theos (theoi)*, or Zeus; the difference of ascription need not have any theological or philosophical significance. There is no evidence to suggest that for
Archilochus it had. It would be a similar misconception to
suppose that Archilochus's contemporary, the iambist,
Semonides of Amorgos, is propounding a monotheistic view
of world governance when he declares that "Zeus the
Thunderer controls the outcome (*telos*) of all things and dis-
poses them at his will" (1).[35]

The same contrast between human helplessness and divine
control, with emphasis on the arbitrariness and omnipotence
of that control, is stated in Fr. 58:

> Τοῖς θεοῖς τ' εἰθεῖ'[36] ἅπαντα · πολλάκις μὲν ἐκ κακῶν
> ἄνδρας ὀρθοῦσιν μελαίνῃ κειμένους ἐπὶ χθονί,
> πολλάκις δ' ἀνατρέπουσι καὶ μάλ' εὖ βεβηκότας
> ὑπτίους κλίνουσ' · ἔπειτα πολλὰ γίγνεται κακά
> καὶ βίου χρήμῃ πλανᾶται καὶ νόου παρήορος.

For the gods all things are easy. Many times they raise
Upright from troubles men who lie on the black earth,
And many times they overturn even those astride good fortune
And lay them prone. Then much evil comes,
And men wander in need of livelihood, unharnessed from
sense.

There is in this statement a good deal in common with the
sense of resignation in the melancholy scene, *Iliad* 24, where
Achilles speaks of the urns of Zeus and the mixture of human
fortunes in which the bad predominates. But in this as in the
other Archilochian lines on the changes of fortune, there is
more emphasis on fluctuation and less on resignation than in
Homer. In *Iliad* 24, man's fortune is unchangingly dominated
by evil; in Archilochus what is unchanging is the fact of change.

In this poetry that stresses the inevitability of change and
the consequent need for personal endurance and balance, one
note is conspicuously absent: there is no acceptance of mutability in the personal relationships of loyalty, love, and friendship. In Sophocles' *Ajax* the fluctuation of friendship and
enmity is recognized, with bitterness by Ajax, with philosophical breadth of view and humane compassion by
Odysseus;[37] in *Antigone* there is the idea of reconciliation and
the abandonment of hatred;[38] and tentatively in Euripides,
firmly in Plato, the principle of returning evil with evil begins
to retreat.[39] These things find no place in archaic Greek
thought. Archilochus sees the need to accept and endure what
the gods bring on men, but the acceptance of evil committed
by another man is no part of his view (66):

> ἓν δ' ἐπίσταμαι μέγα,
> τὸν κακῶς μ' ἔρδοντα δεινοῖς ἀνταμείβεσθαι κακοῖς.[40]

> One big thing I know how to do:
> To requite with terrible evils the man who does evil to me.

With the same total honesty that he shows in refusing to accept

the time-honored outward signs of courage and excellence,
and insists on baring the real value of an action or a man, so
he demands, with ruthless insistency, absolute loyalty in
personal relationships. The harshest and the most animated
of all extant poetry of Archilochus is poetry of hatred for those
who have betrayed him. One of the most powerful of all
archaic poems is a thirteen-line fragment of an epode (79a),
consisting of couplets of iambic trimeters and dactylic dimeters,
in which, in a kind of black *propemptikon*, evil voyage is wished
for a personal enemy.[41] An unknown number of lines precede:

κύμασι πλαζόμενος.
κἀν Σαλμυδησσῷ γυμνὸν εὐφρονέστατα
    Θρήικες ἀκρόκομοι
λάβοιεν — ἔνθα πόλλ᾽ ἀναπλήσει κακά
    δούλιον ἄρτον ἔδων —
ῥίγει πεπηγότ᾽ αὐτόν. ἐκ δὲ τοῦ χνόου
    φυκία πόλλ᾽ ἐπιχέοι,[42]
κροτέοι δ᾽ ὀδόντας ὡς κύων ἐπὶ στόμα
    κείμενος ἀκρασίῃ
ἄκρον παρὰ ῥηγμῖνα κυμαντῷ . . .
    ταῦτ᾽ ἐθέλοιμ᾽ ἂν ἰδεῖν,
ὅς μ᾽ ἠδίκησε, λὰξ δ᾽ ἐπ᾽ ὁρκίοισ᾽ ἔβη
    τὸ πρὶν ἑταῖρος ἐών.

Driven by the sea.
Naked in Salmydessos may the top-knotted Thracians
    Seize him in their gentle way
(With them he will find a full career of hardships,
    Eating the bread of slavery),
As he lies frozen with cold. May seaweed in abundance
    Ooze over him from the brine;
May his teeth chatter as he lies like a dog,
    Helpless on his face
At the very edge of the waves [?] . . .
    All this I would like to see
Because he wronged me and trampled on oaths,
    He who was once my friend.

The combination of the epic cadence of the dactylic dimeters with the conflicting iambic meter of the alternate lines corresponds to the extraordinarily powerful combination of traditional and original in the language and the scene. δούλιον ἄρτον ἔδων ("eating the bread of slavery") recalls the recurrent Homeric phrase, δούλιον ἦμαρ ("the day of slavery"), but its graphic suggestion of the experience of slavery is original; the phrase was later imitated by Hipponax.[43] The scene may be consciously modeled on the casting up of Odysseus on the shores of Scheria; there is some verbal reminiscence of that scene.[44] The implicit contrast between the hospitality of the top-knotted Thracians and that of Nausicaa and Alcinous adds a literary dimension to the personal anger of the lines, and to the irony of the poet's reference to Thracian hospitality, which he may have experienced himself.

Archilochus has moved far from the epic spirit, even though the metrical pattern and the diction are still to some degree tied to those of epic. In this epode we see also another divergence: in the elegiac poem urging endurance and describing man's lot there is a strong vein of that spirit of *paraenesis* that was, at the beginning of the chapter, ascribed above all to the elegiac writers, but here the tone is personal and private, expressive of Archilochus's own experience and views. He does not speak for the community. It is in passages like this that Archilochus appears as the forerunner of the monodists.

The metrical boundaries cannot be dogmatically set. Of the fragments that can with certainty or likelihood be assigned to Archilochus's celebrated quarrel with Lycambes several are from one or more epodes—we shall turn to them presently—but the only extant fragment to Neobule herself is trochaic. Since this fragment is certainly concerned with love, it will be convenient, before continuing with the poems of hatred, to observe along with it other expressions of the poet's experience with love. The trochaic line is Fr. 71:

εἰ γὰρ ὣς ἐμοὶ γένοιτο χεῖρα Νευβούλης θιγεῖν.

Unfortunately, it is impossible to determine whether this is to be taken as a lover's wish:

If only I might touch Neobule's hand!

or as a desire to "lay a hand" on her, in some form of revenge for the poet's rejection:

If only my hand might lay hold of Neobule!

If the first is correct, it gives us a uniquely gentle expression of Archilochus in love. If the second is correct, the line expresses, in much more typical spirit, the animus of the rejected poet, suggesting violent revenge or even a savage violation,[45] akin to the coarse and vigorous lines of Fr. 72, in the same meter:

καὶ πεσεῖν δρήστην ἐπ᾽ ἀσκὸν κἀπὶ γαστρὶ γαστέρα
προσβαλεῖν μηρούς τε μηροῖς

And to fall upon her slavish bag and drive
Belly against belly, thighs against thighs.

Again, the exact meaning escapes us because we do not know for sure the connotations of some of the words. ἀσκός, "wineskin," which I have translated "bag," can hardly be complimentary; the word modifying it, δρήστην, probably means either "runaway" (that is, slavish) or "hardworking." This is language to express contempt or hatred, but its sexual ferocity cannot be separated entirely from the passion of love. There is no proof that Neobule is the girl in this case.

Other fragments that describe the poet's experience with the emotion of love are all in epodic or asynartetic verse, and in all of them there is the same suggestion: the emotion is an unwanted force from without, or a disease that afflicts the poet. One reveals love turned to bitterness (112):

τοῖος γὰρ φιλότητος ἔρως ὑπὸ καρδίην ἐλυσθεὶς
πολλὴν κατ᾽ ἀχλὺν ὀμμάτων ἔχευεν
κλέψας ἐκ στηθέων ἁπαλὰς φρένας.

So strong a passion of love, coiled beneath my heart,
   Cast a thick mist over my eyes
Stealing the soft wits from my breast.

The passage is from an epode, perhaps to be linked with the
poet's love affair with Neobule. What is most remarkable about
the lines is the way in which phrases familiar from Homer, and
which thus evoke Homeric incidents, gain force by the contrast
of the Homeric evocation. Ἐλυσθείς, which here describes
passion, is used by Homer to describe Odysseus coiled beneath
the ram of the Cyclops (*Odyssey* 9. 433), and Priam crouching
at Achilles' feet (*Iliad* 24. 510); ἀχλύς ("mist") and χέω ("pour"),
which here image the effect of love's power, occur together in
a number of Homeric passages describing the mist of death
that descends on a stricken warrior (as in *Iliad* 5. 696); ἀπαλός
("soft") is a regular Homeric description of external parts of
the body, the neck, feet, or hands, and Archilochus's transfer
of application is violent.

Even where there is no apparent question of the description
of a love that has turned to bitterness, the suggestions of pain,
unfulfillment, and coercion are present (104):

δύστηνος ἔγκειμαι πόθῳ
ἄψυχος, χαλεπῇσι θεῶν ὀδύνῃσιν ἕκητι
πεπαρμένος δι' ὀστέων.

Wretched I lie, a prey to longing,
Lifeless, at the will of the gods by bitter pains
   Pierced through the bones.

118:

ἀλλά μ' ὁ λυσιμελής, ὦ 'ταῖρε, δάμναται πόθος.

I am mastered, comrade, by that looser of limbs, desire.

In the highly personal, un-epic statement of Fr. 104, one
phrase, ὀδύνῃσιν . . . πεπαρμένος is straight from Homer (*Iliad*
5. 399). In Homer the pain is physical: Hades is wounded by
Heracles. The Homeric context, like the Archilochian, involves

deity and man; Archilochus has reversed the direction of the injury, as well as internalized its nature or cause. The Homeric words are in Dione's speech of consolation to Aphrodite, who has been wounded by Diomedes.[46]

While there is reason to believe that François Lasserre[47] has greatly overestimated the dimensions and the centrality of the epodes, there can be no doubt that the form and Archilochus's use of it are important steps in the development of Greek lyric poetry. On the purely formal side, the epode marks a compromise between the stichic poetry of hexameter and iambic and the stanzaic poetry of lyric. The elegiac couplet is a step in the same direction, but a less decisive one, because both lines of the couplet retain a close connection with the meter of epic, whereas the combinations in the epodic form are varied and fluid, combining different rhythms as well as unit lengths: iambic trimeter followed by a dactylic unit $(-\cup\cup-\cup\cup-)$ which was an essential unit of the dactylo-epitrite as it is known from later poetry; iambic trimeter followed by iambic dimeter; dactylic hexameter followed by iambic dimeter.

Archilochus has a further rudimentary stanzaic form called variously epode or *asynartêton* ("unconnected"), in which a verse called Second Archilochian, consisting of two metrical units (dactylic tetrameter and ithyphallic) divided by diaeresis, is followed by an iambic trimeter catalectic. This complexity of rhythm and fluidity of combination go far beyond the variety of the elegiac couplet. In this respect Archilochian poetry is, so far as extant poetry goes, the precursor—though not necessarily the progenitor—of the lyric stanza.[48] There is another asynartetic form in Archilochus, the First Archilochian of Frs. 107–11, and there may have been other epodic forms;[49] the evidence is incomplete, though enough to indicate that Archilochus was an important innovator in lyric or proto-lyric forms. The testimony of late critics as to his metrical inventiveness[50] confirms this evidence.

Formally, then, the epodes and *asynartêta* are the most lyrical

of Archilochus's poetry. They include Archilochus's most passionate lines, his most striking transformations of Homeric
language, and most of his boldest innovations in style and
subject.

Assessment of what the epodes were like as poems is extremely hazardous because it is so hard to know how many
poems the extant fragments are from. Fourteen epodes are
reconstructed by Lasserre, largely under the guidance of the
material of Horace's *Epodes*. There are only two of these to
which a substantial number of extant fragments can be convincingly assigned; but almost certainly some of the other
extant epodic fragments are from other poems than these. The
two more or less visible epodes contain fables, and there is
some evidence for the use of other fables—presumably in other
poems and perhaps in other epodes—by Archilochus. These
recoverable epodes both begin with a direct address, and both
present their fables partly in dramatized form, with dialogue.
But from these likenesses between two epodes we cannot make
generalizations about the form. Two other important epodic
fragments have only metrical likeness to these and to each
other. We have already examined them: Fr. 79a, the *propemptikon* to a treacherous friend,[51] and Fr. 104, on the torment of
passionate love. All these epodic fragments are marked by
animation of expression and all are in a mood of anger or
suffering. While these characterizations apply to much of
Archilochus's extant poetry, the epodic lyric form is associated
with a particularly concentrated and personal expression of
emotion. Compared with the tension and passion of 79a and
104, some of the elegiac, trochaic, and iambic fragments seem
relaxed and measured. The contrast certainly applies to the
new, long iambic fragment, POxy 2310; and both the reflective,
tolerant wisdom of the elegiac lines addressed to Pericles (7)
and the sense of balance and restraint perceptible in the
trochaic verses of Fr. 67 seem to be substantially different from
the lyric style.

The fable from its beginning in Greek literature suggests earthiness, simplicity, the non-heroic, non-Homeric. Hesiod, the poet of mainland farm life, gives us our earliest examples; Archilochus comes next. Both predate Aesop by far.[52] Unlike the fables familiar from Aesop, the two Archilochian fables that can be judged bear on specific persons and events in the poet's life; the fable has in his poetry—in its very individualistic way—the function that myth has in later lyric such as the Pindaric epinician. It is more an expansion of a personal theme and has a more emotional application than the moral, paraenetic story ordinarily thought of as a fable. Archilochus is concerned to illustrate not the foibles of mankind but the shortcomings and errors of his personal enemies. At the same time, the illustration by story has the effect of broadening and authenticating the poet's topic and in this it is like the Pindaric and the Sapphic myth.

The better preserved fable epode, called Epode One by Lasserre, and embracing Frs. 88–95 (Diehl), begins with an address to Neobule's father (88):

Πάτερ Λυκάμβα, ποῖον ἐφράσω τόδε;
  τίς σὰς παρήειρε φρένας,
ἧς τὸ πρὶν ἠρήρεισθα; νῦν δὲ δὴ πολύς
  ἀστοῖσι φαίνεαι γέλως.

Father Lycambes, what have you said?
  Who has stolen away the wits
That once were firmly yours? Now you seem
  A laughing stock to your fellow citizens.

The assault is unremitting, and it begins with the sarcastic opening word; Lycambes has already broken the betrothal.

What else preceded the fable is unknown. But its introduction is preserved (89):

αἶνός τις ἀνθρώπων ὅδε,
ὡς ἄρ' ἀλώπηξ καἰετὸς ξυνωνίην
ἔμειξαν.

There is a story told by men
Of how the eagle and the fox once joined
In partnership.

The Aesopian fable of the vixen and the eagle,[53] which tells
how the eagle betrayed the friendship by feeding the vixen's
young to his eaglets and himself, how the vixen cursed the
eagle, and how the eagle was punished, accidentally burning
his eaglets to death by feeding them animal flesh purloined hot
from an altar fire, may reasonably be supposed to have been
the essence of Archilochus's presentation, but the extant fragments suggest some significant differences of version, including
the introduction of a third animal.[54] Dialogue is prominent in
the fragments: Archilochus addresses Lycambes, the vixen
addresses the eagle, some third animal addresses the vixen,
somebody, probably the vixen, addresses Zeus. The theme of
friendship betrayed was presumably the point of contact with
Lycambes.

An epode in which the fable of the ape and the fox was told
seems to have had the same structure: a direct address to the
recipient of the story as introduction, and use of dramatic
dialogue in the presentation of the fable. The beginning, the
only substantial fragment, has the same urgent and bitter tone
as that to Lycambes (81):

> Ἐρέω τιν' ὑμῖν αἶνον, ὦ Κηρυκίδη,
>   ἀχνυμένη σκυτάλη.
> πίθηκος ᾔει θηρίων ἀποκριθείς
>   μοῦνος ἀν' ἐσχατιήν.
> τῷ δ' ἄρ' ἀλώπηξ κερδαλῆ συνήντετο
>   πυκνὸν ἔχουσα νόον.

I shall tell you a fable, Kerykides,
    And I shall be a grievous messenger.
An ape went apart from the beasts,
    Alone in the wilderness.
There came to meet him a crafty vixen,
    With subtle, scheming mind.

Here again an Aesopian fable (Halm 44) probably gives a version of Archilochus's story: the ape, made king of the beasts, is tricked into a trap by the vixen, who then points out to him how little qualified he is to be king. Of the particular application and of the addressee we know nothing. Kerykides, "herald's son," is probably a pseudonym, perhaps ironically chosen in connection with the figure of the "grievous messenger," literally "grievous herald's staff."[55]

The animus, the irony, and the attack on human pretentiousness that these animal illustrations contain are akin to other aspects of Archilochus's manner, and the use of homely animal comparisons is not restricted to the epodes. The brief saying (88a),

τέττιγα δ' εἴληφας πτεροῦ

You have a grasshopper by the wing,

quoted (more or less) and elaborately explained by Lucian as alluding to the unwise rousing of the satirist, is usually catalogued as a fragment of the Lycambes epode, but evidence for this is nonexistent, and there are good reasons for rejecting the assignment.[56] It is at least as likely to be from another type of poem, and the cryptic but stylistically similar reference to the *myrmêx* in line 16 of POxy 2310 shows that Archilochus's animal comparisons are not restricted to the epodes. One other striking animal reference (103),

πόλλ' οἶδ' ἀλώπηξ, ἀλλ' ἐχῖνος ἓν μέγα

The fox knows many things, the hedgehog one, but big,

is said, by one of the late Greek writers who quote it, to be from an epode.[57]

There are, however, some other epodic fragments. 79a and 104 (also 112, but it should perhaps be classed as asynartetic) are the best examples, since—as we have noticed above—they very strikingly combine epic language and highly personal statement, and the effect cannot be altogether separated from the metrical facts of these lines. Fragments 104 and 112, with their transformations of phrases that in epic are purely physical and external to express the suffering of love, and 79a, with its interweaving of epic phrases in epic cadences (lines 2 and 4, and, partially, 6) with a brutal, vivid, intensely personal curse are, with respect to diction, among the most striking of the fragments of Archilochus. They point the way to that combination of factors that creates the particular essence of some of the best archaic Greek lyric poetry: epic evocations, personal intensity, and contrast or parallel between the immediate and the traditional.

The dramatic quality of the epodes, with their dialogues and characters, is found elsewhere. A four-line iambic fragment rejecting the power and riches of a tyrant (22) is spoken by "Charon the carpenter," Aristotle informs us, and the probability of an ironical intent, dramatically achieved, as in the pseudo-moderation of the usurer in Horace, *Epodes* 2, is very high.[58] The lines on the eclipse (74), the first four of which are quoted above in connection with the dating of Archilochus's life, are said by Aristotle, in the same passage, to have been put in the mouth of a father and to have been spoken in censure of his daughter. A recent papyrus discovery (POxy 2313 fr. 1a) confirms that the characters are Lycambes and Neobule. How and why Lycambes is represented as censuring Neobule remain unclear; but the papyrus fragment provides the word "marriage," and it is a natural assumption that the betrothal and its cancellation were directly concerned. Irony on Archilochus's part can hardly be doubted.

The metaphor of the Ship of State has an elaborate history in the poetry of politics from Alcaeus onward, and an antecedent of it appears in Archilochus, Fr. 56. The traces are so slight that without the assurance of Heraclitus, the author of the work *Quaestiones Homericae* (first century A.D.?),

who quotes the lines, we would not suppose them to be
allegorical:

Γλαῦχ᾽, ὅρα · βαθὺς γὰρ ἤδη κύμασιν ταράσσεται
πόντος, ἀμφὶ δ᾽ ἄκρα Γυρέων ὀρθὸν ἵσταται νέφος,
σῆμα χειμῶνος · κιχάνει δ᾽ ἐξ ἀελπτίης φόβος.

Glaucus, look. Already the deep sea is stirred
With waves, and about the Gyrean heights[59] mist rises aloft,
Signal of storm. And suddenly fear comes on.

Heraclitus says that the poet "when threatened in the Thracian
dangers likens the war to a sea wave." The address to Glaucus,
known from epigraphical evidence[60] to have been the leader
of the Parian forces on Thasos, substantiates Heraclitus's
connection of the poem with Thracian matters. In these three
tetrameters no Ship of State appears, but surely the fear in
the third line is that of a person in a ship at sea. The storm
that threatens is the storm of war rather than civic unrest, and
hence we do not yet have the picture that later becomes
familiar. We are at about a halfway point between the Homeric
simile, as at *Iliad* 15. 623–29, comparing the advance of Hector
against the Achaeans to a wave breaking over a ship, and
Alcaeus's elaborate metaphors. A papyrus fragment, apparently
in the same meter (there are no complete lines) and hence
possibly from the same poem, has ships, but not certainly
allegory (56a):

[. . . βαθεῖ φέρο]νται νῆες ἐμ πόντῳ θοαί
[. . . π]ολλὸν δ᾽ ἱστίων ὑφώμεθα
[. . . λύσαν]τες ὅπλα νηός, οὐρίην δ᾽ ἔχε
[ἱκμένην σάου θ᾽ ἑταί]ρους, ὄφρα σέο μεμνεώμεθα.

Our swift ships are (carried) upon the (deep) sea; let us
reef sails, slacken ropes; and you, get a favoring wind (and
save your comrades) that we may remember you.

The problems of meaning in these and four more fragmentary

lines that follow them need not detain us.[61] There is certainly
a picture, in dramatic strokes, of ships and a storm at sea. As
we shall see in the case of Alcaeus's similar pictures, it is not
certain that the scene is metaphorical, though other purposes
for such a dramatization are hard to imagine.

The most conspicuous feature of the poetry of Archilochus
is the participating and vivid presence of the poet himself,
addressing and criticizing his friends and fellow citizens, ex-
plaining and justifying his actions, expressing his views and
emotions. It is the combination of this personal presence[62]
with the traditional epic diction, a combination that is metrically symbolized in the combination of epic with lyric rhythms
in the epodes and *asynartêta*, that gives Archilochus's poetry its
unique character.

A number of passages deserve mention as preeminently
illustrating the poet's power of expression. We have noticed
already the brisk, earthy conciseness of his animal metaphors
—the fox, "a grasshopper by the wing," the "ant" who knows
how to help and how to bite, the hedgehog—and the same
energy abounds in quite different kinds of expression. In Fr. 5,
a remnant from a poem on an incident aboard a ship, Archilochus bids someone—apparently a companion on night watch
—to "rip the lids from the hollow caskets" (κοίλων πώματ' ἄφελκε
κάδων), and to "Seize the red wine down to the very bottom"
(ἄγρει δ' οἶνον ἐρυθρὸν ἀπὸ τρυγός).[63] Another fragment has
words in wry disparagement of Paros (53); he speaks as roughly
of the island he went to, Thasos (18):

> ἥδε δ' ὥστ' ὄνου ῥάχις
> ἔστηκεν ὕλης ἀγρίης ἐπιστεφής.

> Like the backbone of an ass
> It stands up, with a crown of wild woods.

The bluntness and incisiveness of language in these passages
accord very well with the spirit of Fr. 6 (the shield) and Fr. 60
(the generals).

Bluntness is likely to include expressions and figures of speech outside decorum. Ancient Greek satire and comedy lent themselves to fairly uninhibited obscenity, and the language of Archilochus shares this tendency, though it is often hidden by the bowdlerizing effect of preservation in quotations. Fr. 41 exemplifies both the vulgarity of expression and the bowdlerizing. In the indirect tradition, there is one line quoted along with similar phrases from other authors:

ἀλλ' ἄλλος ἄλλῳ καρδίην ἰαίνεται.

But each man's heart's delight is different.

So the fragment stood. But POxy 2310, fr. 1, has added words that expand the thought with Archilochian directness, in specific examples of the generalization. Some illegible type or person is concerned, above all, with his penis; Lasserre-Bonnard, in their translation, not unreasonably guess that the person concerned is "le voluptueux." The next example is "the herdsman," but the fragmentary state of the papyrus prevents our learning what his preoccupation is. The spirit is essentially the same as in the animal images and the fables: earthiness and a tendency to mock human pretentiousness.[64]

The same spirit can, in a different mood, lead to a sharp but not unfriendly criticism of Glaucus (59), and to this characterization of a female of easy virtue (15):

συκῆ πετραίη πολλὰς βόσκουσα κορώνας
εὐήθης ξείνων δέκτρια Πασιφίλη.

The fig tree on its rocks feeds many crows
And easy-going Pasiphile is hospitable to strangers.

It is most unlikely that the reference is as innocuous as it might appear to be. The name Pasiphile, "friend to all," is suggestive, and the comparison is equally so.[65]

Archilochus's power of expression is by no means devoted

only to harsh or depreciative descriptions. There is a delicate
picture of a girl (25):

ἔχουσα θαλλὸν μυρσίνης ἐτέρπετο
ῥοδῆς τε καλὸν ἄνθος
ἡ δέ οἱ κόμη
ὤμους κατεσκίαζε καὶ μετάφρενα.

She held a myrtle branch and a lovely rose
And delighted in them, and her hair
Gave shade for her back and shoulders.

The description is charming and the mood sunny, but since
we are told by Synesius, who quotes the second part,[66] that
the praise is of a *hetaira* it would not be surprising if the context
were satirical. This picture and the poignant phrase in Fr. 12
(quoted above, p. 35), likening sea waves to tresses of hair,
are reminders that Archilochus's power as a creator of strong
pictorial phrases is varied in its scope and application. But
there is more of energy and emotion than of conventional
beauty in the language of Archilochus. Greek lyric begins with
poetry that reflects personal life experienced primarily as
suffering. The poet accepts vicissitude as an inevitable
"rhythmos," but his response to personal misfortunes is one
of rebellion, not acceptance.

CHAPTER THREE

Alcaeus

Both Alcaeus and Sappho are the spiritual successors of Archilochus, because both continue his contemporaneity of subject matter and his intensity of self-expression. They may owe specific debts; there is, as we shall see, some evidence of direct imitation by Alcaeus. But it is a long step from Archilochus's asynartetic verses and epodes to the four-line stanzas of Alcaic and Sapphic strophe.[1] The choral poetry of Alcman and Stesichorus,[2] who wrote contemporaneously or shortly before them, bears no striking similarities to their poetry; any influence, in either direction, can have been only slight. But there were other possible models. Traditional songs associated with work, religion, or social activities, which have been mentioned in Chapter One, may have influenced the poetry of Sappho and Alcaeus; some of the melic forms familiar from them may have been used earlier by forgotten poets; and, finally, there was a history of lyric composition on Lesbos, associated principally with the name Terpander.

From native tradition, the Lesbian poets no doubt inherited their strong dependence on local, non-epic, and presumably non-literary diction. Just as the Aeolic meters of their poetry are further from epic hexameter than other contemporary forms of verse are, so too the dialect and the vocabulary of the monodists are further from epic language. This linguistic difference continues for long to be a dividing mark between the poetic types and a symptom of a difference both of tradition

and of concern, not unlike the medieval distinction in which
Latin was retained for poetic forms and themes consciously
and directly in the public tradition, while the vernacular
languages were more often the vehicles for personal and lyric
expression. In archaic Greece the differences of medium and
origin were less pronounced; Archilochus, who in both forms
and themes straddled the types, tended also to straddle the
linguistic distinction. Alcaeus and Sappho vary in the intensity
of their localism in accordance with the nature of their themes
and to some degree of the forms of their poems.

About Terpander and his place in poetry perhaps the only
important thing is that he existed on Lesbos before Alcaeus
and Sappho. In specific points their debt to him may be small,
for the few remaining lines alleged to be his give little evidence
of an individual poetic style. Heavily spondaic, they are
written in a language much more indebted to Homer than
theirs is. Terpander must have derived much more from the
public, epic tradition than from local art. His subjects were
similarly public and impersonal. Extant fragments that have
been ascribed to him include opening lines of poems praising
Zeus, Apollo, the Muses, and the Dioscuri; and a poem of his
concerning Dionysus was known in antiquity. All the fragments are in a stately style, rich in Homeric epithets. These
lines have questionable value as specific evidence, since they
are not at all likely, in their present form, to have been composed by Terpander;[3] yet they may convey a tradition of what
his poetry was like. If reliance can be placed on ancient
reports, he lived about the middle of the seventh century.[4]
Advances in musical composition[5] and in the form of the lyre[6]
are ascribed to him, and he is credited with inventing various
types of nome.[7] Perhaps his principal contributions were in
music rather than poetry, yet his name was great in poetry
too, and his excellence gave rise to a saying to describe the
second best: "After the Lesbian poet."[8] He may have been
one of numerous poets imported to Sparta,[9] and perhaps his

poem to the Dioscuri can be connected with a Spartan sojourn; one fragment (Bergk, *PLG* 6) is in praise of Sparta, where "the valor of young men flourishes, and the clear-voiced Muse; and Justice, sponsor of noble deeds, walks in wide streets."

There was, then, a famous Lesbian poet before Alcaeus and Sappho, and it would be wrong to entertain the romantic idea of a sudden creation *ex nihilo* of formal lyric poetry at the end of the seventh century, with the emergence of two extraordinary figures using the same poetic forms at the same time. Behind these two remarkable poets there lie a local tradition of artistic literature, a history of ritual and popular songs, and a broad Hellenic stream of iambic, elegiac, epic, and hymnal poetry in varying degrees of relationship to the Homeric fountainhead.

Alcaeus and Sappho share, as a result of their local heritage, a very striking similarity of forms and diction. But they are utterly different in content, spirit, values, and interests. It is possible that Alcaeus occasionally shows some Sapphic influence;[10] Sappho seems to have gone her way as a poet without a trace of influence by Alcaeus. It is not known which was the elder, but it is convenient to begin with Alcaeus because some account of the politics of Lesbos in the seventh century B.C. is necessary for an approach to his poetry.

The political life of the island of Lesbos revolved largely around that of its principal city, Mytilene, and it is only of Mytilene that we have any substantial political information. Until about the middle of the seventh century the city had apparently been ruled by hereditary monarchs of the family of the Penthilidae, whose eponymous founder, Penthilus, was reputedly a son of Orestes. The Penthilidae were notorious for arrogance and cruelty; Aristotle in the *Politics* (1311b26) tells us that they dispensed arbitrary beatings to the citizens, and it was partly at least because of their bad behavior that they were reduced, in time, to a position of equality with other aristocratic families. At the end of the seventh century B.C.,

when Alcaeus was in young manhood, they still had enough
prestige to make an alliance with them valuable for a politically
ambitious man.

Thus in Alcaeus's earliest years the state was under the un-
stable rule of an aristocratic oligarchy. The forms of government already in force in Mytilene long enough to count as
traditional were the council and assembly usual in archaic
Greek politics.[11] This pattern was broken at least three times
during Alcaeus's life by the elevation to power of a tyrant or
single ruler of similar powers. Three such rulers were attacked
by Alcaeus in poetry; the same three were conspired against
by a faction, probably aristocratic, to which Alcaeus belonged.
The first was Melanchrus, about whom very little is known.
He is named in one brief fragment of Alcaeus (331),[12] and is
mentioned in a passage of Strabo, who tells us that Melanchrus
was one of the tyrants of that period of civil unrest that forms
the subject matter of Alcaeus's *Stasiôtika* or "Partisan Songs."[13]
The second tyrant known from Alcaeus's poetry and Strabo's
account was Myrsilus, who held power at some point in the
period between 605 and 590. From poems of Alcaeus and some
other supporting evidence it appears certain that after Myrsilus
had seized power a conspiracy of *hetairoi*, literally "companions"
but in this context clearly political confederates, was formed
against him, of which Alcaeus and Pittacus were members.
Thereafter Pittacus left the conspiracy and was allied in power
with Myrsilus. The only further fact known about Myrsilus is
his death, exulted in by Alcaeus in a classic shout of joy at
the fall of the tyrant (332):

> νῦν χρῆ μεθύσθην καί τινα πρὸς[14] βίαν
> πώνην, ἐπεὶ δὴ κάτθανε Μύρσιλος.

Now it is right to get drunk, a man must drink
With all his might, for Myrsilus is dead.

The third in the series of rulers is a much more substantial historical figure and one whose period of dominance in Mytilene is generally reputed to have been both beneficial and welcome to most of the citizens. This is Pittacus, one of the Seven Sages, and the traditional source of numerous utterances of political and moral wisdom. His early career was perhaps not altogether admirable. To his credit, it is recorded that he was the leader in deposing the tyrant Melanchrus.[15] Also, in the Sigean War, fought between Lesbos and Athens in a dispute as to who should have control over the promontory of Sigeum, the northwest tip of the Troad, Pittacus was the leader of the Lesbian forces, and won a temporary advantage for his fellow citizens over Athens when he defeated in single combat the Athenian champion, an Olympic victor named Phrynon. This Homeric victory for possession of Homeric territory was nullified shortly thereafter, when Periander of Corinth, called in as arbitrator, awarded Sigeum to Athens. But we are told that Pittacus's later appointment as ruler of Mytilene was made in gratitude for his services on this occasion. Against these favorable points in Pittacus's early history, we must set two questionable actions: Pittacus broke away from the conspiracy against Myrsilus and was then associated in power with that tyrant; and, it seems, he made a marriage alliance with the hated house of Penthilus, even as Cypselus married a Bacchiad and became tyrant of Corinth. Since both these points about Pittacus are conveyed to us by the hostile report of Alcaeus, it may be that they reflect less discredit than Alcaeus would have us believe. At any rate, the rest that is known of Pittacus is admirable. At some point, in all likelihood after the death of Myrsilus, he was given a position of dictatorial power, the position called by Aristotle *aisymnêtês*. The exact nature of it is not clear, but it was certainly conferred by those to be ruled, not seized in the traditional tyrant fashion. Aristotle calls it "tyranny by choice."[16] After ten years of rule Pittacus voluntarily surrendered his power. So far as is known, the state went back to its aristocratic form of government.

Alcaeus's position has been indicated, but there are a few points to add. His aristocratic place in Lesbian society is strongly suggested by his reference, in Fr. 130, to the possessions and rights of his father and grandfather. A notice in Diogenes Laertius[17] and a fragment of Alcaeus (75) have been put together to suggest that at the time of the overthrow of Melanchrus Alcaeus was still a child.[18] The earliest action that we know him to have been concerned in is the Sigean War; at this point, 607/6, he must have been of military age, for on this occasion he lost his shield (428). That he was in exile at Pyrrha, a place in Lesbos, is certified by his own reference to it (130). Whether he himself was ever exiled beyond Lesbos, as some of his contemporaries were, is uncertain but probable. He was exiled more than once; a commentary (to 114) speaks of his "first" exile and says that it was to Pyrrha; another commentary refers to "the second exile."[19] That Alcaeus was regarded as a force to be reckoned with is apparent from Aristotle,[20] who says that Pittacus was given unlimited power against the exiles, of whom Alcaeus and his brothers were the leaders. Pittacus is reported to have spared Alcaeus on one occasion.[21] Finally, it appears that Alcaeus lived long enough to have become gray (50), but it is uncertain whether he was then in exile. Perhaps Pittacus's voluntary resignation of dictatorial powers after a decade indicates that the storm that led to Alcaeus's exile had then spent itself sufficiently for him and his friends to be safely tolerated in the state.[22]

Alcaeus's political life cannot be disregarded in the study of his poetry, because his political fortunes occupy a large place in it and appear to affect its spirit profoundly. It is therefore exasperating to discover that it is impossible to arrive at a satisfactory judgment of his politics. Traditionally, it has been supposed that the poet's professions of idealism and concern for the *damos*, the Lesbian body politic, are to be taken seriously, that he and his companions were high-minded fighters against tyranny, and that the political lyrics are calls to a higher and more universal concept of life.[23] But there are difficulties. All sources of information except Alcaeus are unanimous in finding Pittacus's rule beneficial to the state. Yet Alcaeus is as blindly hostile to him and as convinced that his rule is ruinous as he is concerning the tyrants Melanchrus and Myrsilus. There is no sign that he ever learned to value Pittacus more justly. A number of recent critics have concluded that Alcaeus was a hot-headed partisan with a thoroughly undeveloped sense of political progress, and that the *Stasiôtika* were what they were called and nothing more: songs of a partisan. "All through his stormy life he had neither might nor right on his side," is Denys Page's verdict;[24] and another recent critic speaks of "the violent and largely empty-headed politics of Alcaeus."[25]

Alcaeus was certainly on the wrong side, in some ways at least, but cynicism is not justified. We have no intrinsic grounds for finding Alcaeus's protestations of concern for the *damos* and for political freedom insincere or wrong in aim. There is, in some of the odes, a suggestion that he sought concord and an end of strife; in one celebrated poem (326 and 208) representing the state as a storm-tossed vessel, he can quite reasonably be thought to be writing of the danger of civil strife. And from a fragment of a commentary (305) which contains *lemmata* from poems on political matters, we know that Alcaeus, addressing a certain Mnemon, who had "provided a skiff for the return of Myrsilus," declared that "he did not blame him or take issue with him on that account." One *lemma* in the commentary consists of the words "let there not be war." There is nothing here that seems either violent or empty-headed.[26]

The impression of Alcaeus's ill-tempered pugnacity comes from one matter, his ceaseless abuse of Pittacus, who as *aisymnêtês* no doubt ruled by the will of the people and ruled beneficently. We know that Alcaeus had special reason to nourish a deep and undying hostility toward Pittacus. Rightly or wrongly, Alcaeus thought that Pittacus's conduct in betraying his friends, selling out to the tyrant Myrsilus, and marrying

into the house of Penthilus was all for political advantage. It
would be too much to expect a man of passionate nature (and
such, beyond doubt, Alcaeus was) to feel anything but ever-
lasting hatred for such an adversary. Moreover, as will appear
in the course of this examination of Alcaeus's poetry, a unifying
factor throughout the poet's work is a tendency to decided
moral judgments, with strong emphasis on the virtue of loyalty.
To the treachery of Paris and Helen he reacted as he did to the
treachery of Pittacus—with poetry that expresses a hatred of
disloyalty. It was Alcaeus's misfortune that Pittacus was with
the tide of history and he himself against it.

It is hard to estimate how much poetry Alcaeus wrote. The
number of books in the Alexandrian edition of his works is
unknown; the highest number referred to is ten. The organization of the books is also unknown. It cannot have been by
meter, as it was in the edition of Sappho's poetry, since Poem 1
of Book 1 began with the first line of an Alcaic strophe, while
1. 2 was in Sapphic strophes. Since both were hymns, it is
possible that arrangement was by type, as in the edition of
Pindar's works. Papyrus finds have given no information about
books, and no papyrus fragment is assignable to a specific
book. The passage already cited from Strabo (13. 617) indicates that the political poetry, or some of it, may have formed
a unit, since it was designated *poêmata stasiôtika*.

Few of the extant fragments even give a clear idea of the
form of the poems from which they survive. Seldom is it
possible to conjecture reasonably what their length was, apart
from the likelihood that most of Alcaeus's poems, as Sappho's,
were short, from eight to thirty-two lines.[27] It is a matter of
some importance: if ten lines remain, it makes a difference to
one's comprehension of the poetry if it can be known whether
what remains was ten of twelve or ten of thirty-two or a
hundred and thirty-two lines. Only one poem, 42, on Helen
and Thetis, is complete enough to be studied with entire
confidence concerning its form.[28]

The patterns of structure are not readily apparent in most fragments of Alcaeus's poetry. Two Sapphic strophes, describing an otherwise unkown incident in the political or military career of Alcaeus, illustrate this structural indefiniteness (69):

Ζεῦ πάτερ, Λύδοι μὲν ἐπασχάλαντες
συμφόραισι δισχελίοις στάτηρας
ἄμμ᾽ ἔδωκαν, αἴ κε δυνάμεθ᾽ ἴραν
ἐς πόλιν ἔλθην,

οὐ πάθοντες οὐδάμα πῶσλον οὐδ᾽ ἒν
οὐδὲ γινώσκοντες · ὀ δ᾽ ὠς ἀλώπαξ
ποικιλόφρων εὐμάρεα προλέξαις
ἤλπετο λάσην.

Father Zeus, the Lydians were troubled at our misfortunes and gave us two thousand staters if we could make our way to the (holy?) city,

Though they had never had any good from us, or known us. But he, like a crafty-minded fox, foretelling an easy issue, thought he would deceive us.

It is a reasonable guess that the fox is Pittacus, that "we" are in exile, and that the Lydians, perhaps to divide and conquer, are backing the exiles in an assault on a city of Lesbos which may have been Mytilene or a city, otherwise unknown, named Hiera or Ira. The nature of the fox's deceit is obscure, but the general point of the eight lines is obvious enough: to contrast the straightforward cooperativeness of the Lydian strangers with the double-dealing of the fox. The two strophes may be a whole poem. The sense seems complete, the structure implies no connection with anything following, and papyrus evidence reveals that nothing preceded these lines.[29] The end coincides with the bottom of a roll and lacks the usual indication, by the *coronis*, that this is the end of the poem. It is tempting to assume that these eight lines, with their succinct dramatic and moral picture, are the entire poem; and both the brevity and the dramatic, contrastive form would accord very well with what appears to be Alcaeus's style in poems on mythological matters. But since in fact the political poems whose dimensions can be judged are substantially longer it is hard to be confident of such brevity here, and the stanzas themselves offer no guidance.

The most obvious feature of Alcaeus's poetry is the degree to which it is concerned with politics. In this characteristic it continues the intensely personal and self-centered spirit of Archilochus. Sappho's expression of this aspect of the lyric tradition is as intense, but very different in content. There is barely a word in the whole range of Sappho's remaining poetry that can be connected with politics. Though she must surely have been aware of the turmoil going on, since she was, apparently, materially affected by it, politics did not stand in any central position in Sappho's emotional life.

A second outstanding feature of Alcaeus's poetry is its range. Though politics fills probably half the substantial surviving pieces, the variety of the rest is still very striking: convivial songs of various types and moods, literary hymns to deities and other objects of real or nominal veneration, poems on a variety of mythical topics, a few poems of love, and poems of friendship and moral or philosophical reflection. Variety of form is substantial; in addition to the Alcaic and Sapphic strophes, which are the most commonly used in what remains, there are several four-line strophe forms of other Aeolic cola and one in Ionic (10), several two-line strophes of Aeolic cola, and some iambic and dactylic meters. There is also an impressive variety and, it seems, independence in the treatment of themes. The use of allegory is extensive and varied.[30] Alcaeus's treatment of myth includes a wide choice of standard stories. There are Trojan War themes such as Helen and Paris (283), Thetis and Achilles (44), Ajax and Cassandra (248); there is a probable reference to the story of Perseus (255); the stories of Sisyphus (38), the

Hydra (443), Endymion (317),[31] and the Dioscuri (34) occur. There is also a good deal of rather learned, special, localized material, such as a hymn to an obscure Thessalian form of Athena (325).

A particularly striking example of Alcaeus's apparent originality in composition is provided by Fr. 10, of which only three lines, not consecutive, preserve more than single words. In the first line of the poem, a speaker of feminine gender refers to herself in desperate terms:

ἔμε δείλαν, ἔμε παῖσαν κακοτάτων πεδέχοισαν . . .

Wretched me, participant in every sorrow . . .

The other preserved lines, known from papyrus evidence to have been the fourth and fifth of the poem, are too uncertain in exact meaning to justify inclusion, but there is a very good likelihood that they give the reason for the speaker's distress, and that it is the mating cry of a stag, inspiring fear in the breast of the speaker, presumably a doe. Both form and content are most unusual. The pure Ionic meter is a striking and relatively rare rhythm, especially in verses as long as this; the nearest parallel in monody occurs in a part-line of Alcaeus which may come from this poem. The use of the first person, in the first line of the poem, by a speaker who cannot be identified with the poet, introduces a style of dramatic presentation unique in early poetry. Archilochus had already introduced speaking animals, in his fables, but the analogy is not very close, nor is that of the passage (Fr. 22) in which Archilochus ascribes words of apparent wisdom to "Charon the carpenter." In none of these Archilochian fragments is there evidence of the apparent emotional empathy that makes this passage so remarkable.

One more general characteristic to be noted is Alcaeus's penchant for literary imitation. Surprising though it is in a poet whose work so often seems to reflect his immediate life,

and whose life seems so active and impulsive, this literary
quality is a substantial fact in the poetry of Alcaeus. The most
striking of these imitations is a summons to an unnamed friend
to drink; the summer heat and the consequent general thirst
provide the occasion (347):

> τέγγε πλεύμονας οἴνῳ, τὸ γὰρ ἄστρον περιτέλλεται,
> ἀ δ᾽ ὤρα χαλέπα, πάντα δὲ δίψαισ᾽ ὑπὰ καύματος,
> ἄχει δ᾽ ἐκ πετάλων ἄδεα τέττιξ . . .
> ἄνθει δὲ σκόλυμος, νῦν δὲ γύναικες μιαρώταται
> λέπτοι δ᾽ ἄνδρες, ἐπεὶ . . . κεφάλαν καὶ γόνα Σείριος
> ἄσδει . . .

Wet your lungs with wine, for the star returns
And the cruel season; everything thirsts from the heat.

The grasshopper chirps sweetly from the leaves . . .

The artichoke blooms, and now women are a plague
And men are weak, when Sirius burns head and knees . . .

These lines are a close imitation, in places only a rendering
from hexameters to Asclepiads, of Hesiod, *Works and Days*
582–87. But it is no mere copy. There is ingenuity, for instance,
in the echoing of ἠχέτα τέττιξ by ἄχει . . . τέττιξ, preserving
the sound as well as the sense, even though wording and syntax
have to be changed. The transformation from Hesiod's picture
of a hot summer day, fit for a shady seat, wine, milk, and
curds—essentially a pastoral picture—to what is in essence an
invitation to drink, is both reminiscent and original in tone
and effect. Alcaeus changes Hesiod's women from μαχλόταται,
"most lustful," to μιαρώταται, literally "most foul," his men
from ἀφαυρότατοι, "most feeble" to λέπτοι, literally "thin," or
"slight." The point is not clear, because we do not know
exactly the tone and connotations of Alcaeus's words, both of
which seem oddly chosen in relation to context and to Hesiod's
words. I assume that the words were meant to be surprising,

especially in relation to the Hesiodic model, and that their
effect is that of light satire.

Less extreme but still clear instances of literary imitation are
the Hymn to the Dioscuri (34), which has echoes of a *Homeric
Hymn* to the Dioscuri, a version of Thetis's plea to Zeus in
Iliad 1. 44, and an account of how Alcaeus—like Archilochus—
abandoned his shield.[32] It is reasonable to assume that Alcaeus
really lost his shield, and did not simply pretend to have,
because of Archilochus's poem. The abandonment of a shield
must have been a common phenomenon of battle, but most
men did not write poems on the subject, and it seems probable
that Alcaeus was led to write about the incident because
Archilochus had done so. From Archilochus he took also the
political allegory of storms at sea, some phraseology for an
attack on the traitor Pittacus,[33] and perhaps the use of animal
imagery with moral connotations, as in the fox of Fr. 69. The
likelihood of Sapphic influence has already been mentioned.[34]

Alcaeus, a man of action and the poet of those actions, is,
like Archilochus, also a man of the Muses, though he was not,
to our knowledge, moved to declare himself so, as Archilochus
was. This responsiveness to literary influence fits with Alcaeus's
learnedness about the forms of myth that he follows—the rare
Itonian Athena, the western version of the story of Endymion,
the unusual parentage (Iris and Zephyrus) he gives for Eros—
either a learned allegorical sally or a reflection of an obscure
version.

Though Alcaeus apparently had a reputation as a poet of
love, including the love of boys, there is remarkably little
evidence of it in the fragments. Of the poems addressed to
boys there is little or no trace;[35] we have only Horace's declaration that Alcaeus "sang of Lycus, beautiful with his dark
hair and dark eyes" (*Odes* 1. 32. 10). Only three fragments
certainly deal with love, and not one of them is a personal
love poem of Alcaeus. One is a mere scrap in which "the
wiles of the Cyprian born" are mentioned (380); another

perhaps concerns the love experience of a friend,[36] and is
chiefly memorable for a fine phrase descriptive of nature, "The
gates of spring" (296b); the third (10), which we have already
examined, forms part of a dramatic poem, whether monologue
or dialogue.[37]

A number of fragments reveal a warm and articulate feeling
for nature. In addition to the phrase just quoted from 296b
there are several other fragments like it. A single-line fragment
speaks of (319)

βλήχρων ἀνέμων ἀχείμαντοι πνόαι

The stormless breaths of gentle breezes,

and another short passage (345) describes the arrival of various
birds from Oceanus and the limits of the earth. The beginning
of a poem (45) addressed to the river Hebrus suggests the
poet's interest in nature and, though the fragment is in bad
condition, there is enough to suggest that its description of girls
bathing in the Hebrus—possibly a reminiscence of the incident
of Nausicaa and her attendants at the beginning of *Odyssey* 6—
was a vivid scene. A papyrus fragment (286), badly broken,
has something about "much flowering," "harsh frost," and
"calm over the surface of the sea;" perhaps it was a song
celebrating the return of spring, and it may, as Page suggests,[38]
be imitated in Horace's *solvitur acris hiems*. One other fragment
of nature description (115a) has words reminiscent of Sappho's
ostrakon hymn (LP 2), and possibly owes something to it in
phraseology. It is striking how often the evidence of papyrus
fragments differs from that of the indirect tradition. We had
been led to expect much on love; we find little on love, and
that little not as personal and emotional as we should expect.
In a man who spent his life in the excitement of political strife
the storms that drive the Ship of State are appropriate enough,
but we do not expect to find sensitivity to the quiet charm and
the flowering of nature.

In this variety there are four dominant topics or types: poems on political themes, poems of fellowship and wine, hymns, and poems on themes of mythology. If we examine the principal fragments in each group, it will, I think, help to illuminate some formal qualities of Alcaeus's poetry, to the extent that form can be determined, as well as illustrate his ways of handling different themes.

Two fragments, 129 and 130, are the longest examples of Alcaeus's political poetry, and they exemplify most of the qualities of Alcaeus's poetry in general. 129 is in Alcaic strophes; the length of the original poem is unknown, but it is not improbable that the thirty-two lines of which the papyrus gives evidence were the entire poem. The first twenty-four lines (if the first line apparent on the papyrus is in fact the first line of the poem) are, apart from the beginnings of the first two lines and a few gaps elsewhere, intact:

> . . . τόδε Λέσβιοι
> . . . εὔδειλον τέμενος μέγα
> ξῦνον κάτεσσαν, ἐν δὲ βώμοις
> ἀθανάτων μακάρων ἔθηκαν
>
> κἀπωνύμασσαν ἀντίαον Δία
> σὲ δ' Αἰολήαν κυδαλίμαν θέον
> πάντων γενέθλαν, τὸν δὲ τέρτον
> τόνδε κεμήλιον ὠνύμασσαν
>
> Ζόννυσσον ὠμήσταν. ἄγιτ' εὔνοον
> θῦμον σκέθοντες ἀμμετέρας ἄρας
> ἀκούσατ', ἐκ δὲ τῶνδε μόχθων
> ἀργαλέας τε φύγας ῥύεσθε ·
>
> τὸν Ὕρραον δὲ παῖδα πεδελθέτω
> κήνων Ἐρίννυς ὥς ποτ' ἀπώμνυμεν
> τόμοντες ἄ . . .
> μηδάμα μηδ' ἔνα τὼν ἑταίρων
>
> ἀλλ' ἢ θάνοντες γᾶν ἐπιέμμενοι
> κείσεσθ' ὐπ' ἄνδρων οἳ τότ' ἐπικ . . . ην

ἤπειτα κακκτάνοντες αὔτοις
δᾶμον ὑπὲξ ἀχέων ῥύεσθαι.

κήνων ὁ φύσγων οὐ διελέξατο
πρὸς θῦμον ἀλλὰ βραϊδίως πόσιν
ἔμβαις ἐπ᾽ ὀρκίοισι δάπτει
τὰν πόλιν ἄμμι δέδ . . . αις

οὐ κὰν νόμον

. . .

. . .

Μύρσιλ . . .

. . . This the Lesbians built as a great and far-seen shrine,
to be shared by all, and in it they set altars of blessed immortal
gods,

And called upon Zeus as the god of suppliants, and upon
you, glorious Aeolian goddess, as the parent of all, and this
third one, treasured deity, they called

Dionysus the devourer of raw flesh. Now with propitious
spirit hear our prayer, and deliver us from these toils and from
the grief of exile;

But as for the son of Hyrrhas, may the Erinys of those
men pursue him, because once we swore a solemn oath . . .
never to forsake any one of the companions,

But either to die, and clad in earth to lie, downed by those
men who then held power, or else to kill them and deliver
the state from its woes.

But that pot-belly took no account of *their* will, and readily
trampled upon the oaths, and snaps at the city . . .[39]

There are small fragments of one further strophe, probably
containing the name of Myrsilus, and the presence of a *coronis*
shows that the poem ended one strophe beyond that. For the
political and religious history of Lesbos it provides evidence of
great importance. The son of Hyrrhas is Pittacus, and we have

here first-hand confirmation of the exile of Alcaeus and the
defection of Pittacus from the party to which Alcaeus belonged;
the assumption can hardly be resisted that the conspiracy
referred to was against Myrsilus. The trinity of Zeus, Hera,
and Dionysus is apparently a local Lesbian cult, mentioned
also in a poem by Sappho (17).[40]

The spirit and the general trend of thought are clear: a
solemn invocation of the Lesbian trinity is followed by the
poet's supplication to the deities of that trinity; the supplication
is in two closely linked parts, a prayer for deliverance from
exile, balanced by a curse upon the son of Hyrrhas, with the
rest of the fragment giving the reason for the curse by describing the conspiracy and Pittacus's betrayal of it. The
language is simple, with scarcely any kind of striking metaphor.
Here as elsewhere in Alcaeus's poetry a vividly evoked scene—
here the sanctuary of the trinity, elsewhere sometimes a vignette
from mythology—has the force often provided by poetic
imagery; the emotional center of the poem is the curse which
embodies the reminiscence of the conspiracy, and the emphasis
on the shrine and the trinity lends solemnity to the curse. The
closeknit organization of invocation, prayer, and imprecation
lends dramatic energy, and is supported by the repeated
κήνων ("those men," lines 15 and 21), each time at the beginning
of the verse, with its stress on the remote but powerful presence
of those of the conspirators who died (for surely Erinys in line
14 ensures that "those men" are in fact dead); they remain a
general (such is the effect of the pronoun) and menacing force
to underline and justify the intensity of the poet's hatred.

The abuse of Pittacus after the solemn oath is somewhat
unfortunate in emotional effect. There is power in the steady
movement from the description of the sanctuary to the prayer
to the curse; but in the climactic expression Alcaeus gives to
his anger there is more violence than power. Violence of statement is not necessarily bad, but here it damages the impression
of the passage as a whole. A deeply serious, religious atmosphere

has been created; with the abusive and not particularly relevant word φύσγων ("pot-belly") the tone changes at once. The image created is comic, we are suddenly in the realm of satire, and Alcaeus's anger runs the risk of appearing to have more personal animus than political idealism.

The other long papyrus fragment of political poetry (130) consists of very broken scraps of fifteen lines, a section of twenty lines fairly well preserved, scraps of four more lines, and the *coronis* indicating that the thirty-ninth line of the fragment was the final line of a poem. It is probable that a new poem begins at line 16.[41] If it does, then we again have much the largest part of a poem. The meter is a four-line stanza with a combination of cola not found elsewhere though entirely within the normal range of Aeolic metrical form. Once again the poet is in exile:

> . . . ὀ τάλαις ἔγω
> ζώω μοῖραν ἔχων ἀγροϊωτίκαν
> ἰμέρρων ἀγόρας ἄκουσαι
> καρυζομένας ὦγεσιλαΐδα
>
> καὶ βόλλας · τὰ πάτηρ καὶ πάτερος πάτηρ
> καγγεγήρασ' ἔχοντες πεδὰ τωνδέων
> τὼν ἀλλαλοκάκων πολίταν
> ἔγωγ' ἀπὺ τούτων ἀπελήλαμαι
>
> φεύγων ἐσχατίαισ', ὠς δ' Ὀνυμακλέης
> ἔνθαδ' οἶος ἐοίκησα λυκαιμίαις
> . . . ον πόλεμον · στάσιν γὰρ
> πρὸς κρ . . . οὐκ ἄμεινον ὀννέλην
>
> . . . μακάρων ἐς τέμενος θέων
> . . . μελαίνας ἐπίβαις χθόνος
> . . . συνόδοισι μ' αὔταις
> οἴκημμι κάκων ἔκτος ἔχων πόδας,
>
> ὄππαι Λεσβίαδες κριννόμεναι φύαν
> πώλεντ' ἐλκεσίπεπλοι, περὶ δὲ βρέμει

ἄχω θεσπεσία γυναίκων
ἴρας ὀλολύγας ἐνιαυσίας
. . .

. . . Unhappily I live, enduring a rustic lot, longing, O son of Agesilaos, to hear the assembly summoned,

And the council. What my father and my father's father grew old possessing among these citizens who destroy one another, from those things I am driven away,

And as an exile at the fringes I live here alone, like Onymacles, in wolf thickets (?) . . . planning war, for to destroy our faction against (those who are stronger) is not the better choice.

. . . Near the shrine of the blessed gods, . . . treading the black earth . . . in the assemblies . . . I dwell, keeping my steps free of trouble,

Where the Lesbian women in contests of beauty go to and fro in their trailing robes, and the marvellous cry of women fills the air, the sacred yearly chant . . .

Here the poem breaks off, with only scraps of the last stanza visible.[42]

Alcaeus, we are here told, had an inherited preeminence in the state; the "assembly" and the "council" are most unlikely to have had the democratic inclusiveness of the fifth-century Athenian institutions of like name.[43] The council, at least, would have been restricted to an aristocratic minority. Nothing is known about the son of Agesilaos. The beauty contests of Lesbos, formerly known only from later writers,[44] took place at a shrine of Hera, and hence it is probable that Alcaeus's place of exile is the same as in 129, the shrine of the trinity.[45]

The simplicity and directness of the poet's emotions, as expressed in the first part of the poem, are given some depth by the evocation of lost dignity, and the reminiscence of Achilles in Book 1 of the *Iliad*, longing for the cry of battle and staying away from "the assembly that brings glory to men," whether or not the echo is deliberate, adds dimension to this. Alcaeus becomes, for the moment, a reflection of Achilles. At the end there is another sharply imagined scene, full of localism and particularity, and with it the Homeric epithet ἑλκεσίπεπλοι ("with trailing robes"), which continues, slightly but definitely, the more remote, epic tone introduced by the evocation of Achilles. The combination of longing for the past and the poet's emotional and aesthetic reaction to the ceremonial beauty contest has some of the dramatic quality that is found elsewhere in Alcaeus's poems. The contrast of scenes is made sharp by the contrast between the herald's summons and the religious cry of the women in the ceremony. The sense of resignation of the intervening reflection, "To destroy our faction is not the better choice," forms a bridge from the poet's despair to a perception of the beauty of the scene around him. But it cannot be said that the fragment conveys any concerted, organized sense, beyond the mere fact of its sensitive report of Alcaeus's emotional experiences.

Alcaeus's abuse of Pittacus was celebrated. A sentence in Diogenes Laertius[46] tells us that "he called him 'flat-foot' . . . and 'chap-foot,' because of the cracks on his feet . . . and 'prancer,' . . . and *physkôn* (the same word as occurs in Fr. 129. 21) and *gastrôn* because he was fat, and 'him who sups in the dark' as being without lamps (presumably a reference either to stinginess or uncouthness) and 'swept up' because he was slovenly and dirty." The list is not notable for any suggestion of subtlety or elegance in Alcaeus's attack. It reads rather like a reference to Aristophanic passages; Alcaeus's words are comically abusive rather than seriously critical. The words are also graphic, and this is the manner also of the two most legible papyrus fragments that illustrate Alcaeus's abuse of Pittacus. Fr. 72, extremely uncertain in meaning, appears to be an attack on Pittacus's forebears:

πίμπλεισιν ἀκράτω . . . ἐπ᾽ ἀμέρᾳ
καὶ νύκτι παφλάσδει . . .
ἔνθα νόμος θάμ᾽ . . .

κῆνος δὲ τούτων οὐκ ἐπελάθετο
ὤνηρ, ἐπεὶ δὴ πρῶτον ὀνέτροπε,
παίσαις γὰρ ὀννώρινε νύκτας,
τὼ δὲ πίθω πατάγεσκ᾽ ὀ πύθμην.

σὺ δὴ τεαύτας ἐκγεγόνων ἔχῃς
τὰν δόξαν, οἴαν ἄνδρες ἐλεύθεροι
ἔσλων ἔοντες ἐκ τοκήων . . .

. . . fills (the cups) with unmixed wine . . . day and night
foams . . . where custom often . . .

But that man did not forget these things when first he
brought disorder, for he roused up all the nights, and the
bottom of the wine cask kept ringing.

But you, sprung from such a woman, are you to have the
same repute as free men, men from goodly parents?

"That man" may be Pittacus's father, Hyrrhas, and his
reputed Thracian origin[47] would provide a ready basis for
attack on him as a rowdy drinker, since Thracians traditionally
had this reputation.[48] (The "ringing" presumably means that
the cask kept being emptied.) The "you" is then Pittacus, but
there is no clue as to why Alcaeus refers thus to his mother, of
whom our only other information is that she was "a woman of
Lesbos."[49] The strain of vigorous personal abuse is about all
that is clear in this puzzle. The contrast and confrontation
suggested by "But that man . . ." and "But you . . ." are in
their terseness and dramatic vigor like the sudden turn to "the
son of Hyrrhas" at line 13 of Fr. 129, but here the drama is
hard to see in the midst of general textual confusion. A tone of
aristocratic exclusiveness is conspicuous in the adjectives ἔσλων
and ἐλεύθεροι.

Fr. 70 is another attack on Pittacus, combined with a call

for unity and an end to strife among kindred. Twelve lines
remain, three four-line stanzas of an Aeolic combination of cola.
The first preserved stanza is apparently concerned with the
carousing of Pittacus, for it refers to "the lyre, feasting with
idle braggarts,"[50] and then the poet continues:

κῆνος δὲ παώθεις Ἀτρεΐδαν . . .
δαπτέτω πόλιν ὡς καὶ πεδὰ Μυρσίλω
θᾶς κ' ἄμμε βόλλητ' Ἄρευς ἐπὶ τεύχεσι[51]
τρόπην · ἐκ δὲ χόλω τῶδε λαθοίμεθ' . . .

χαλάσσομεν δὲ τὰς θυμοβόρω λύας
ἐμφύλω τε μάχας, τάν τις Ὀλυμπίων
ἔνωρσε, δᾶμον μὲν εἰς αὐάταν ἄγων
Φιττάκω δὲ δίδοις κῦδος ἐπήρατον.

> But let that man, become kin with the Atridae, snap at the
> city as he did with Myrsilus, until Ares is pleased to turn us to
> our weapons. But would that we might forget our anger,

> And let us end soul-devouring strife and battle among
> kindred, which some one of the immortals has raised,
> bringing the state to ruin[52] but giving Pittacus the glory he
> prayed for.

Apparently Alcaeus is calling for a closing of the ranks of his
own group, no doubt largely the same group as in the conspiracy of Poem 129. Perhaps the defection of Pittacus caused
general dissension in the party; but there is likely to have been
some lapse of time, since this poem clearly comes after the
death of Myrsilus, whereas 129 appears to have been composed
immediately on the defection of Pittacus from the *hetairia*.
Though "Atridae" is a legitimate title for descendants of
Orestes, there is obviously mockery in this Homeric allusion
to Pittacus's politically expedient marriage. But the Homeric
suggestions of the disastrous quarrel raised by an immortal are
grimly earnest, like the reminiscence of Achilles in Poem 130.
The contrastive, dramatic style (from κῆνος, "that man," to

the "we" of χαλάσσομεν, "let us end," and the particles μέν . . .
δέ at the end) is like that of 129, 130, and 72.

Political poetry contains several examples of Alcaeus's use
of what was to become the most familiar of political allegories,
the Ship of State. Fr. 326 is quoted by the commentator
Heraclitus (first century A.D.?) in the *Quaestiones Homericae*. It
is the beginning of a poem (two stanzas of Alcaic strophe and
a line of a third remain), and Heraclitus says that it has to do
with Myrsilus and "the tyrannical conspiracy being raised
against the Mytileneans":

ἀσυννέτημμι τὼν ἀνέμων στάσιν,
τὸ μὲν γὰρ ἔνθεν κῦμα κυλίνδεται,
τὸ δ' ἔνθεν, ἄμμες δ' ὂν τὸ μέσσον
νᾶϊ φορήμμεθα σὺν μελαίνᾳ

χείμωνι μόχθεντες μεγάλῳ μάλα ·
πὲρ μὲν γὰρ ἄντλος ἰστοπέδαν ἔχει,
λαῖφος δὲ πὰν ζάδηλον ἤδη,
καὶ λάκιδες μέγαλαι κὰτ αὖτο,

χόλαισι δ' ἄγκυραι, τὰ δ' ὀήϊα . . .

I do not understand the set[53] of the winds,
For on this side one wave rolls up
And on that another, and we in the midst
Are carried along in our black ship

Much distressed by the great storm.
Shipped water rises about the mast stand,
The sail is now torn through,
Great rents appear in it,

The anchors are loose,[54] and the rudders . . .

There is not enough to tell us much about the application of
the image. The scene is not as effective in suggesting political
troubles as the beetling cliffs and black clouds of Archilochus'
political allegory (56). Alcaeus appears less interested in the
appropriateness of the image than in its intrinsic expressiveness

and pictorial vividness. The emphasis is like that of the Homeric simile, with its tendency to independent development.[55] There is also an analogy in some of Sappho's poems, notably Fr. 96.[56]

There appears to be political meaning in a small papyrus fragment (73), likewise in Alcaics:

καὶ κύματι πλάγεισα
ὄμβρῳ μάχεσθαι . . .
φαῖσ' οὐδὲν ἰμέρρην . . .
δ' ἔρματι τυπτομένα

κήνα μὲν ἐν τούτ . . .
τούτων λελάθων ὦ . . .
σύν τ' ὔμμι τέρπ . . .
καὶ πεδὰ Βύκχιδος . . .

τὼ δ' ἄμμες ἐς τὰν ἄψερον . . .

Wave-beaten, she declares that she has no desire to fight the storm, but striking a reef . . .

She, then . . . in this . . . forgetting these things . . . (I would) take my pleasure, and be festive with you and with Bycchis,

But we for the next (day) . . .

A ship is represented as declaring itself (or, with a slightly different restoration, having somebody declare it) ready to give up the struggle and dash itself upon a reef. Then the poet seems to turn from the ship and speak in his own person. The fragment may suggest something like this: the ship is too completely shattered to continue her voyage, that is, our immediate cause is lost (Myrsilus has succeeded in seizing power?); but, friends, let us not lose our ability to enjoy life; tomorrow we shall try some new approach for our cause.[57]

The resilience of spirit and the absence of abusiveness are refreshing, but of course abuse may be lacking only because we do not have the whole poem.[58] The turn from the wrecked

ship to the survivors has, in wording and spirit, something of
the dramatic contrast that we have noticed frequently in
Alcaeus. The ship is sometimes taken, needlessly, to mean only
the faction of Alcaeus, not the whole state. I see no grounds for
thinking that Alcaeus distinguished between disaster for Lesbos
and disaster for his faction. In 326 the ship can well be the
state as a whole, and it seems also to be such in one further
example of the Ship of State that deserves special mention.
Fr. 6, in Alcaics as are all the political metaphors metrically
identifiable, again is concerned with the upheaval caused by
Myrsilus:

> τὸ δ᾽ αὖτε κῦμα τὼ προτέρω νόμω[59]
> στείχει, παρέξει δ᾽ ἄμμι πόνον πόλυν
> ἄντλην, ἐπεί κε νᾶος ἔμβα
> . . .
>
> . . .
>
> . . .
> φαρξώμεθ᾽ ὡς ὤκιστα νᾶα
> ἐς δ᾽ ἔχυρον λίμενα δρόμωμεν,
>
> καὶ μή τιν᾽ ὄκνος μόλθακος
> λάβη · πρόδηλον γάρ . . .
> μνάσθητε τὼ πάροιθε . . .
> νῦν τις ἄνηρ δόκιμος γενέσθω ·
>
> καὶ μὴ καταισχύνωμεν
> ἔσλοις τόκηας γᾶς ὔπα κειμένοις . . .

Here again a wave like the one before
Comes on, and we shall have much toil
To bale it out, when it enters the ship . . .

Let us shore up our ship as quickly as we can
And run into a secure harbor,

And let no soft hesitation come
Upon us; clear before us . . .
Be mindful of the former . . .
Now let each man be steadfast

>   And let us not put to shame
>   Our brave forebears lying underground . . .

Traces of another seventeen lines remain, but they yield
nothing consecutive, and only one word, "monarchy," that
helps the interpretation of the poem. Only that word gives any
internal indication of allegory. But there is no reasonable
doubt;[60] the references to the ancestors, the mention of hesitation, the thought of the forebears lying under the ground, all
sound more like a call to battle than to save a ship in
distress.

   Other fragments introduce the same or a closely related
metaphor. In 249 Alcaeus warns, "One must look from
the land before a voyage; once at sea, he must obey the wind
that prevails." In 167 the name Phrynon and the word "ship"
appear in close proximity. But these and other scraps of
political poetry, though they provide glimpses of Alcaeus's
emotions and experiences and no doubt would deserve close
attention in a biographical essay,[61] add little to our picture of
Alcaeus's poetry.

   It is tempting to try to chart the voyage of Alcaeus's Ship by
reconstructing a time-table of political events out of the statements and moods of the political poems. One might guess at
the following: 249 gives the first warning against the troubles
the poet foresees; 6 and 326 (plus 208) are rallying cries against
the imminent threat of Myrsilus, with the second describing a
later and more desperate state of affairs than the first. Fr. 73
comes after Myrsilus has seized power and the ship of the
Lesbian state has run on the rocks. To this period belongs
another fragment of political poetry, 114, which gives us
nothing more than a dozen intriguing line beginnings, with
the words "well," "may they grant," "thus . . . a man . . .
bravery . . . now," and "others . . . this land" (we may yet
fare well; may the gods grant us aid; thus with bravery may a
man win out, though now others hold this land[?]), but is

accompanied by a commentary which says that the poem was
written during Alcaeus's first exile, when, after Alcaeus and
his group had plotted against Myrsilus and the plot had been
revealed, they escaped before harm came and fled to Pyrrha.
The first three of these poems show a relatively self-contained
though urgent mood. Then, in 73 and 114, an encounter has
been lost, Myrsilus is in power, Alcaeus and his group are in
exile; courage remains, and a zest for life, and hope of future
success. This is the period of the aristocratic conspiracy against
Myrsilus, and perhaps the songs of conviviality are from it.
Where precisely the death of Myrsilus fits into the pattern is
unknown. Disaster struck when Pittacus, and perhaps others
less notable, defected, whether justifiably and even nobly, or,
as Alcaeus thought, basely. 129 must come early in this period,
when the wound of Pittacus's betrayal is very fresh. Then come
the poems of bitterness, the attacks on Pittacus and his family
(70, 72), the endless words of abuse, and the anguish and
loneliness of 130. But this is of course all speculation.[62]

Poem 73 is political, but it is also a poem of conviviality;
Alcaeus bids his friends join him in festiveness. The surviving
fragments and the witness of Horace let us know that Alcaeus
was noted for poetry on convivial themes. Before we turn to
some other poems on this topic a further word on Alcaeus's use
of allegory is necessary. In 73, as in the other examples we have
looked at, the meaning is political, but allegory is used in
other contexts too. A fragment of commentary (306, fr. 14,
col. ii) explains an elaborate image in a poem not preserved
except in a few lemmata of the commentary. The state does
not appear, but a ship does, and is likened to an aging courtesan. Which was metaphor and which objective reality is not
certain, but some phrases in the commentary seem to say that
points concerning the ship stand for aspects of the woman,
and so it seems more likely that the ship is here again the
image, the woman the real subject. If she is, the poem was
perhaps the model for Horace's unkind poems on aging

mistresses (*Odes* 1. 25; 4. 13). Whichever is the metaphor,[63] the evidence of the commentary suggests that Alcaeus pursued it with a good deal of ingenuity and, it would seem, originality.[64]

The Ship of State is Alcaeus's most conspicuous contribution to the language of poetry, and to a remarkable degree he is, apparently, responsible for the development of this metaphor. He may have been familiar with Archilochus's metaphors in Frs. 56 and 56a, but there is no evidence that the particularity and realism that mark his use of it have any precedent. There are, of course, similes of the sea and ships in the *Iliad*, the *Odyssey* is full of voyages and storms, and Archilochus—apart from Fr. 56—has poetry on shipwreck, the savage *dyspemptikon* (79a), the elegy on the loss of his brother-in-law at sea, and the new iambic fragment (POxy 2310, fr. 1), the latter part of which is concerned with a voyage and shipwreck. For an islander like Alcaeus the language of ships is natural, not only because he is likely to be experienced in ship travel and its perils, but because he is in daily life kept aware of the sea and its moods. Alcaeus's ship-pictures are dramatic and intense reflections of his political experience. It is suggestive for Alcaeus's affinities that in Greek literature the fullest development of the Ship of State subsequent to his use of it is in the drama of the fifth century.

Although Alcaeus's Ship is usually called an allegory, the term is a bit misleading; it is not so explicitly allegorical as the figure later became, as in Horace's Ship of State, *Odes* 1. 14.[65] Allegory is clearly the appropriate term for Theognis 667–82, where, though the figure of the ship in a storm is drawn with care, even more care is taken to ensure that the reader is aware of the political events that are being illustrated. Some of the alleged shipboard activities are more germane to the city of Megara than to a voyage (677–80):

χρήματα δ' ἁρπάζουσι βίῃ, κόσμος δ' ἀπόλωλεν,
δασμὸς δ' οὐκέτ' ἴσος γίνεται ἐς τὸ μέσον ·

φορτηγοὶ δ᾽ ἄρχουσι, κακοὶ δ᾽ ἀγαθῶν καθύπερθεν.
δειμαίνω, μή πως ναῦν κατὰ κῦμα πίῃ.

They seize our property with violence, order is destroyed.
No fair and common division of tribute is made;
Our rulers are dealers in cargo; the low are above the noble.
I fear that a wave will drink down the ship.

The ship in line 680 is an afterthought to bolster the allegory. Objective reference is carefully maintained, but the image is dulled by the introduction of such non-nautical words as χρήματα ("money") and δασμός ("tribute"). To Alcaeus the state becomes the ship; "the reality is quite subordinated to the image,"[66] just as in Fr. 96 of Sappho the distinction between a beautiful girl and a moonlit night-scene is hardly maintained and the two concepts blend. As in the political contexts of 129 and 130, Alcaeus's imagination is gripped by a vivid and familiar scene. His myths, as we shall see, are like this, and the same precision, detail, and realism mark his description of a hall full of armor that awaits use in battle (357).

This delight in vivid and detailed description of the world of the poet's experience—ships, armor, familiar Homeric stories—has its parallel in Sappho's poetry, though Sappho's range is narrower, more personal, and more sensuous. Both poets are close in this respect to Homer. Alcaeus is closer because of the similarity of matter; Homer's descriptions, both the detailed precision of the similes and the repeated incidents of arming, sacrifice, embarkation, and the like, have the same concern for accuracy and the particular. In Alcaeus these detailed scenes are the principal adornment of the poetry. There is very little of the varied imagery that is so strikingly prevalent in Pindar's poetry.

Athenaeus, to whom we owe so much Greek convivial poetry, preserves this example of Alcaeus's symposiac art (346):

πώνωμεν · τί τὰ λύχν᾽ ὀμμένομεν; δάκτυλος ἀμέρα ·
κὰδ δ᾽ ἄερρε κυλίχναις μεγάλαις, οὔατα ποικίλαις ·

οἶνον γὰρ Σεμέλας καὶ Δίος υἶος λαθικάδεα
ἀνθρώποισιν ἔδωκ'. ἔγχεε κέρναις ἔνα καὶ δύο
πλήαις κἀκ κεφάλας, ἀ δ' ἀτέρα τὰν ἀτέραν κύλιξ
ὠθήτω.

Let us drink. Why wait for the lamps? Only a finger of the
   day is left.
Lift down the large drinking cups with decorated ears.[67]
For the son of Semele and Zeus gave wine to man to bring
Surcease from care. Mix one of water with two of wine
And pour and fill the cups to the brim, and let one cup
Crowd another.

The lines are in the long greater Asclepiadean meter; the style
and language are informal and dramatic; asyndeton abounds,
strengthening the air of abrupt urgency in this call to pleasure.
The cups are to be festive, large, well-filled, and frequent, the
mixture unusually strong;[68] the justification, with its creden-
tials from myths, is naive and plain. Other fragments dedicated
to the pleasure of the symposium are 322, with its allusion to
the *kottabos* ("The last drops flying from Teian cups"), a game
in which the last drops of wine were thrown at a target,[69] and
338, with its picture of storm without, comfort and wine within,
which Horace imitates at the start of *Odes* 1. 9, *Vides ut alta
stet.* In the same context with 346, Athenaeus gives us one
Alcaic strophe, almost certainly the first of a poem, in much
the same mood, but more lyrically, less dramatically, expressed (335):

οὐ χρῆ κάκοισι θῦμον ἐπιτρέπην,
προκόψομεν γὰρ οὐδὲν ἀσάμενοι
ὦ Βύκχι, φαρμάκων δ' ἄριστον
οἶνον ἐνεικαμένοις μεθύσθην.

To yield the spirit to sorrows is not right;
Grieving gets us nothing;
The best of remedies, my Bycchis, is
To bring wine and get drunk.

There is less gaiety here, and more tension; it sounds as though
Alcaeus were seeking relief from political disappointments, of
which he had an abundance, and in which Bycchis apparently
shared, to judge from Fr. 73.

In 73 we saw the themes of wine and politics brought together; another small fragment, 206, seems to combine a call
for courage in battle with the setting up of the mixing bowl,[70]
and another, famous as a Horatian model, is the cry of joy at
Myrsilus's death, already quoted, which brings wine into a
frantic celebration of triumph. Alcaeus unites conviviality also
with an artful literary *tour de force*, in his imitation of a Hesiodic
passage.[71] Almost the only detail in these lines that is not taken
from Hesiod is the abrupt and authoritative opening command:

τέγγε πλεύμονας οἴνῳ, τὸ γὰρ ἄστρον . . .

Moisten your throat with wine, the star (is here) . . .

But this detail transforms the piece into a drinking song for
summer. The venerable and didactic Hesiod lends an authority
that parallels the justification by mythology in Fr. 346. The
most finished and complex of the extant drinking songs combines conviviality with reflections on the meaning of life. The
poem is in couplets of lengthened glyconics; the sense is complete in twelve lines and so may the poem be (38):[72]

πῶνε καὶ μέθυ' ὦ Μελάνιππ' ἄμ' ἔμοι · τί φαῖς
ὄταμε . . . δινάεντ' 'Αχέροντα μέγ . . .

ζάβαις ἀελίω κόθαρον φάος ἄψερον
ὄψεσθ'; ἀλλ' ἄγι μὴ μεγάλων ἐπιβάλλεο ·

καί γὰρ Σίσυφος Αἰολίδαις βασίλευς ἔφα
ἄνδρων πλεῖστα νοησάμενος θανάτω κρέτην.

ἀλλὰ καὶ πολύιδρις ἔων ὑπὰ κᾶρι δὶς
δινάεντ' 'Αχέροντ' ἐπέραισε, μ . . .

αὔτῳ μόχθον ἔχην Κρονίδαις βασίλευς κάτω
μελαίνας χθόνος · ἀλλ' ἄγι μὴ τα . . .

... τ' ἀβάσομεν αἴ ποτα κἄλλοτα ...
... ην ὄττινα τῶνδε πάθην τάχα δῶ θέος.

Drink (and get drunk), Melanippus, with me. Why (do you
    fancy)
That when once (you have) crossed eddying Acheron

You will see again the pure light of the sun?
No, do not (aim at) great things;

Why even Sisyphus, Aeolus's son, a king,
Wisest of men, who thought to cheat death,

Even he, for all his cunning, twice by order of fate
Crossed over eddying Acheron, ...

And the king, Cronus's son, (caused) him to have toil
Below the black earth. But come, do not (have such hopes).

While we are young, if ever, (it is right)
(To take) whatever of these things the gods give.

The mutilation is great, but the general movement of the poem
is clear.[73] The Horatian theme of *carpe diem* is set forth with a
proof from mythology, a proof that contrasts the toil and gloom
of what inevitably follows life with the pleasures of the moment.
The repetition of the phrase "eddying Acheron" does not have
the effect of ring composition which we will find often in
Sappho's poems, but only of the naïveté of Lesbian lyric style,
which shows no hesitation about casual repetition of words
and phrases. The fact that the lines have several Homeric
phrases (ποταμῷ ἐπὶ δινήεντι, Ξανθῷ ἐπὶ δινήεντι, etc.) perhaps
lends them a degree of special solemnity justifying repetition.
"Black earth" is of course Homeric, but it has also the particular force of emphasizing the contrast between the darkness
of the world below and the bright pleasure of this one.[74]

Of the other two categories that exemplify Alcaeus's range
of subject and style, the hymns need only brief mention,
because only one remains in any substantial form. We know

of hymns to Apollo, a Thessalian form of Athena, Eros, Hermes, the Dioscuri, and, if hymn is the appropriate word, to the river Hebrus. The hymn to Hermes is said to have been the model for Horace's ode to Hermes,[75] and the incident of the stealing of Apollo's quiver (9–12) is specifically said to have come from Alcaeus. Only the first strophe of Alcaeus's poem, a Sapphic strophe, has been preserved (308). In phraseology, it is like the openings of the two *Homeric Hymns* to Hermes; deliberate imitation seems a reasonable assumption.[76] Of the rest of the poem we know only that it celebrated the birth of Hermes, as we should have supposed, and was the second poem of Alcaeus's first book. The first poem of the first book was a hymn to Apollo, of which only the opening line remains (307), the first line of an Alcaic strophe. The principal source of information about this poem is an extensive paraphrase of it given by Himerius,[77] from which it is clear that Alcaeus, surprisingly for an eastern Greek, tells the story of the Delphic Apollo; that Alcaeus is, in spirit, in accord with the Delphic part of the *Homeric Hymn* to Apollo; and that, in details, he is strikingly independent of it and of any known picture of Apollo. Once again we find in Alcaeus's poetic procedure a breadth of interest beyond the local stories and versions of the Aeolian world, an affinity for the Homeric tradition, and a good deal of special knowledge in the detailed treatment of his subject. In the hymn to Hermes too, in spite of the likeness of the opening to the tradition of the *Homeric Hymns*, his story was different in details from the usual tradition.

The one hymn remaining to us with enough of its form preserved to provide substantial evidence of what the poem was like is the hymn to the Dioscuri (34). What remains is the first three of what were originally six stanzas, in Sapphic strophe. It is a "cletic," that is, an invocatory hymn[78] but there is no way of knowing the occasion of its composition. It may have been composed for a festival in honor of Castor and

Pollux, but it may equally well have had a less formal occasion.
Perhaps it served as a petition for the patronage of the Dioscuri
on the occasion of a voyage to be undertaken. The preserved
part is as follows:[79]

δεῦτέ μοι νᾶσον Πέλοπος λίποντες
παῖδες ἴφθιμοι Δίος ἠδὲ Λήδας,
ἰλλάῳ θύμῳ προφάνητε Κάστορ
καὶ Πολύδευκες,

οἳ κὰτ εὔρηαν χθόνα καὶ θάλασσαν
παῖσαν ἔρχεσθ᾽ ὠκυπόδων ἐπ᾽ ἴππων,
ῥῆα δ᾽ ἀνθρώποις θανάτω ῥύεσθε
ζακρυόεντος

εὐσδύγων θρῴσκοντες ὂν ἄκρα νάων
πήλοθεν, λάμπροι πρότον᾽ ὀντρέχοντες
ἀργάλεα δ᾽ ἐν νύκτι φάος φέροντες
νᾶϊ μελαίνᾳ.

Come to me, leaving the island of Pelops,
Valiant sons of Zeus and Leda,
Appear, Castor and Polydeuces,
With favoring spirit;

Who over the broad earth and all the sea
Journey, borne on swift-footed horses,
And easily deliver men from
Death that chills,

As you leap upon the masts of their well-benched ships
From afar, and, climbing on the forestays, shine,
Bringing light in the grievous night
To the black ship.

What is striking in these stanzas is the combination of tradition
and originality. There are two brief *Homeric Hymns* to the
Dioscuri, 17 and 33. To 17 Alcaeus's poem bears no resemblance; with 33 it shares a few phrases, and the general theme
of the Dioscuri as saviors in storms at sea. Alcaeus's phrase-

ology is thoroughly Homeric (*broad* earth, *swift-footed* horses, *well-benched* ships, *black* ships, the gods coming from afar); the reference, in the invocation, to a place where the worship of the invoked powers is prevalent is a feature also of one of Sappho's hymns to Aphrodite (Fr. 2) and several of the *Homeric Hymns* begin with similar references. The phenomenon of phosphorescent fire, "St. Elmo's fire," which was in antiquity thought to herald the arrival of the Dioscuri and rescue from the storm, is possibly alluded to in the Homeric hymn, but the emphasis given to it is probably Alcaeus's own idea.[80] It is really this picture, along with the transformation of Homeric language into Sapphic strophe, that gives the passage its character. The brightness of the arriving deities and their easy leap onto the riggings of the distressed ship contrast with the labor of the mariners. The last phrase preserved interweaves the two contrasting elements of the scene: the ship is black not just because Homer's ships are black, but as a part of the poet's picture, contrasting a dark storm with the bright and benign power of the Dioscuri. Once again, the art of the poem lies principally in the felicity of a sharply and dramatically drawn scene and event.

Mythological references occur in a number of short fragments. We have already looked at the drinking song addressed to Melanippus (38), where the fate of Sisyphus illustrates the inevitability of death and the fragility of human powers in a passage, probably a whole poem, just twelve lines long.[81] A poem (44) which was complete in eight verses, four Asclepiadean couplets, apparently alludes to the appeal of Achilles to Thetis and Thetis's consequent appeal to Zeus, as in *Iliad* 1. The few words that remain of this small poem suggest that it was Homeric in phrasing as in matter. About another mythological poem, Fr. 255, we know still less. Scraps of eight lines survive, with half a dozen decipherable words and no meaningful phrases. One of the words is *kibisis*, which virtually ensures that the poem dealt with the story of Perseus and Medusa,

88 EARLY GREEK MONODY

since *kibisis*, a Cyprian word, according to Hesychius, is the usual word for the wallet in which Perseus carries the Gorgon's head, and is not likely to have got into Alcaeus's vocabulary in any other context.

In these meager fragments we have no way of telling whether the myth was used as an illustration for a specific contemporary scene or occasion, as it is in Poem 38, or used in no immediate connection with the contemporary world. We know, however, that Alcaeus wrote at least one poem, apart from his hymns, in which the content is purely mythological. Fragments of two poems concerning Helen remain. One, Fr. 42, is complete in sixteen verses, four Sapphic strophes, of which only the line endings are missing:

ὡς λόγος, κάκων ἄχος ἔννεκ᾽ ἔργων
Περράμῳ καὶ παῖσί ποτ᾽, Ὦλεν᾽, ἦλθεν
ἐκ σέθεν πίκρον, πύρι δ᾽ ὤλεσε Ζεῦς
Ἴλιον ἴραν.

οὐ τεαύταν Αἰακίδαις ἄγαυος
πάντας ἐς γάμον μάκαρας καλέσσαις
ἄγετ᾽ ἐκ Νήρηος ἔλων μελάθρων
πάρθενον ἄβραν

ἐς δόμον Χέρρωνος · ἔλυσε δ᾽ ἄγνας
ζῶμα παρθένω · φιλότας δ᾽ ἔθαλε
Πήλεος καὶ Νηρεΐδων ἀρίστας,
ἐς δ᾽ ἐνίαυτον

παῖδα γέννατ᾽ αἰμιθέων φέριστον
ὄλβιον ξάνθαν ἐλάτηρα πώλων ·
οἱ δ᾽ ἀπώλοντ᾽ ἀμφ᾽ Ἑλένᾳ Φρύγες τε
καὶ πόλις αὔτων.

The story goes that sorrow in return for evil deeds
Once came on Priam and his sons, O Helen,
Bitter sorrow, through you, and Zeus destroyed
Holy Troy by fire.

Not such a bride the great son of Aeacus
Calling to his wedding all the blessed ones,
Took from Nereus's halls and led,
A tender virgin,

To Chiron's home. He loosed the girdle
Of a pure virgin; and the love of Peleus
And the best of the Nereids flourished.
In a year

She bore a son, strongest of demigods,
Illustrious driver of tawny horses;
But for Helen the Phrygians were destroyed,
They and their city.

The exact wording is questionable in some places,[82] but of
the scope, meaning, and structure of the poem there can be no
doubt. Here alone we have a poem of Alcaeus in which we
can discern a unified whole, in which the relationship of the
parts is clear and comprehensible. The contrast with Fr. 130,
lines 16–39 of which probably contain a poem nearly as complete as 42, is conspicuous; in 130 there is no clear unity, in 42
the unity is striking. The poem is built on a contrast between
the ruin brought on Troy by Helen and the glory that came
from the marriage of Thetis. That Helen came to Troy as no
bride but a runaway wife is alluded to clearly enough by the
emphasis on Thetis's virginity. The connection of the two
women with the destruction of Troy links the contrasting
themes, and the poem ends as it begins, with the fall of Troy.[83]
The style is simple, as in the hymn to the Dioscuri. The
language is strong in Homeric echoes ("sacred" Troy, the
patronymic Aiakidas and Nereides, the phrase "driver of
horses") yet much modified by non-Homeric, Lesbian forms
(*Perramus, iran* in place of *hieran, Cherronos, aimitheon*); the combination gives a pleasant blend of local poetic dialect and epic
tradition. The material follows Homeric mythological tradition, and squeezes a good deal of myth—a miniature history

of the Trojan War—into its small space. It is not a profound
thought; the irony of the destructiveness of Achilles is ignored
and the awkwardness that Thetis is hardly more a model wife
than Helen is disregarded. But the vivid, dramatic confrontation, achieved with economy of description, and the somber
illustration of moral consequences give this poem shape and
substance.

The other Helen poem is harder to judge. It is on a similar
theme, but there is no indication of length, and both beginning
and end are lost. It may have had contemporary references.
The surviving fragment (283) consists of four Sapphic strophes,
with bits remaining both before and after:[84]

κ'Αλένας ἐν στήθεσιν ἐπτόαισε
θῦμον 'Αργείας, Τροΐω δ' ὐπ' ἄνδρος
ἐκμάνεισα ξενναπάτα 'πὶ πόντον
ἔσπετο νᾶϊ,

παῖδα τ' ἐν δόμοισι λίποισ' ἐρήμαν
κἄνδρος εὔστρωτον λέχος, ὠς F' ὐπείκην
πεῖθ' ἔρῳ θῦμος διὰ τὰν Διώνας
παῖδα Δίος τε

. . .

. . . κασιγνήτων πόλεας μέλαινα
γαῖ' ἔχει Τρώων πεδίῳ δάμεντας
ἔννεκα κήνας,

πόλλα δ' ἄρματ' ἐν κονίαισι . . .
ἤριπεν, πόλλοι δ' ἐλίκωπες . . .
. . . 'στείβοντο, φόνῳ δ . . .
. . . 'Αχίλλευς

And roused to passion the spirit of Argive Helen
Within her breast, and she, driven mad by the Trojan,
The host-deceiver, followed him in his ship
Over the sea,

And left her daughter deserted at home
And her husband's bed of fair coverlet, because
Her spirit bade her yield to love, through the daughter
Of Zeus and Dione

. . .
. . . many brothers the black earth
Holds in the Trojans' plain, fallen
On her account,

And many chariots overturned in the dust
And many glancing-eyed . . .
. . . trampled . . . slaughter . . .
. . . Achilles.

The moral earnestness is like that in 42. The emotion is somewhat more intense; there, the contrast between Helen's fault
and Thetis's virtue was mostly implicit, and the emphasis was
on Thetis's virtue. Here the descriptions are rather livelier:
Helen is "roused"—the word is apparently the same as in
Sappho's famous description of her violent symptoms of love[85]
—and "maddened," and Paris is clearly a figure of evil, not
only as "host-deceiver," but in that he is responsible for the
death of "many brothers," presumably his own brothers, as
in *Iliad* 6, where Hector speaks of his "many goodly brothers,
who may fall in the dust at the hands of their foes" (452–53).
The precise connection of Achilles with the rest of the poem is
not clear; perhaps there was again, as in 42, a specific contrast
between Paris and Achilles, but Achilles may stand only for
the avenging might of the Achaean besiegers. Homeric reminiscences are at least as profuse as in 42. The fragments are
much alike in style; both are strongly moralistic, with an
urgent and dramatically framed insistence on cause and effect.
The difference in spirit between this poem and Sappho 16,
where Helen's flight is also mentioned, is a measure of the
difference between the two poets. Alcaeus uses the incident to

create a dramatic scene that vividly makes a moral generalization. Sappho, though she acknowledges the moral point, is
not concerned with it; in her poem the flight of Helen exemplifies the power of love, and forms a mythological excursus on
an immediate, specific situation and feeling.

In both these mythological poems of Alcaeus we find the
same combination of epic theme and language with Lesbian
forms. Both have the same clarity and precision of style and
outlook. It seems unnecessary to look elsewhere than to
Alcaeus's own moral view to understand them. The influence
of Stesichorus as a link between epic and lyric is by no means
improbable.[86] It is likely, however, that the practice of treating
epic themes in lyric form is Alcaeus's main debt to the Sicilian
poet; the outlook and the dramatic presentation are so consistent and so well in keeping with what we know otherwise of
Alcaeus that they seem certainly to be his own.

We have arrived at something of a paradox in the poetry of
Alcaeus. If we take the political poems on the one hand,
especially the two relatively long pieces, 129 and 130, and the
two poems on mythological topics, 42 and 283, on the other
hand as representing two discernible extremes in the way that
they illustrate the style and spirit of Alcaeus's art, we find that
each group has certain qualities that the other is without. In
the political poems there is the excitement of partisan struggle,
the emotional intensity of conspiracy and enmity, the pathos
of loss and loneliness, and there is vivid description, as in the
scene of the beauty contest, and in the Ship of State, but there
is little evidence of general, formal unity, or of a unifying
theme in any one poem. There is, apparently, a tendency to
sacrifice overall design to the scenes and emotions of the
moment; anger and invective take command. The myth-
poems have a gemlike orderliness of form and a clear point
of view, but because they are set entirely in the world of myth
(so far as we can tell), they have a spirit of relative detachment.
In the political poems Alcaeus shows himself to be an absorbing

witness and an intense participant in an age and place that
were full of excitement, but as a creator of formal expressions
of his ideas he is on the whole disappointing. His sense of
organization, his range of style, and his learning are more
evident in the poems of mythology.

Perhaps the scattered and informal impression of the political
poems is deliberate. But their spirit is of such wholehearted
concern that it is hard to believe in the degree of objectiveness
that a contrived informality would require. The serial quality
that marks these poems, with scenes or ideas strung along, and
no apparent over-arching unity,[87] is a frequent characteristic
of archaic Greek poetry, corresponding in its way of presenting
ideas to the serial style of syntax typical of archaic writers,
called by Aristotle (*Rhetoric* 1409a29) λέξις εἰρομένη, "run-on
style." Much early elegy is in this style, particularly the
political and martial elegy of Tyrtaeus and Solon. Where
Solon's elegy is least prone to such looseness, as in the poem
to the Muses (Fr. 1 D), he is farthest from political poetry.
Alcaeus, with his sensitivity to various poetic traditions, may
in his political poems have been drawn toward the manner of
expression that had been used for such material. Also, the
abusiveness that seems to have been a feature of Alcaeus's
political poems is usually associated with satire. Perhaps
Alcaeus was using lyric form for material that had no lyric
tradition and was therefore less successful in organizing this
material than that which had already been put in this form by
other poets, by Alcman, by Stesichorus, and perhaps by Sappho.

In the poems of mythology that we have examined, Alcaeus
does not do, essentially, what Alcman and Sappho do. These
poems of Alcaeus have no frame or parallel drawn explicitly
from the contemporary world; in Alcman's Partheneion
(*PMG* 1), and in a number of Sappho's poems, the combination of mythological and contemporary world is conspicuous and, in the poetry of Sappho as later in the poetry
of Pindar, artistically essential. What Alcaeus does instead, in

these poems, is to interweave two incidents or themes, two
contrasting parts of a picture combining to present, by their
contrast, a moral point. Where Sappho's use of myth has the
effect of expanding or universalizing the immediate, contemporary incident or scene, Alcaeus's method is dramatic; it is
the method of confrontation and contrast, for example, Helen
against Thetis. Instead of the myth as poetic center, as in
Sappho and Pindar, we have the dramatic suggestiveness and
allusiveness that are found later in the dithyrambs of Bacchylides. So far as can be known, Alcaeus is here an innovator.
That he was highly experimental in another kind of essentially
dramatic poetry appears certain from Fr. 10. Elsewhere in his
poetry we find indications of the more usual employment of
myth as an illustration paralleling contemporary experience,
as in 38, where the story of Sisyphus creates justification for
seeking the pleasures of life, specifically the pleasures of the
symposium.

One more fragment of mythological poetry, again epic-
inspired, remains to be mentioned, and it apparently introduces, in a political context, the combination of contemporary
setting and extended mythological reference that is elsewhere
absent from the poetry of Alcaeus. The poem has come to
light in two separate papyri, first in POxy 2303, which consists
of partial lines of three Alcaic stanzas, providing enough intelligible phrases to permit the general sense to be made out;
it tells the story of the rape of Cassandra by Oïlean Ajax and
of his consequent punishment. A Cologne papyrus first published by Reinhold Merkelbach in 1967[88] adds four preceding
stanzas in a poor state of preservation; it provides a small
amount of further information for the earlier-known stanzas,
and continues, in a second column, with twenty-two additional
line-beginnings. There are a few not very illuminating marginal
notes. Neither beginning nor end is present, nor is there any
indication of how much longer than the forty-nine detectable
lines the poem was. The new papyrus fragment adds signifi-

cantly to what we can tell about Alcaeus's handling of the
myth. Even more important for the general picture of Alcaeus's
poetry is the indication, slight but inescapable, that there was
a contemporary political framework.

Nearly all the preserved lines are or may be concerned with
the story of Ajax. Three extremely fragmentary lines at the
beginning seem to express a generalization to the effect that
"one who has done shameful and unjust things ought to be
executed," and apparently transition is then made to the story
of Ajax as an example of the generalization: "Just so, it would
have been better for the Achaeans had they stoned Ajax." (In
the *Iliou Persis*, as we know from Photius's summary of the
Chrestomathy of Proclus, the Achaeans intended to stone Ajax,
but he escaped by fleeing for refuge to the altar of Athena.)
Then follows, in the main body of the fragment, the story of
the rape and the punishment. The last twenty-two lines add
only one piece of information, in the letters ωυρραδον at line 47.
There seems little choice but to interpret these letters as
addressing "the son of Hyrrhas,"[89] and thus to conclude that
the poet has moved from myth to the contemporary world
and to politics.

It then becomes a probable supposition that the words at
the beginning of the fragment refer to the same contemporary
situation, and that in fact Alcaeus is urging that Pittacus be
executed for his villainous behavior; it is altogether likely that
the context is again Pittacus's betrayal of the ἕταιροι, the conspirators against Myrsilus.

It must be recognized that the evidence for contemporary
allusion is very restricted. The opening part need not be so
interpreted, and could instead be a moral generalization,
perhaps about the inevitability of punishment for iniquity; it
is only the part-line fragment at the end that provides real
evidence.[90] On present information, however, it seems right to
believe that Pittacus is addressed and that the poem combines
myth and a contemporary reference.

What we have of the poem is essentially still the myth. The
intelligible part is as follows (Page, *LGS* 138. 6–27):[91]

> . . . παρπλέοντες Αἴγαις
> . . . ἔτυχον θαλάσσας
>
> . . . ἐν ναύῳ Πριάμω πάις
> . . . Ἀθανάας πολυλάιδος
> . . . ἐπαππένα γενήῳ
> . . . νέες δὲ πόλιν ἔπηπον
>
> . . . Δαΐφοβόν τ' ἄμα
> . . . οἰμώγα δ' ἀπὺ τείχεος
> . . . καὶ παίδων αὔτα
> . . . πέδιον κάτηχε.
>
> . . . λύσσαν ἦλθ' ὀλόαν ἔχων
> . . . ἀγνας Παλλαδος ἀ θέων
> φώτεσσι θεοσύλαισι πάντων
> δεινοτάτα μακάρων πέφυκε.
>
> χείρεσσι δ' ἄμφοιν παρθενίκαν ἔλων
> . . . παρεστάκοισαν ἀγάλματι
> . . . ὀ Λόκρος οὐδ' ἔδεισε
> . . . ος πολέμω δοτέρραν
>
> γόργωπιν · ἀ δὲ δεῖνον ὐπ' ὄφρυσιν
> σμ . . . πελιδνώθεισα κὰτ οἴνοπα
> ἆιξε πόντον ἐκ δ' ἀφάντοις
> ἐξαπίνας ἐκύκα θυέλλαις.

> . . . as they sailed by Aegae
> . . . found the sea (smoother)
>
> . . . Priam's child in the temple
> Of Athena, giver of rich spoils
> . . . touched her chin
> . . . seized the city
>
> Deiphobus . . .
> . . . A groan from the walls

> ... and the wail of children
> ... held the plain
>
> ... came, possessed of deadly madness
> ... of chaste Pallas, who of all
> The gods is fiercest against the violence
> Done by men to sacred shrines;
>
> And seizing with both hands the maiden
> As she stood before the (holy) statue
> The Locrian (took her) and did not fear
> ... the giver of war,
>
> The grim-eyed; but she glared with a dark
> And frowning look, and over the sea
> Wine-hued she swooped, and stirred
> A sudden dark tempest of winds ...

As in the other poems about myths, there is an animated description of wickedness and its punishment. The theme is epic, but only partially Homeric; the incident of the rape was in the *Iliou Persis;* the punishment of Ajax is mentioned in the *Odyssey* (4. 499–511) and very briefly in the *Nostoi* in Proclus. There is a good deal of traditional epic diction, as in *oinopa ponton* ("wine-hued sea") and *hup' ophrusin* ("frowning"), but one of the most striking phrases, *polemou doterran* ("giver of war"), uses a word found not in Homer but in Hesiod, in the grim phrase (*Works and Days* 356) *thanatoio doteira.* "Giver of death" is precisely what Athena is in this poem, although in the reference to the death of Ajax in *Odyssey* 4 it is Poseidon who brings his doom. The transfer of agency to Athena is quite natural, since the crime of Ajax was a desecration of her shrine and image; this directness of moral consequence fits well with what we see in Alcaeus's other mythological poetry, and the point may have been his own innovation.[92] Once again dramatic compression and mythological allusiveness give an impressive forcefulness and liveliness. So rapidly and intensely does divine anger follow *hybris* that it is striking to remember that Alcaeus is here condensing what in epic narration occupies a considerable period of time. The rapidity with which the poet moves from the picture of the returning Greek fleet, off the Euboean promontory Aegae, to the scene in the temple of Athena, with a glance at the general picture of disaster at the fall of Troy, and back to the main event, the storm and (presumably) the death of Ajax, gives far the best extant example of Alcaeus's skill in compressed dramatic narrative. It has the intensity and drama of the best of Browning's short poems, and gives a new dimension to the earliest Greek lyric.

What is most remarkable about this fragment, in terms of its revelation of Alcaeus's range and tendencies as a poet, is the fact that even if—as appears—it arises from a contemporary, political context, one concerning which, to judge from the other evidence in Alcaeus's poetry, Alcaeus was deeply emotional, nevertheless the treatment of the myth shows the same brilliant, objective skill that we saw in the poems in which there seems to be no contemporary frame. The intrusion of the hated Pittacus is so controlled that the specific contemporary application of the myth is not even apparent. The gist is not, "the Greeks should have punished Ajax," which would be the expected lesson-analogue for urging action against Pittacus, but "deity punishes the wicked." Rather than a specific, propagandistic case illustration, Alcaeus gives a general moral observation, and does so with a picture drawn from mythology with admirable skill.

We now have a poem that bridges the gap between the other dramatic poems on mythological subjects and the political poems. Elsewhere the gap seems very wide. But the dramatic manner, featuring succinct, vividly drawn scenes and strong contrasts, is eminently characteristic also of the political poems. There are a number of stylistic features that bear this out: Alcaeus's way of making a sudden transition with a demonstrative pronoun—the κήνων of 129. 14 and 21, the κῆνος of 70.

6 and 72. 7, the ὀ δέ of 69. 6; evocative passages like the description of the Lesbian beauty contests (130. 32–35) and, in the same poem, the poet's longing for the life of political activity (16–18); and the vivid scenes in the metaphors of the Ship of State. These are essentially dramatic devices, though the effect of some of them is marred by the fragmentary condition of their contexts.

Like Archilochus, Alcaeus was a man of violent feelings, strong friendship, implacable enmity. On the whole, his political passions are not as successfully transmuted into poetry as are the emotions of Archilochus, but his adaptation of political material to fully developed lyric forms constitutes a significant broadening of the range of lyric poetry. Like Sappho, he wrote poems in which myth plays an integral, effective part in the form and the meaning of the poetry, but generally the worlds of myth and contemporary life remain separate. He is one of the most varied of archaic Greek writers. With his extraordinarily wide range of interests and his openness to the influences both of literature and of personal experience, he has an important and perhaps even momentous role in the development of lyric poetry.[93]

CHAPTER FOUR

Sappho

Alcaeus and Sappho are alike in the apparent intensity of their involvement in much of what they write about and in many external features of poetic form, but they are utterly different in the subject matter of their poetry and in outlook. Alcaeus is political and moral, Sappho apolitical, and her primary concern with human emotions and the activities that express them gives moral judgment only an incidental place.

The first point of contrast is in the background necessary for understanding their poetry. Because Sappho's poetry is essentially nonpolitical, the framework of local history can largely be forgotten for her. There are a few facts about Sappho and a few fragments of her work with probable political implications: she was exiled at some time between 605 and 591 and went to Sicily;[1] she makes a reference, seemingly unfavorable, to a woman of the family of the Penthilidae (71); the name Cleanactidae (which was probably connected with Myrsilus[2]) and the word "flight" appear near each other, in Fr. 98b; the name Archeanassa occurs in a passage that may be abusive, Fr. 213; the Archeanactidae were probably among Alcaeus's political adversaries.[3] There is enough in these slight indications to suggest that Sappho was in the same political group as Alcaeus.[4] We do not know whether she was exiled simply because she was by family a member of this group, or because her expressions of dislike of members of politically powerful families were enough to bring punishment. She may have written much more than we have evidence of in this vein, but it is unlikely; Sappho was much talked about in antiquity, but never for this, so far as we know.

She was probably a native of the small town of Eressus, on the west side of the island and hence far from the political excitement of the city; this may be a reason for her apparently nonpolitical outlook. Yet it is likely that she lived in Mytilene much of her life. Her family was one of means: her husband was a wealthy man from the island of Andros; her youngest brother served as wine-pourer in the Prytaneion of Mytilene, a role usually reserved for youths of the best families.[5] We know of a daughter, Cleis, and of Sappho's affection for her (132). A second brother is addressed in a poem that will be mentioned below; a third is known only through his being named by later writers.

If the political background is less important for Sappho than for Alcaeus, the relationship of the poet to her friends is crucial.[6] Both the fragments and the indirect tradition contain ample evidence of Sappho's intense relationships with other women. It appears certain that Sappho had about her a circle of women, probably for the most part younger than herself, and that she felt some kind of rivalry with other women about whom there existed similar circles.

Beyond these inconclusive but basic points of evidence it is difficult to proceed with certainty. In later antiquity the opinion was widespread, though by no means universal, that Sappho's relations with her associates were homosexual.[7] But there was another story of Sappho's erotic adventures, similarly extreme in its presentation of Sappho's emotional nature, but seemingly at variance with a propensity to "Lesbian" love. Sappho is alleged, by some later writers, to have thrown herself from a cliff, in grief over an unsatisfied passion for a beautiful youth named Phaon. There is in Greek tradition an Adonis-like figure named Phaon, associated not with Lesbos but with Leukas, on the west coast of mainland Greece. The story of

Sappho's passion for this mythological figure probably took its rise from the fact that Sappho wrote poetry to be used at a ritual honoring a year-spirit either identical with or like Phaon. The story of Sappho and Phaon is a legend, arising most likely from material in Sappho's poetry, expanded by comic burlesque in the fourth century B.C., and perpetuated by Ovid's *Heroides*. The tradition of Sappho's homosexuality is no doubt likewise an inference arising from her poetry. The question remains whether it is a correct inference. The point that matters is clear from the poetry: Sappho expressed an intensity of emotion that is complete. Whether that feeling was expressed in physical relationship as well as in poetry can only be conjectured, and concerns the historian of morals rather than the student of Sappho's poetry. Whoever chooses to is free to suppose that passionate expression in poetry reflects only an intensity of the spirit and offers no proof of homosexual practice. To be avoided above all is the artificial and obviously inaccurate picture of Sappho's group which was created in the nineteenth century, and which continued until recently to command a credence it never deserved. This is the picture of a kind of young ladies' seminary, where Sappho dispenses lessons in music, deportment, and marriage preparation. There is scant evidence for any closely organized group, and there is no evidence for any such curriculum. The fabrication would be harmless enough were it not that it leads to a false interpretation of a number of Sappho's poems. The idea that a large proportion of the poetry is marriage poetry has gained wide belief, and this, as the newer fragments reveal, is contrary to the evidence of Sappho's work.

Something is known about the arrangement of Sappho's poetry in the standard Alexandrian edition, but there is a certain amount of confusion. There were probably nine (possibly eight) books, organized mostly on the basis of meter. Book One, consisting entirely of poems in Sapphic strophes, had a total of 1320 lines of verse.[8] Book Two consisted of poems

in a stichic or stanzaic[9] Aeolic meter, a glyconic lengthened
by two inset dactyls, which is sometimes called Aeolic dactylic
pentameter; Fr. 44, on the wedding of Hector and Andromache,
is the only substantial surviving fragment certainly from this
book. Books Three and Four, from which no extensive examples
remain, were in Asclepiadean and a related unit respectively.
Some of these poems were in two-line stanzas, as Frs. 62, 63,
and 65 reveal. Book Five, from which the long fragments 94,
96, and 98 may come, had apparently several different verse
forms, all marked off in three-verse units. Phalaeceans, lesser
Asclepiadeans, and glyconics are attested. Nothing is known of
Book Six. Of Book Seven one two-line fragment remains, in a
basically iambic meter. Book Eight is virtually a blank.[10] Book
Nine perhaps consisted of epithalamians in a variety of meters.
There is evidence that in some edition a book was entitled
Epithalamia,[11] but it may have been in an edition where ar-
rangement was throughout by type rather than by meter. It
is clear from the fragments that the epithalamian poetry of
Sappho was in various meters.[12]

The metrical range is, then, quite broad. The variety of her
subject matter is less impressive, and is substantially less extensive than in the poetry of Alcaeus. Nevertheless, the newer
fragments have a wider range than the traditionally famous
fragments had suggested. Love, as would be expected, dominates, with far more fragments, large and small, devoted to
this theme than to any other. A dozen or so fragments are
concerned with Sappho's circle of women, perhaps ten have
to do with her family, another dozen may be epithalamian.
There are about eight fragments whose burden is a moral or
general reflection, and some fifteen pieces remain that are
concerned with myth. Moreover, the tone of the pieces dealing
with Sappho's circle and her family is not always the same.
Some, like the lines to her daughter (132) show only affection,
but elsewhere there is a critical, even a sharp tone, as in the
fragment concerning her brother's affair with the courtesan

Doricha (5, 15), and in passages concerning her rivals for the
attention and affection of the young women of Lesbos. This
variety of material and tone may be important not only in
helping to fill out the picture of Sappho's life and to assess her
traits of character, but also in helping to assess the character
of her poetry. Most studies of Sappho emphasize the biographical element; our aim is to concentrate largely on the
form and range of the poems.

Can we speak of a typical Sapphic poem? There is good
evidence to suggest that there is a recognizable type, familiar
from the two long-known poems, the hymn to Aphrodite preserved by Dionysius of Halicarnassus (1), and the description
of Sappho's passion, preserved by the author of *On the Sublime*
(31), and seemingly especially characteristic of the poems of
Book One. The clearest and simplest example is Fr. 16. Though
we are under the disadvantage of not being certain that lines
1–20 are a complete poem, there is the compensating advantage
of relative clarity of meaning and adequacy of text in those
lines:[13]

οἰ μὲν ἰππήων στρότον οἰ δὲ πέσδων
οἰ δὲ νάων φαῖσ᾽ ἐπὶ γᾶν μέλαιναν
ἔμμεναι κάλλιστον, ἔγω δὲ κῆν᾽ ὄτ-
τω τις ἔραται ·

πάγχυ δ᾽ εὔμαρες σύνετον πόησαι
πάντι τοῦτ᾽, ἀ γὰρ πόλυ περσκέθοισα
κάλλος ἀνθρώπων Ἐλένα τὸν ἄνδρα
τὸν πανάριστον

καλλίποισ᾽ ἔβα ᾽ς Τροΐαν πλέοισα
κωὐδὲ παῖδος οὐδὲ φίλων τοκήων
πάμπαν ἐμνάσθη, ἀλλὰ παράγαγ᾽ αὔταν
. . .

. . . αμπτον γαρ . . .
. . . κούφως . . .
. . . με νῦν Ἀνακτορίας ὀνέμναι-
σ᾽ οὐ παρεοίσας,

τᾶς κε βολλοίμαν ἔρατόν τε βᾶμα
κἀμάρυχμα λάμπρον ἴδην προσώπω
ἢ τὰ Λύδων ἄρματα κἀνόπλοισι
πεσδομάχεντας.

Some say an army of horsemen, some say
Infantry or a fleet is the fairest thing
Upon the black earth; but I say it is
Whatever you love.

And very easy it is to make
This known to all; for she who far
Surpassed mankind in beauty, Helen,
Leaving the noblest

Of men, her husband, sailed off to Troy,
With no thought at all for her child or for
Her own dear parents; she was drawn astray
. . .

        . . . bent . . .
     . . . lightly . . .
Now recalled to me Anactoria
Who is not here;

Whose lovely step and the sparkling glance
Of whose face I had rather look upon
Than Lydian chariots and infantry
Fighting in armor.

In the papyrus (POxy 1231) that chiefly preserves the poem
there are parts of lines following 20. There is no apparent
connection of thought in what follows, and there can be no
presumption that what follows is from the same poem, since
this poem is preceded by a fragmentary passage clearly belonging to another poem and yet separated from this one by
no extra space between verses (which is the normal but far
from consistent practice). Since the left side is missing there is
no possibility of the guiding presence of a *coronis*, marking the
end of a poem, in either place. If 20 is the last line of a poem,

the poem that follows is of twelve lines, and there are just twelve lines in the part of the papyrus column that precedes Fr. 16. With a length of twenty verses, and in view of the sense of completeness that the passage presents, there is a high degree of probability that we have here the full extent of the poem.[14]

If the poem ends at line 20, the thought and organization are simple and closely unified, proceeding from an initial proposition (the fairest thing is whatever you love) to a demonstration or expansion of the proposition, by the mythical example of Helen, and back to a conclusion in the personal realm of the initial statement: to Sappho the radiance of Anactoria's face would be a finer sight than the brilliance of a Lydian army. The circular pattern is lightly emphasized by the verbal similarity of the end to the beginning.

The simplicity and unity are like the Helen poems of Alcaeus. But there is also a striking difference. In Alcaeus's poems the myth is self-contained, and the meaning depends on the moral point that the poet exemplifies in the myth. Sappho's poem combines the contemporary world with the mythical world of Helen and the Trojan War. In Sappho's poem myth illustrates the contemporary world; in Alcaeus's, contrasting elements of the myth illustrate each other. Illustration of a contemporary theme by a scene or an incident drawn from something or somewhere different is, we shall see, a recurrent feature in Sappho's poetry.

What kind of meaning has the poem? In Alcaeus's poems on myth we find a moral generalization. The wrongness of Helen's desertion of Menelaus and the wickedness of Paris's behavior are basic to Alcaeus 283. The moral point unifies the poem and gives it an air of purpose and completeness. Sappho's poem has as its basis Sappho's longing for Anactoria. It is this that makes her know, with such firmness, that the fairest thing on earth is "whatever you love."[15] In Sappho, then, the unifying element is a personal emotion, but the appearance of

simplicity and naïveté is partially deceptive. For so small a
poem it is very complex; and every strand of its complexity
lends force to the poem's argument, the compelling force of
the emotion of love.

The poem opens with the rhetorical device of Priamel:[16]
"Some say an army of horsemen, some say Infantry or a fleet
is the fairest thing . . . but *I* say . . . ." It is a conventional
device in ancient poetry, familiar to us from Horace (*sunt
quos* . . . in *Odes* 1. 1, and *laudabunt alii* . . . in 1. 7); that it
was not uncommon in archaic Greek literature is suggested by
its presence a number of times in Pindar (as in the opening
lines of *Olympians* 1 and 2) and in Tyrtaeus (9) and Theognis
(699–718). Then follows the demonstration of the proposition
that "whatever you love" is the fairest thing on earth, by the
mythical example of Helen. The example is strangely chosen.
Why should Helen, who is famous not as a lover but for her
beauty, be the example of one who has treasured "what she
loved" above all else? Then, in a transition lost because of a
gap in the text, Sappho returns from myth to the contemporary
world and to the closing statement that the absent Anactoria
is prized by her beyond the panoply of an army.[17]

The device of Priamel is common, and Sappho's use of it
lacks the brilliance and force of such Pindaric examples as the
beginning of *Olympian* 1. But its use here is far from banal,
because of the way in which its components are integrated
with the rest of the poem. There is an element of paradox
that a comparison that starts out with various kinds of armies
culminates with a mention of "whatever you love." The last
strophe provides clarification: what Sappho thinks of when she
pictures Anactoria is her "lovely step" and "sparkling glance."
With Anactoria's step and glance Sappho at once compares,
in the closing stanza, the *look* of chariots and men in armor.[18]
The gleam of the beloved is fairer than the gleam of armor;
the graceful motion and radiance of Anactoria are set beside
the action and sheen of armies, and the contrast and analogy

of the realms of love and warfare are suggested. Also, the
soldiery of the contemporary picture has its implied counter-
part in the armament of the Trojan expedition, which the story
of Helen suggests.

The choice of Helen is strange and naive, and it is effective.
What more arresting proof of her proposition could Sappho
have chosen than that the very woman who was most desirable,
who was herself "the fairest thing" to so many, should abandon
all that her beauty had brought her (her husband, noblest of
men, and her child, and the devotion of her parents) in misled
pursuit of what she loved? Sappho subsumes, within her
demonstration of the power of love, the moral point that
occupies Alcaeus's attention in 283. The word-fragment
paragag-, though its sense is incomplete, succinctly conveys
Sappho's opinion that Helen's action was wrong, though it
leaves open the question of responsibility. Above all, it heightens
the impression of the irresistible attraction of love.[19]

The power of love and the combination of beauty and
warfare fill all three parts of the poem, and the link between
contemporary concern and mythical example is close. The
principal subject of the poem is not left behind but expanded
in the course of the circling movement. It is a very concentrated
poem, yet for one so short it is complex in suggestion and
allusion. Its complexity leaves us with the impression of having
been told about an emotional experience that is not merely
Sappho's own but is valid for all. Yet we realize that this
universalizing through myth is in essence only a use of
poetical rhetoric to emphasize Sappho's intensely personal
statement.

The poem that is most familiar as a representative of
Sappho's art is Fr. 1, to Aphrodite:

> ποικιλόθρον᾽ ἀθανάτ᾽ ᾽Αφρόδιτα,
> παῖ Δίος δολόπλοκε, λίσσομαί σε,
> μή μ᾽ ἄσαισι μηδ᾽ ὀνίαισι δάμνα,
> πότνια, θῦμον,

ἀλλὰ τυίδ' ἔλθ', αἴ ποτα κἀτέρωτα
τὰς ἔμας αὔδας ἀίοισα πήλοι
ἔκλυες, πάτρος δὲ δόμον λίποισα
χρύσιον ἦλθες,

ἄρμ' ὑπασδεύξαισα · κάλοι δέ σ'ἆγον
ὤκεες στροῦθοι περὶ γᾶς μελαίνας
πύκνα δίννεντες πτέρ' ἀπ' ὠράνωἴθε-
ρος διὰ μέσσω ·

αἶψα δ' ἐξίκοντο · σὺ δ', ὦ μάκαιρα,
μειδιαίσαισ' ἀθανάτῳ προσώπῳ
ἤρε' ὄττι δηὖτε πέπονθα κὤττι
δηὖτε κάλημμι

κὤττι μοι μάλιστα θέλω γένεσθαι
μαινόλᾳ θύμῳ · τίνα δηὖτε πείθω
ἄψ' σ' ἄγην ἐς σὰν φιλότατα; τίς σ', ὦ
Ψάπφ', ἀδικήει;

καὶ γὰρ αἰ φεύγει, ταχέως διώξει,
αἰ δὲ δῶρα μὴ δέκετ', ἀλλὰ δώσει,
αἰ δὲ μὴ φίλει, ταχέως φιλήσει
κωὐκ ἐθέλοισα.

ἔλθε μοι καὶ νῦν, χαλέπαν δὲ λῦσον
ἐκ μερίμναν, ὄσσα δέ μοι τέλεσσαι
θῦμος ἰμέρρει, τέλεσον, σὺ δ' αὖτα
σύμμαχος ἔσσο.

Deathless Aphrodite, elaborate-throned
Child of Zeus, guile-weaving, I pray you
Master not with pain and anguish
My soul, o revered one;

But come to me, if ever before
Hearing my voice from afar and
Heeding, you left the golden
House of your father

Yoking your chariot; and fair swift
Sparrows drew you close to the black earth,

Whirring on rapid wings from heaven
Through the middle air,

And straightway were come; and you, blessed one,
Smiling with deathless countenance
Asked what again I had suffered and why
Again I was calling,

And what I most wished for myself
In my frenzied soul. "Whom again shall I bring
By my persuasion to love you? Who,
Sappho, wrongs you?

Know, if she flees, she soon will pursue,
If gifts she refuses, gifts she will give;
If she loves not, soon she will love,
Though she would not."

Come again to me now, free me from bitter
Anguish, and all the fulfillment desired
By my soul, fulfill; with your own presence
Be my ally.[20]

The general formal similarity to 16 is apparent: a short
poem in Sapphic strophes, concrete in expression, with a
strongly personal content. Here alone we know for sure that
we are dealing with a complete poem by Sappho.[21] Its formal
likeness to 16, lines 1–20, is extremely close and this fact is
not without weight as evidence for the completeness of that
poem. There are several no less apparent and important differences. Though the language is again simple, the cast of
thought is not so. The irony and self-analysis of this poem are
foreign to the spirit of 16; and it has a more strictly personal
and self-centered content. Fr. 16 takes its rise from personal
experience and emotion, but generalizes them; here we appear
to be concerned throughout with Sappho's own experience in
love. The language of this poem, though the syntax is still
naive, is richer and more rhetorically elaborated than that of
16. In 16 there are just four epithets, all of them simple, two

of them, "black" (earth) and "dear" (parents), traditional and
familiar; there is no ingenious transfer of meaning of conventional words, such as we find in Alcaeus's poetry. The other
two both describe Anactoria, "lovely" (gait) and "bright"
(radiance), thus in a modest way putting what rhetorical
emphasis the poem contains on the description of Anactoria.
In Poem 1 there is, relative to this simplicity, an abundance
of epithets. Aphrodite is "elaborate-throned" and "guile-
weaving" (both single, sumptuous words); the house of Zeus
is "golden," the sparrows "fair" and "swift," the earth "black";
the wings of the sparrows flutter, and Aphrodite smiles with
"deathless" countenance on Sappho whose soul is "frenzied."
Nine epithets in the first twenty lines make this a more formal
and elaborate poem than 16.

The poem is the one complete example we have in monodic
lyric of the cletic hymn, an apparently traditional form in
which a deity is addressed or invoked, then described or
praised by the recital of a story illustrating the divine power,
and invoked again at the end.[22] In the present poem the
pattern is invocation, picture of the goddess as she came to
Sappho before, and renewed invocation for the present emer-
gency. Clearly the poem is not a real hymn, written for use
at a religious occasion, because no religious occasion is suggested. Fr. 2 may be such, but the tone and the matter of Fr. 1
are alien to worship. The subject is not religious devotion but
the power of love. It is a highly personal poem, and Sappho's
attitude is by no means detached or dispassionate. The
"anguish" of strophe 1 and the "frenzied soul" in strophe 5
are evidence of the depth of Sappho's feeling and the genuine-
ness of her involvement. But though in a broad sense a love
poem, it is not chiefly concerned with a loved girl, as 16 is
concerned with Anactoria. This time the subject is rather the
phenomenon of love in Sappho's life, personified by Aphrodite
and conceived of as her power. It is on the borderline between
poetry of love and poetry in worship of Aphrodite.

The occasion of the poem is clearly a specific event. Sappho
has been rejected and is suffering. But without supposing that
Sappho does not take her immediate situation seriously, we
can tell by the poem's emphasis that what Sappho wants
mainly to express is the relationship between Sappho and
Aphrodite. Sappho can treat her present predicament as part
of the picture of that relationship. It is wrong, however, to
think that, because Sappho makes her present unhappiness
appear as one in a series of *contretemps* for which she needs the
recurrent help of Aphrodite, Sappho is laughing at herself, or
taking her plight lightly, or supposing that Aphrodite is
laughing at her. The repeated *dêute*, which has been taken as
a sign that Sappho is amused at her plight, is a commonplace,
in archaic poetry, in descriptions of the onset of love.[23] Sappho
does not use commonplace words to signify indifference; they
are part of the naïveté of diction and syntax that characterizes
all her poetry and that suggests simplicity, candor, and earnestness of attitude. There are other naive repetitions in this poem:
otti in 15 (twice) and 17, and *tacheôs* in 21 and 23; and in
Poem 2 there is a threefold repetition of *en de*.

In effect, two Sapphos are present. One of them is Sappho
the woman; to deny that she is involved we must deny the
validity of Sappho's own words in the poem. There is also
Sappho the poet, who is able to analyze her emotions with a
degree of detachment, and to concentrate on the poetic form
in which the experiences of Sappho the woman are described.
This combination of personal involvement and artistic detachment creates much of the basic pattern of the poem.

The main thing, whether it is measured by the proportion
of the poem devoted to it, by the elaboration with which it is
described, or by the degree to which it dominates our impression of the poem, is the picture of Aphrodite. The most
striking epithets describe Aphrodite, and in fact she permeates
the whole poem. Far more vivid than the situation at the
beginning and end, where Sappho's appeal to Aphrodite for

the present moment is expressed, is the intervening picture (line 6 to line 24) of the goddess who has in the past heeded her devotee, has descended in a chariot drawn by sparrows, has smiled upon her worshipper and spoken words of encouragement to her. The goddess's smile is not a smile of indulgent amusement. It expresses the approval and support of a beneficent power, and while the description recalls the Homeric "laughter-loving" (*philommeidês*) Aphrodite, the divine figure is far more dignified and potent than the Homeric Aphrodite. The momentary situation at the end is a mere conclusion to the main theme, and we have no vivid impression about the girl or the incident. The epiphany occupies four of the seven strophes and is, quite clearly, the essence of the poem. If we regard the description of Aphrodite as an intrusion and an "irrelevant flight of fancy"[24] we can only find the poem lacking in sense. But this is a capricious judgment. The present plight and prayer are the occasion; within this framework Sappho as artist is creating a picture of the beneficent sway of Aphrodite over the loves of Sappho.

In 16 the unity of the poem is ensured by the unity of imagery and by the complex relationship of the mythological example to the immediate situation. Here in Poem 1 the momentary incident gets taken into a larger picture, and the unity of the poem is contingent upon this absorption. But the moment has a more permanent and important force in the poem than just to introduce and be lost in the general theme of Aphrodite and Sappho. There is a sense of urgency and aliveness that the poem could not have without the need and doubt raised by Sappho's present rejection. The contrast between Sappho as sufferer and Sappho as reflective observer and artist depends on this double reference. The relationship between the immediate moment and the picture that fills the center of the poem is analogous to that between present experience and mythical example in 16. We can reasonably say that the epiphany of Aphrodite in Poem 1 serves as the "myth" of the poem. The form and balance of these two poems represent the same basic structure.[25]

Poem 2 is also a cletic hymn to Aphrodite. While probably not a cult hymn,[26] it has a formal and public quality that sets it off from Poem 1:

> . . . ρανο-
> θεν κατίοισα
>
> δεῦρύ μ’, αἰ Κρήτεσσί περ, ἔλθ’ ἔναυλον
> ἄγνον, ὄππαι δὴ χάριεν μὲν ἄλσος
> μαλίαν, βῶμοι δὲ τεθυμιάμε-
> νοι λιβανώτῳ ·
>
> ἐν δ’ ὔδωρ ψῦχρον κελάδει δι’ ὔσδων
> μαλίνων, βρόδοισι δὲ παῖς ὀ χῶρος
> ἐσκίαστ’, αἰθυσσομένων δὲ φύλλων
> κῶμα κατέρρει.
>
> ἐν δὲ λείμων ἰππόβοτος τέθαλεν
> ἠρίνοισιν ἄνθεσιν, ἐν δ’ ἄηται
> μέλλιχα πνέοισιν . . .
> . . .
>
> ἔνθα δὴ σύ γ’ ἔλθ’ ὀνέλοισα Κύπρι
> χρυσίαισιν ἐν κυλίκεσσιν ἄβρως
> ὀμμεμείχμενον θαλίαισι νέκταρ
> οἰνοχόεισα.

                                        . . . from
. . . descending,

Come for me, as you come to the Cretans, to a sacred
Sheltered place, where there is a graceful grove
Of apple trees, and altars smoke,
Fragrant with incense;

In it cool water through apple branches
Sounds, with roses all the place
Is shadowed, and from flickering foliage
Slumber flows down.

In it a meadow, pasture for horses,
Blooms with spring flowers, and the breezes
Fragrantly blow . . .
    . . .

Come, Cyprian, come to this place, and
Gracefully in wine cups of gold
Bring nectar blended with feasting;
Be our wine-pourer.

Let us suppose that the poem is all here except the first stanza and the end of the fourth.[27] What remains is at least a complete unit, in the same circular style as 1 and 16. As in 1, there is invocation, expansion by means of a picture deriving from the invocation, and return to an invocation at the end. The text is too fragmentary for us to be sure that the return was marked by a verbal echo. The expansion in Fr. 16 takes the form of a mythical example to prove the point raised at the beginning; in 1, there is a description of the appearance and words of the invoked goddess when she appeared on previous occasions; in Poem 2, the expansion consists of a word picture of the place of worship. Aphrodite is bidden to come to a place where her worshipper, presumably Sappho herself, is situated, a place that is called, with Giulia Lanata's reading, an ἔναυλος, a shelter; the word is used by Hesiod, *Theogony* 129, to describe the mountains which earth brought forth to be "Graceful haunts of the goddess nymphs." The haunt or sanctuary is then described in detail. The connection between this central expansion and the return to the invocation at the end is extremely close, for the last strophe, in addition to its framing effect created by the return to direct address of the goddess, provides (by its picture of the goddess herself pouring nectar into golden cups) a climax to the luxuriance and color of the sanctuary. The unity and meaning are in the same pattern as in the other two poems: here the fragrance, bloom, and brilliance of the grove expand and symbolize the spirit of the goddess and of the relationship between her and her worshipper.[28]

This poem is fully as ornate as 1 in its epithets: the sanctuary is "holy," the grove "graceful," the altars "fragrant," the water "cool," the foliage "flickering," and so on down to the golden cups that Aphrodite is to fill with nectar. Clearly one function of all this is to enhance the picture of the grove, which, along with the goddess herself, is as central to this poem as the description of Aphrodite's previous appearance is to 1. But it is noticeable that the epithets of 2 are less suggestive than those of 1 of an intimate personal link between Sappho and the goddess. They are highly traditional and impersonal; there is nothing to lend an immediate and special feeling, as "guile-weaving" Aphrodite and Sappho's "maddened" spirit do in 1. Poem 2 is closer to being a public poem than either 1 or 16; there is less tension and less dramatic quality, and, I think it is fair to say, less appearance of deep personal feeling than in 1 and 16. Just as the epithets have a standard and impersonal aspect, so the whole poem is less immediate. The description of the grove is sensually beautiful; there is movement as well as color, not only through word choice but by the use of participles as epithets (*tethumiamenoi, aithussomenon*); but is has nothing to compare with the urgency of Poem 1 and the naive earnestness of 16.

The three poems have the same metrical pattern, are roughly the same length, and have the same structural type: each begins with an occasion or a reflection that concerns Sappho personally and that is contemporary and immediate; this is followed by an expansion or development, which in some way illustrates the beginning; each ends with a return to the immediate situation. The three poems represent three different kinds of experience; in style and tone they show a great deal of individuality; in form they are closely similar, even though two are, formally, hymns and the third is not.

If we turn to a different metrical form, we find poetry with

the same structural pattern and the same individuality of
occasion, style, and meaning. Poem 96 is in three-line strophes,
with all the lines basically glyconic but varying in length:[29]

          ... Σαρδ ...
   ... πόλλακι τυίδε νῶν ἔχοισα

ὦσπ ... ὤομεν ... χ ...
σε, θέᾳ σ᾽ ἰκέλαν ἀρι-
γνώτᾳ, σᾷ δὲ μάλιστ᾽ ἔχαιρε μόλπᾳ

νῦν δὲ Λύδαισιν ἐμπρέπεται γυναί-
κεσσιν ὤς ποτ᾽ ἀελίω
δύντος ἀ βροδυδάκτυλος σελάννα

πάντα περρέχοισ᾽ ἄστρα · φάος δ᾽ ἐπί-
σχει θάλασσαν ἐπ᾽ ἀλμύραν
ἴσως καὶ πολυανθέμοις ἀρούραις ·

ἀ δ᾽ ἐέρσα κάλα κέχυται, τεθά-
λαισι δὲ βρόδα κἄπαλ᾽ ἄν-
θρυσκα καὶ μελίλωτος ἀνθεμωδής ·

πόλλα δὲ ζαφοίταισ᾽, ἀγάνας ἐπι-
μνάσθεισ᾽ Ἄτθιδος ἰμέρῳ.
λέπταν ποι φρένα ... ... βόρηται

          ... Sardis ...
   ... many times turning her thoughts hither

As ...   ... regarded
You as a goddess manifest,
And in your music took greatest delight.

And now among the women of Lydia
She is conspicuous, as when the sun
Goes down, the moon, rosy-fingered,

Excels all the stars, and its light
Spreads alike over the salt sea
And over the fields, covered with flowers,

And lovely dew is shed, and roses
Bloom and soft chervil too,
And the blossom-filled melilot.

As she walks to and fro
She thinks of gentle Atthis with longing . . .
(With grief) consumes her tender heart . . .

I take it that a poem ends after one stanza beyond what I
have quoted, at line 20 of the fragment; 18–20 are so fragmentary that restoration is mere guessing, yet enough can be
seen in them to make it very probable that they belong with
what precedes them.[30] As line 21 of the fragment stands,
partially restored, in the text of Lobel and Page and in other
editions, there is no apparent connection in thought between
it and what precedes. The context is too uncertain for this to
be a decisive point. What is more persuasive is that there is no
sign of a grammatical connective. Within a poem, this would
be almost unique in Sappho:[31] while connectives are regularly
simple, they are always there; a new sentence lacks a connective
only when it begins a new poem. There is, then, some evidence
that the poem ends at line 20. How much is lost from the
beginning is not indicated by the papyrological evidence, but
the progression of thought in the fragment suggests that not
much is missing.

Judgment is necessarily tentative, but the evidence for a
similarity of form to that of the poems just observed is enough
to merit consideration. There is no doubt that the beginning
describes a contemporary situation; a girl who loved Atthis
and misses her[32] has gone away to Lydia, probably to Sardis.
The absent girl's beauty is then compared with that of the
moon, and the simile is extended into a general description of
a moonlit evening. Then, suddenly, it is again the girl who is
described, as she "walks to and fro, thinking of gentle Atthis."
Lines 18–20 are almost total darkness, but they have something about "to go to that place," and "a great . . . gives

voice . . . in between." Perhaps the passage has to do with
going between Lesbos and Sardis and how long the distance
seems when it separates lovers. This thought would represent
a return to the theme at the beginning where Sardis and
"turning her thoughts hither" also suggest the separation of
lovers. The longing for Atthis in 15–16 returns to the theme
of 4–5. If we accept the long intervening simile as the "myth"
of this poem, the formal pattern of 16, 1, and 2 is recognizable.

There are two motifs in the poem, the absent girl's devotion
to Atthis, at the beginning and end, and the absent girl's
beauty. This second theme begins in line 6 and presently slides
into the graphic simile that by its length, color, and beauty
dominates the poem. We do not find the same degree of unity
here, where there are two contemporary themes, as in 1, 2,
and 16. The poem is addressed to Atthis, yet mostly concerns
neither her nor Sappho, but another girl. This is necessarily a
looser and less intense poem. Perhaps the relative looseness of
the metrical form, with each line of the stanza in a different
metrical length, is deliberately chosen for such a combination
of themes.

But what about the simile? A simile of the moon and moonlit
nature standing for a woman's beauty is not inappropriate.
And the analogy of the other poems we have observed suggests
the structure and emphasis of the poem. In Poem 1, for example, not the immediate occasion but the picture of Aphrodite
and the relation between Sappho and Aphrodite bear the
main emphasis of the poem. Here, analogously, it is misleading
to think of the simile as an incidental patch of decoration
breaking in on the real subject matter; the simile implies the
universality of that beauty of which Atthis's beloved is a
particular, contemporary, and momentary fulfillment. The
return from nature to the girl is then only a turn from one
aspect to another of the same topic. Even the gender of the
participle need not change.[33]

In Alcaeus's descriptions of the Ship of State, especially in

Fr. 326, the picture is so fully elaborated that it is hard to find analogies in the underlying political events for all the details of the ship; and there would, if we were not clearly instructed, be some reason to doubt whether the poetry was in fact allegorical. Like Alcaeus in his metaphor, Sappho is willing, in this poem, to allow the simile to develop far beyond its strictly comparative function. In both poets this form of expression can be ascribed in part to a delight in specific descriptions that is characteristic of archaic Greek thought and is apparent in Homeric scenes of arming and sacrifice, in Alcaeus's list of weapons (Fr. 357), and in other poems of Sappho (94 and 98 seem to show traces of the same appetite for details). But in this poem the thematic importance of the simile and its virtual identity with its context provide a structural explanation. Different kinds of reality join in a unity of poetic theme; the union is perhaps a blur rather than a blend.

Sappho's remarkable analysis of her symptoms of passion at the sight of a beloved girl in conversation with a man has been admired deeply and variously. The author of *On the Sublime*, to whose quotation of the poem we owe its preservation, describes it as a "congress of emotions," selected with extraordinary discrimination of what is important and blended into a unity. One modern critic finds neither selection nor unity in the description of emotions, but admires Sappho's objectivity and the accuracy and vividness of her description.[34] Another finds the peculiar strength of the poem in the combination of passion and detachment, which is essentially the opinion expressed by "Longinus."[35] The text is as follows (31):[36]

> φαίνεταί μοι κῆνος ἴσος θέοισιν
> ἔμμεν' ὤνηρ, ὄττις ἐνάντιός τοι
> ἰσδάνει καὶ πλάσιον ἆδυ φωνεί-
> σας ὑπακούει
>
> καὶ γελαίσας ἰμέροεν, τό μ' ἦ μὰν
> καρδίαν ἐν στήθεσιν ἐπτόαισεν ·

ὼς γὰρ ἔς σ᾽ ἴδω βρόχε᾽, ὥς με φώναι-
σ᾽ οὐδ᾽ ἒν ἔτ᾽ εἴκει,

ἀλλὰ κὰμ μὲν γλῶσσα ἔαγε, λέπτον
δ᾽ αὔτικα χρῷ πῦρ ὐπαδεδρόμηκεν,
ὀππάτεσσι δ᾽ οὐδ᾽ ἒν ὄρημμ᾽, ἐπιρρόμ-
βεισι δ᾽ ἄκουαι,

κὰδ δὲ μ᾽ ἴδρως κακχέεται, τρόμος δὲ
παῖσαν ἄγρει, χλωροτέρα δὲ ποίας
ἔμμι, τεθνάκην δ᾽ ὀλίγω 'πιδεύης
φαίνομ᾽ ἔμ᾽ αὔτᾳ.

He seems to me the equal of the gods,
That man who sits before you
And listens close by you to the sweet
Sound of your voice

And the charm of your laughter, that
Sets flying the heart in my breast.
As soon as I look at you, so soon do I lose
All power to speak;

My tongue lies broken, and a subtle
Flame at once runs under my skin,
My eyes see nothing, a roar
Sounds in my ears,

Sweat pours down me, trembling
Seizes all of me, I am paler
Than grass, only a little short of death
I seem to myself.

Modern criticism is now, after an interlude of absurd mis-
interpretation, able once more to take the meaning of the
poem to be what it seems to be, a description of the symptoms
of Sappho's passionate love for a girl, occasioned by Sappho's
witnessing the girl *tête à tête* with a man. A number of critics
in the early years of this century contrived to interpret it as a
song sung at a wedding, with the man and the girl bridegroom

and bride. There is no evidence for this. It is simply the most
extreme piece of the conjectural fabric in which Sappho's
relationship to the girls she wrote about was likened to that of
teacher to pupils, and in which the interest of Sappho in the
girls was to prepare them for marriage. This view, though it
lingers among the sentimentally inclined, has been system-
atically and thoroughly demolished by Denys Page, and can
be confidently dismissed.[37] It is a poem of passion, far the
most emotional and intense poem that we have from Sappho.

Neither the man nor the girl really matters much in the
poem. The new papyrus evidence discussed in note 36 allows us
to see more clearly than before what the place of κῆνος ἄνηρ
("that man") is in the poem. He is a contrast figure for Sappho;
by his privileged position close to the girl he emphasizes to
Sappho her own inability to sustain the sight of the girl's
beauty without acute suffering. The identity of the girl is un-
important. She is the cause of the poem, and her conversation
with the man is its occasion, but its essence is the description
of Sappho's emotional experience. Similarly, in Poem 1, it is
not the immediate occasion of Sappho's invocation that
matters most, but the picture of Aphrodite and of the relationship between her and Sappho. Is there, then, a similarity of
form between this poem and the others that we have found to
resemble one another? The echo of the opening *phainetai* in the
φαίνομ᾽ ἐμ᾽ αὔτᾳ ("I seem to myself") of line 16 is strong evidence
that the circular pattern was present.[38] The poem proceeds,
like the others, from an opening scene to an to expansion of it
—this time by a detailed and vivid description of Sappho's
passion. Sappho has used herself as the illustrative equivalent
of a simile or myth in her poem: the girl's beauty is made
important by the description of its overwhelming effect on
Sappho. It is a curious feature and not insignificant for the
controlled nature of Sappho's art that she can thus become her
own poetic subject; artistic detachment is combined with
intense personal involvement.

In the foregoing discussion of certain poems of Sappho, I have used the word "myth" for that constituent of a poem's structure that corresponds to the myth that is common in poems of Pindar. Of the five poems analyzed, only one has an actual myth. If the proportion of poems in which the central elaboration or example were only one in five, its designation as myth would be somewhat precious. But the case was probably quite different. These particular poems show that the same structural pattern, including the same type of elaboration, is present even when there is no real myth to force the pattern upon our attention. These five poems are, moreover, the most complete and hence the most satisfactory examples of this type of Sapphic structure. There are other poems in which the combination of myth and contemporary scene is beyond question, even though most of them are too fragmentary to permit more than a guess as to the poetic form. Sappho's practice in the poems examined makes it reasonable to suppose that some at least of the instances of myth plus contemporary scene are from poems of this circular structure.

In Fr. 58 the story of Eos and Tithonus is surrounded by references that are contemporary and personal. Since only the ends of the lines are preserved in the relevant part of the fragment, information is incomplete, but it seems likely that Sappho told, in six or seven lines, how "rosy-armed Eos" snatched up someone (the name Tithonus is not preserved in the fragment), "bearing" him to "the ends of the earth" to be "her husband."[39] The immediately preceding lines, concerned with the symptoms of old age, end with the question, "What could I do?" The fate of Tithonus in the story exemplifies, presumably, the inevitability of old age: if even the goddess Eos did not avail to save Tithonus from old age, what can mankind do? The use of the myth would then be something like that in the Sisyphus poem of Alcaeus. The poem ends with two lines following the Tithonus-Eos story. They are too dubious in meaning to contribute clearly to an understanding of the fragment, but they return, beyond doubt, to the contemporary world, for they begin with the statement "I love luxury" (or "soft delicacy").[40] If a new poem begins at 13, then in magnitude at least, the myth dominates the poem.[41]

In Fr. 23, Hermione is mentioned and someone addressed in the second person is likened to Helen. Here again contemporary references enclose a myth. In this case space indicates that the myth is very brief.

The story of Niobe and her children was treated by Sappho, and it is easy to see how this story of pride and jealousy might illustrate a personal incident. Our evidence for Sappho's use of this myth, however, is slight. One line (142) of Sappho's announces that Leto and Niobe were very good friends; Fr. 205 consists of Aulus Gellius's statement that Sappho said Niobe had nine sons and nine daughters, while Homer said six and six, Euripides seven and seven. This is meager but not insignificant. First, the one line of Fr. 142 is very likely to have been the first of a poem, since it lacks a connective and has the particle *men*. Fr. 205 suggests that Sappho told the usual story, presumably including the death of Niobe's children under the arrows of Apollo and Artemis. That would mean that there is irony in the stress on the "friendship" of Leto and Niobe. Since the story apparently began the poem in which it was told, this may not be a parallel to the structure and the use of myth that we have hitherto noticed. But a further fragment, which has not, to my knowledge, been brought together with these, but perhaps concerns the same story, may shed a different light on Sappho's use of this myth. Fr. 90, part 10, is a piece of POxy 2293, a commentary, in extremely fragmentary condition, on some poems of Sappho. In part 10, which consists of eighteen lines, none containing more than four syllables, one line has the letters λατως (the correct Lesbian genitive form of Leto)[42] and another, well separated, has the genitive case of Atthis. One might guess that these lines had to do with a poem in which the rivalry of Sappho and Andromeda, to whom we know from Fr. 131 that Atthis defected from Sappho, was likened to the rivalry of Leto and Niobe. Andromeda-Niobe is made to pay for her breach of friendship with Sappho-Leto; and no doubt the runaway Atthis suffered in verse for her defection. Did Andromeda have a larger group than Sappho? We can only conjecture, but the two names strongly suggest a combination of myth and contemporary scene.

Fr. 68a joined the Tyndarids with Sappho's rival Andromeda. The context is too uncertain to show more than that there was again a combination of myth and Sappho's immediate circumstances. (Perhaps in the letters -μεγαρα, at the end of what is preserved, the name of a girl of Sappho's group occurs;[43] this would suggest the circular pattern, since mention of Andromeda precedes that of the Tyndarids.) If, as suggested above, line 20 of Fr. 96 ends a poem, then the following part of that fragment may be a further example of this illustrative use of myth. It begins with some kind of personal reference (the pronoun "us" is fairly certain), then there are the names of Aphrodite and Peitho, something about pouring nectar and "from golden," (27–28), and at the end the Euboean promontory of Geraestium is named, bringing us back to earth, though not necessarily back to Sappho.

Two more examples of this structure in which myth or similar material is centrally used by Sappho remain to be mentioned. The first of these, Fr. 17, provides an excellent contrast, in poetic style, with Alcaeus, since it touches subject matter used by him, and handles it altogether differently. The poem is addressed to Hera:

πλάσιον δή μ . . .
πότνι' ῞Hρα σὰ   . . .
τὰν ἀράταν 'Aτ[ρεῖδαι . . .
τοι βασίληεs ·

ἐκτελέσσαντεs . . .
πρῶτα μὲν πὲρ ῎I[λιον . . .

τυίδ᾽ ἀπορμάθεν[τες . . .
οὐδ᾽ ἐδύναντο

πρὶν σὲ καὶ Δί᾽ ᾽Αντ[ίαον . . .
καὶ Θυώνας ἰμε[ρόεντα παῖδα ·
νῦν δὲ . . .
κὰτ τὸ πάλ[αιον . . .

Near to me . . . Lady Hera, your . . . which the Atridae, . . .
kings, invoked in prayer, having accomplished . . . first
around (Troy?) . . . departing hither . . . were not able . . .
until you and Zeus Antiaeus and Thyone's desired (son?)
. . . now too . . . according to the old . . .

The general meaning is clear, and probable supplements
have been made. The phrases above are from lines 1 to 12.
The poem was complete in twenty lines, and in line 20 the
word "arrive" is probable. Thus the poem seems to be Sappho's
prayer to Hera for a safe arrival, with lines 3–10 referring to
the myth of how the Atridae had to put in at Lesbos and pray
to the Lesbian trinity of Hera, Zeus Antiaeus, and Dionysus
before they could make their way home. The form is virtually
certain, the function of the myth as illustration and sanction is
probable. As in Alcaeus 129, in the mention of the trinity
chief emphasis is on Hera. But the differences between the
poems of Alcaeus and of Sappho, in this religious context, are
striking. Alcaeus's poem is strictly contemporaneous, immediate, and bound up with political strife; and it is rather
sprawling and loosely organized. Sappho's is a neatly formed
unit, beginning and ending with a personal prayer, but containing a mythical reference that expands the theme. Sappho
stabilizes and authenticates the moment by the introduction
of a myth-analogue.[44] The form of the story she gives is local,
non-Homeric: in Homer only Menelaos stops at Lesbos, not
Agamemnon.[45]

Fr. 95 is too fragmentary to be categorized. But one passage in it, on the underworld, gives it something in common with the form we are now concerned with. Only a few phrases are certain, and there is no way of knowing what proportion of the poem is represented. The part preserved begins with a contemporary reference, naming Gongyla, who according to other evidence was one of Sappho's girls.[46] The next three lines are obscure, but say something about a "sign" and the fact that someone, possibly Hermes, came, and Sappho addressed him (lines 8–13): "Master, . . . for by the blessed one . . . I have no desire to be raised up . . . a yearning for death (holds me?), and to see the banks of Acheron, lotus-clad, bedewed . . . ." No more remains. Perhaps Sappho is expressing a wish for death because of her unfulfilled longing for Gongyla, in which case Hermes is addressed in his role as psychopomp. A point of structural interest is that Sappho's wish for death takes the form of a sort of myth, a picture of the underworld. Instead of lingering over the wish to die, Sappho mythicizes the condition of death. On the basis of analogy, it may be supposed that the picture of Acheron was more central and had more emphasis than a description of Gongyla. This does not mean that Sappho is impassive or does not really care about Gongyla. It means that her way of expressing her feelings in some poems is by myth, by a generalization of the immediate moment and fact.

This poem touches on another feature of Sappho's art, though not a major one. So far as its fragmentary preservation permits judgment, the description here of Acheron, while not lacking in delicacy and vividness, nor in originality—neither epithet is so used elsewhere—seems conventional. Sappho's depiction of nature appears generally conventional. The pictures she draws are often colorful, precise, and apt, but they seldom strike the reader as unexpected or as the manifestation of a deep personal concern with the phenomena of nature. In Sappho's extant poetry, only the moonlit scene of 96, full of color and detail, offers impressive evidence of the

128   EARLY GREEK MONODY

poet's very real ability to observe and describe nature. The
sumptuous garden of Poem 2 is so reminiscent of other literary
paradises that it has been supposed to reflect a formal, eschat-
ological depiction of paradise.[47] A three-line fragment on a
night scene (34),

ἄστερες μὲν ἀμφὶ κάλαν σελάνναν
ἂψ ἀπυκρύπτοισι φάεννον εἶδος
ὄπποτα πλήθοισα μάλιστα λάμπῃ
γᾶν . . .

The stars that surround the beautiful moon
Hide away their lovely form at once
Whenever she shines full upon the earth

is not detailed enough to be striking as a description of nature;
in fact nature is almost certainly here an analogy for human
beauty, just as the garden in 2 is a symbol of Aphrodite. The
well-known fragment numbered 94 in Diehl's *Anthologia Lyrica
Graeca*, and omitted by Lobel and Page as not being Sappho's,[48]

δέδυκε μὲν ἀ σελάννα
καὶ Πληΐαδες, μέσαι δὲ
νύκτες, παρὰ δ' ἔρχετ' ὤρα ·
ἐγὼ δὲ μόνα κατεύδω.

The moon is down
And the Pleiades, and the middle
Of the night is here. The time goes by
And I lie alone,

uses a night scene to suggest loneliness and disappointment.
Nature's role is again secondary, its portrayal slight. Whether
by Sappho or not, the lines are certainly on a traditional theme
of folk poetry. In all these cases, and even in 96, where the
description is detailed and striking, nature is a means of
suggestion, not a subject of intrinsic interest.[49]

Most of the familiar poems and fragments of enough length

to justify analysis have been examined. There are, however, several interesting poems which are without the dimension of myth or its equivalent and are concerned with subjects that depart little from immediate experience.

One of the most substantial of these poems on purely immediate subjects is formally a *propemptikon*, that is, a poem in which a person about to make a voyage is wished good fortune. The recipient of Sappho's wishes is her brother, and the poem is Fr. 5:

Κύπρι καὶ Νηρήϊδες ἀβλάβην μοι
τὸν κασίγνητον δότε τυίδ᾿ ἴκεσθαι
κὤσσα Ϝοι θύμῳ κε θέλῃ γένεσθαι
πάντα τελέσθην,

ὄσσα δὲ πρόσθ᾿ ἄμβροτε πάντα λῦσαι
καὶ φίλοισι Ϝοῖσι χάραν γένεσθαι
κὠνίαν ἔχθροισι, γένοιτο δ᾿ ἄμμι
πῆμ᾿ ἔτι μήδ᾿ εἶς ·

τὰν κασιγνήταν δὲ θέλοι πόησθαι
. . . τίμας, ὀνίαν δὲ λύγραν
. . . πάροιθ᾿ ἀχεύων

(Cyprian goddess and) daughters of Nereus,
Grant that my brother return here unharmed,
(And all that) his heart most wishes fulfilled,
Grant that it happen,

And give him release from all his sins
Of the past, and let him bring (to his friends)
Delight (and sorrow) to his foes, and to us let
No one be a sorrow.

And his sister—let him wish to do
Some honor to her, and the bitter sorrow
. . . grieving before . . .

Fragments of two stanzas follow.

The poem has some resemblance to a cletic hymn, in that divinities are addressed and their aid is invoked. It may, like two other hymns which we have examined (Frs. 1 and 2), have had ring form, but there is considerable doubt as to details. It is not certain, though it is rather likely, that the five stanzas of which there are fragments preserved constitute the whole poem. The word "Cyprian" probably occurs in the last stanza, but it is only partially preserved, while the two words at the beginning of the poem are a modern restoration. Still, we have enough of the poem to be able to make out its main lines.[50] It is clear that in this case the invocation does not serve as a frame for an expansion by myth or vision or simile; the invocation here is only a means of presenting Sappho's words on her brother, which combine good wishes for his safety and happiness with the hope that his past undesirable behavior may end. The nature of his behavior is not revealed in what remains, nor was it unveiled much, if at all, in the poem if line 20 is its end. From other authors, chiefly Herodotus, we know of an incident in the life of Sappho's brother Charaxus, an incident that exercised Sappho much and can reasonably be supposed to underlie this poem. Charaxus, while trading in wine between Lesbos and Naucratis in Egypt, became enamored of a celebrated and beautiful Thracian courtesan named Doricha and nicknamed Rhodopis ("Rosy"), whose freedom he bought at a high price. Herodotus says that Sappho in her poetry reproached her brother for his behavior.[51] The important point for Sappho's poetry is that what seems to be an entire poem is on this purely personal plane. The introduction of Aphrodite and the Nereids does nothing to alter the immediacy of the poem.

In its simplicity and earnestness of style it is like the other poems examined; its unrelieved attention to the present and the tangible is different. As a piece of historical or biographical information, it is fully as valuable as the other poems, but as a treatment of a theme it has less depth and less force. Its use

of the *propemptikon* form for a content that is not really
"propemptic" but a moral exhortation recalls the poem of
Archilochus (79a) that uses the same form for a fierce attack
on a personal enemy. Sappho's poem is considerably less
powerful.

Apparently Sappho devoted at least one other poem to the
affair of Charaxus and Doricha; Fr. 15b is fairly certainly the
final stanza of another poem:

> Κύπρι καί σε πικροτέραν ἐπεύροι
> μηδὲ καυχάσαιτο τόδ᾽ ἐννέποισα
> Δωρίχα, τὸ δεύτερον ὡς πόθεννον
> εἰς ἔρον ἦλθε.

> Cyprian, and may she find you bitterer,
> And may she not boast, may Doricha
> Not say that a second time he came
> To her longed-for love.

Herodotus's reference to the incident indicates that Sappho
reproached Charaxus after his return to Mytilene. Therefore
Poem 5 cannot be the poem he is referring to; 15b may be
from it.

Sappho may have written a good deal of poetry on this level
of simple, personal communication. Short fragments tell nothing
of the character of the poem from which they are torn, but
there are several passages that may be from similar poems,
such as the lines in which Sappho refers to her daughter (132):

> ἔστι μοι κάλα πάις χρυσίοισιν ἀνθέμοισιν
> ἐμφέρην ἔχοισα μόρφαν Κλέις ἀγαπάτα,
> ἀντὶ τᾶς ἔγωὐδὲ Λυδίαν παῖσαν οὐδ᾽ ἐράνναν . . .

> I have a beautiful daughter, my lovely Kleis,
> Who looks like golden flowers. For her
> I would not (take) all Lydia or charming . . .

Apparently on a personal level is a sharp-toned piece (57)
aimed at Sappho's rival, Andromeda:

τίς δ' ἀγροΐωτις θέλγει νόον . . .
ἀγροΐωτιν ἐπεμμένα σπόλαν . . .
οὐκ ἐπισταμένα τὰ βράκε' ἔλκην ἐπὶ τῶν σφύρων;

What rustic girl holds you spell-bound . . .
Clad in rustic garments . . .
Who has not learned to draw her skirts about her ankles?

Just as personal, and distinctly gentler, is 98, the only one of
the relatively new fragments that seems to illustrate this
domestic side of Sappho's poetry:

                . . . ἀ γάρ μ' ἐγέννατ' ἔφα . . .
σφᾶς ἐπ' ἀλικίας μέγαν
κόσμον, αἴ τις ἔχῃ φόβαις
πορφύρῳ κατελιξαμένα . . .

ἔμμεναι μάλα τοῦτο δή ·
ἀλλ' ἀ ξανθοτέραις ἔχῃ . . .
ταῖς κόμαις δάιδος προ . . .

στεφάνοισιν ἐπάρτια
ἀνθέων ἐριθαλέων ·
μιτράναν δ' ἀρτίως . . .

ποικίλαν ἀπὺ Σαρδίων . . .

          . . . For my mother (said) . . . that in her youth it was a
great adornment if a girl could bind her hair with a
purple . . . but a girl who has hair yellower than a torch . . .
fastened with wreaths of blooming flowers . . . just now a
colorful band from Sardis . . .

The piece is too fragmentary for a clear judgment of the
poem, of unknown length, that contained it.[52] There is no
suggestion of anything beyond the level of verse-conversation.
Whether three additional lines, from the same papyrus and
apparently in the same meter, belong in the same poem is
uncertain (98b):

σοὶ δ' ἔγω Κλέι ποικίλαν —
οὐκ ἔχω πόθεν ἔσσεται —
μιτράναν · ἀλλὰ τῷ Μυτιληνάῳ

... for you, Kleis, I have no way of getting a
colorful head band; but for the Mytilenaean ...

If the lines belong with the foregoing, an argument which
makes the poem rather more than conversation, begins to
emerge, and there is a degree of organization: the naive
repetition of words gives the familiar ring form, and the talk
about hair-dressing takes on more substance if it is centered
in a motherly wish of Sappho's for her daughter. But we are
probably still on the level of immediate, personal matters, as
in Fr. 5. If the rest of 98b, which is fragmentary, is added,
we have some more indications of content ("Cleanactid" and
"flight" occur, and "colorful" comes once more to strengthen
the possibility of connection with the rest of 98) but we gain
little in knowledge of the form or scope of the poem.[53]

Poem 94 may belong in this category of poems on immediate
experience only, but there are grounds for thinking that it is
closer in form to Poem 96, where the simile of the moon
removes the poem as a whole from the purely immediate level.
Poem 94 is also in three-line stanzas, this time of two glyconics
followed by a lengthened glyconic. A passage of nine consecutive verses is preserved, followed by twenty very fragmentary verses. The beginning is lost and there is no way of
knowing how much preceded:

τεθνάκην δ' ἀδόλως θέλω ·
ἄ με ψισδομένα κατελίμπανεν

πόλλα καὶ τόδ' ἔειπε ...
ὤμ' ὡς δεῖνα πεπόνθαμεν ·
Ψάπφ', ἦ μάν σ' ἀέκοισ' ἀπυλιμπάνω.

τὰν δ' ἔγω τάδ' ἀμειβόμαν ·
χαίροισ' ἔρχεο κἄμεθεν
μέμναισ', οἶσθα γὰρ ὥς σε πεδήπομεν ·

αἰ δὲ μή, ἀλλά σ᾽ ἔγω θέλω
ὄμναισαι . . .
          . . . καὶ κάλ᾽ ἐπάσχομεν.

πόλλοις γὰρ στεφάνοις ἴων
καὶ βρόδων   . . . τ᾽ ὔμοι
          . . . πὰρ ἔμοι περεθήκαο

καὶ πόλλαις ὐπαθύμιδας
πλέκταις ἀμφ᾽ ἀπάλᾳ δέρᾳ
ἀνθέων   . . . πεποημμέναις

καὶ   . . . μύρῳ
βρενθείῳ . . .
ἐξαλείψαο καὶ βασιληίῳ

καὶ στρώμναν ἐπὶ μολθάκαν
ἀπάλαν
ἐξίης πόθον . . .

κωΰτε τις . . .
ἴρον οὐδ . . .
ἔπλετ᾽ ὄπποθεν ἄμμες ἀπέσκομεν

οὐκ ἄλσος . . .
          . . . ψόφος
. . .

. . . I honestly wish I were dead. Weeping much as she left me

She said this . . . "Alas we have suffered such pains; Sappho, truly it is not by my will that I leave you."

And I answered her thus: "Farewell, go and remember me, for you know that we have cherished you;

And if you do not, still I wish to remind you . . . and we have known joys.

For many (wreaths) of violets and roses and . . . for you, and . . . you put around you beside me,

Many woven garlands, made of blossoms, around your
tender neck

And ... with rich myrrh ... you anointed yourself, and
with royal ...

And upon soft beds ... tender ... you have satisfied your
desire ...

And neither any ... holy ... no ... was, from which we
were absent,

No grove ... sound ...

There is necessarily a good deal of doubt about some aspects
of the meaning of this fragment.[54] Apart from the opening
clause, we might explain it as a narration by Sappho of a
tender leave-taking, in which the actual event is chiefly an
occasion for Sappho to depict the intimacy and luxury that
have in the past been shared. The voluptuousness of the description is in keeping with Sappho's use, elsewhere as here,
of terms of strong sensuousness to express emotional intensity,
as in Poem 2. The plural, "we have cherished you," suggests
that the poem stressed the intimacy not of Sappho and the
girl but of the group. We may guess almost with certainty that
in the fragmentary part at the end of what is preserved, the
words "holy," "grove," and "sound" described in sensuous
terms some shared religious or quasi-religious experience. On
the assumption that the deity of the holy place is Aphrodite,
the poem has a good deal of similarity to Poem 2; the depiction
of the erotic intimacy of the group[55] replaces the description,
in Poem 2, of the goddess's shrine.

To the two levels of concern, the parting and the intimacy,
the opening clause, "I honestly wish I were dead," adds a
third.[56] There is a sudden change in apparent mood between
the desperate sorrow of this clause and the grave and controlled
tone of Sappho's address to the girl. The change suggests that
the recollection of past joy not only served as a consolation to

the departing girl, but serves again now as a consolation to
Sappho.

No other fragment tells us nearly as much as this one about
the emotional intimacy of Sappho's group, though it does not
give as telling a picture of the emotional power of Sappho
herself as Poem 31. It is more like Poem 96. There the physical
beauty of a moonlit scene is used to symbolize the beauty of
an absent girl. Here the material that is used to convey the
intimacy is drawn from the circumstances of the intimacy
itself, as in the garden of Aphrodite in Poem 2. There is even
a double frame for the central expansion which, as in the
other comparable poems, constitutes the main body of the
poem.

There are two small fragments in which Sappho speaks of
herself, in circumstances in which it is hard to know whether
her poetry went beyond a mere statement. Fr. 120 is two
partial lines: "I am not one of the stubborn ones in temper;
my mind is gentle." How seriously we are to take the assertion
is doubtful; Sappho's severity with her errant brother and her
sharpness toward her rival Andromeda suggest that her assurance of mildness is rather like Catullus's occasional de-
clarations of indifference: possibly true at a given moment,
but unlikely to remain valid for long. Fr. 121 is similarly
personal, and yet has a reflective tone also:

> ἀλλ' ἔων φίλος ἄμμι
> λέχος ἄρνυσο νεώτερον ·
> οὐ γὰρ τλάσομ' ἔγω συνοί-
> κην ἔοισα γεραιτέρα . . .

> If you are my friend
> Seek a younger woman's bed:
> I cannot endure a union
> Where I am the older partner.

(The lover addressed here is a man.) In several other fragments
of varying kinds there is, more clearly than here, an almost

didactic thoughtfulness, which suggests that Sappho must have written poetry more pervasively ethical and reflective than is apparent in the longer fragments. In Fr. 55, for example, lines said to have been addressed by Sappho to a woman who was without poetic talent,[57] there is, along with a measure of invective that may have sprung from personal hostility, a general reflection on the power and permanence of poetry:

κατθάνοισα δὲ κείσῃ οὐδ' ἔτι τις μναμοσύνα σέθεν
ἔσσετ' οὐδέποτ' εἰς ὕστερον · οὐ γὰρ πεδέχῃς βρόδων
τῶν ἐκ Πιερίας · ἀλλ' ἀφάνης κἀν 'Αίδα δόμῳ
φοιτάσῃς πεδ' ἀμαύρων νεκύων ἐκπεποταμένα.

When you lie dead there will be no memory of you,
In time to come, because you have no roses,
Pieria's flowers. Unseen in Hades' house too,
Your place will be with the dim dead, when you have flown
    from here.

Different in tone, yet with something of the same pride in the dignity of song, are two lines said to be addressed by Sappho, at the point of death, to her daughter, who is weeping in distress (150):[58]

οὐ γὰρ θέμις ἐν μοισοπόλων οἰκίᾳ
θρῆνον ἔμμεν' · οὔ κ' ἄμμι πρέποι τάδε.

In the house of those who serve the Muses
Lament is wrong. It would not befit us.

What context there may have been for such passionate fragments as 47, "Eros whirls my mind like a wind on a mountain, falling on oaks," and 48, "You came . . . and I was maddened, and you inflamed my mind, burning with desire," can only be guessed. Similarly lacking in context must remain the curious fragment preserved in Aristotle's *Rhetoric* (Fr. 137), purporting to be a dialogue between Alcaeus and Sappho, but very doubtful in form and application.[59]

There are many more fragments that may come from poetry with a purely or primarily immediate and personal content, but such fragments, ranging as they do from the haunting, emotion-laden mention of Atthis in Fr. 49 ("I loved you once, Atthis, long ago . . . you seemed a little graceless child to me"), to the sharp-toned references to Irana (91: ". . . never found a girl more annoying than you") and Sappho's rival Andromeda (131, 133), to the mere name-dropping scraps in which we hear of Micca (71) and Mnasidicca (82), potentially valuable as they are for biographical information, reveal little about Sappho's poetry.

We have examined poems of Sappho that combine the personal and immediate with a "myth" element that expands them beyond the purely immediate, and we have looked at poems that seem to stay at the level of personal information. Sappho wrote also some poetry that moves entirely on a non-personal and "mythic" level. Before turning to an example of this type of poetry, something should be said about a familiar category of Sapphic poetry that I have scarcely mentioned. This category contains poems at once impersonal and immediate. I refer to the marriage songs.[60]

It was noted above (p. 103) that there is evidence for a separate book of epithalamians, and that apparently some marriage songs were placed elsewhere in the collection too, perhaps in whatever book was metrically appropriate. Thus Frs. 27 and 30, both in Book One, are, as phrases in them reveal, from marriage poems. It was also suggested above (p. 102) that the importance of the marriage poems in the works of Sappho has generally been exaggerated. The misconception has arisen partly because of the widely held notion that Sappho was concerned with preparing members of her group for marriage,[61] and partly because the epithalamians, being in a great variety of metrical forms, made a convenient quarry for ancient scholars in search of metrical examples. It was once reasonable to say that the preserved fragments contained a high proportion of epithalamia. With the recovery of a partial book text of Sappho, such a statement is no longer permissible. Epithalamians play only a slight part in the preserved book text. No certainly complete examples of epithalamian poetry are extant. The pieces that can be identified with assurance as epithalamians do not deserve a conspicuous place in a discussion of Sappho's poetry.

If we restrict attention to what is certainly epithalamian, the range is exceedingly small—twenty verses (Frs. 110–17) of not very distinguished poetry. Ten of these verses are scraps addressed to bride and bridegroom, praising one or both, such as Fr. 112,[62]

ὄλβιε γάμβρε, σοὶ μὲν δὴ γάμος ὡς ἄραο
ἐκτετέλεστ᾽, ἔχῃς δὲ πάρθενον ἂν ἄραο . . .

Fortunate bridegroom, the marriage for which you prayed
Has now come to pass, the bride for whom you prayed is
    yours . . .

and Fr. 115,

τίῳ σ᾽, ὦ φίλε γάμβρε, κάλως ἐικάσδω;
ὄρπακι βραδίνῳ σε μάλιστ᾽ ἐικάσδω.

What, good bridegroom, shall I say you are like?
A slender sapling I shall say you are like.

One fragment (114) is a mock-dialogue between bride and maidenhood:[63]

παρθενία, παρθενία, ποῖ με λίποισ᾽ ἀποίχῃ;
οὐκέτι ἥξω πρὸς σέ, οὐκέτι ἥξω.

"Maidenhood, maidenhood, do you leave me and go?"
"Not again shall I come to you, never again."

Fr. 111 is of special interest because it is the only identifiable example of poetry written by Sappho for choral performance:

ἴψοι δὴ τὸ μέλαθρον.
ὑμήναον.
ἀέρρετε τέκτονες ἄνδρες ·
ὑμήναον.
γάμβρος ἐσέρχεται ἶσος "Ἀρευι
ἄνδρος μεγάλω πόλυ μέζων.

Let the hall be high;
Hymenaeus!
Raise it high, carpenters;
Hymenaeus!
A bridegroom like Ares will enter,
Taller by far than a tall man.

The refrain and the general stylistic resemblances to Catullus
61, which is clearly a choral poem, make it appear that this
piece (which there is no reason to think complete) was for
performance by a chorus. Fr. 110, on the analogy of other
marriage poetry, may also be choral:

θυρώρῳ πόδες ἐπτορόγυιοι,
τὰ δὲ σάμβαλα πεμπεβόηα,
πίσσυγγοι δὲ δέκ᾽ ἐξεπόναισαν.

The doorman's feet are seven fathoms long,
His sandals are of five ox hides,
Ten shoemakers worked hard to make them.

The matter of both poems appears to be traditional, and so
does the form. Both the possible sexual suggestiveness of
"tallness" in 111 and the burlesque of the doorkeeper in 110
are in the spirit of much ancient wedding poetry.[64] The importance of these fragments in an account of Sappho's poetry
is that they (probably) show that Sappho wrote some choral
poetry; we are likely to continue to think of her as a monodist.

Frs. 27 and 30, both in Book One and hence in Sapphic
strophes, have a fairly strong claim to be regarded as
epithalamian, for they contain clear references to the celebra-

tion of a marriage. Both are too fragmentary to justify examination here.

Six more small fragments (104-9) are usually called epithalamian, but the designation is questionable. The evidence is purely circumstantial; some of them served as models for the epithalamian poetry of Catullus, and two of them are quoted by Himerius, who perhaps quoted only from a special collection consisting exclusively of marriage poetry of Sappho.[65] Two of these fragments, seven verses in all, are important both because of their intrinsic value as poetry and because they are conspicuous representatives of what Lobel has called the "abnormal" poems of Sappho, those poems written in a less strictly Lesbian-Aeolic dialect admitting some Homeric forms, and influenced more than Sappho's other poetry by Homeric language. These poems are in dactylic hexameter or in meters closely related, and contain a number of instances of Attic correption.[66] It is conspicuous that none of the poetry that is certainly epithalamian is in the "abnormal" style. But epithalamian or not, the points of interest about these fragments do not concern their connection with weddings; they concern their rhythm and their elegance of description, both of which are quite distinct from all that we have seen elsewhere in Sappho's poetry. Fr. 105a is a good example:

οἶον τὸ γλυκύμαλον ἐρεύθεται ἄκρῳ ἐπ' ὕσδῳ,
ἄκρον ἐπ' ἀκροτάτῳ, λελάθοντο δὲ μαλοδρόπηες,
οὐ μὰν ἐκλελάθοντ', ἀλλ' οὐκ ἐδύναντ' ἐπίκεσθαι.

Even as an apple reddens at the end of a bough,
At the end of the highest bough, and the pickers have
    forgotten it,
No, not forgotten it, they could not reach it . . .

Himerius, who quotes the lines, says that the comparison in this passage is with a girl (apparently a bride). Two other passages, similar in form and spirit, are Fr. 104, on Hesperus

(which Catullus imitates in No. 62, beginning "Vesper adest")
and Fr. 105c, in which something—in Catullus 62. 38–47, it
is the loss of maidenhood—is likened to a hyacinth crushed
underfoot. (In Catullus 11. 21–24, the same metaphor is used
differently.) If these fragments are epithalamian, they are the
best of what we have of Sappho's in this genre.[67] The combination of vividly conceived and subtly suggestive metaphor
with the pleasantry and informality of the "correction" in line
3 gives this fragment a unique place in Sappho's poetry; in its
relative lightness and detachment and in its cleverness of
imagery it points toward the poetry of Anacreon.

One more major fragment demands attention. Fr. 44, often
classed with the epithalamian poetry, is one of the longest
pieces of Sapphic poetry that we have. There are grounds for
regarding this poem not as an epithalamian but as simply an
example of lyric-narrative poetry on a mythological subject.
It narrates, in "abnormal" dialect, a mythical scene, with a
degree of detail and story-emphasis much greater than in most
other fragments; the meter, though it is a type of glyconic and
therefore lyrical, is long of line and reminiscent of epic verse.
It is, moreover, apparently stichic, not stanzaic,[68] and this too
is like epic form.

The poem contains thirty-four lines, which include the end
of the poem but not the beginning. In addition to the in-
completeness at the beginning, there is a break of indeter-
minable length in the middle of the fragment. I translate the
first eleven lines and the last five:

Κυπρο . . .
κάρυξ ἦλθε . . .
῎Ιδαος . . .   . τάχυς ἄγγελος
. . .
τάς τ᾽ ἄλλας ᾿Ασίας . . . κλέος ἄφθιτον ·
῎Εκτωρ καὶ συνέταιροι ἄγοισ᾽ ἐλικώπιδα
Θήβας ἐξ ἱέρας Πλακίας τ᾽ . . .
ἄβραν ᾿Ανδρομάχαν ἐνὶ ναῦσιν ἐπ᾽ ἄλμυρον

πόντον · πόλλα δ' ἐλίγματα χρύσια κάμματα
πόρφυρα καταΰτμενα, ποίκιλ' ἀθύρματα,
ἀργύρα τ' ἀνάριθμα ποτήρια κἀλέφαις.
ὣς εἶπ' · ὀτραλέως δ' ἀνόρουσε πάτηρ φίλος ·
φάμα δ' ἦλθε κατὰ πτόλιν εὐρύχορον φίλοις ·
αὔτικ' Ἰλίαδαι σατίναις ὐπ' ἐυτρόχοις
ἆγον αἰμιόνοις, ἐπέβαινε δὲ παῖς ὄχλος
γυναίκων τ' ἄμα παρθενίκαν τ . . . σφύρων
χῶρις δ' αὖ Περάμοιο θύγατρες . . .
ἴπποις δ' ἄνδρες ὔπαγον ὐπ' ἄρματα . . .
. . . ἠίθεοι μεγάλωστι
. . . ἀνίοχοι
. . .
[unknown number of lines missing]
. . .   ἴκελοι θέοις
                          ἄγνον ἀολ . . .
ὄρμαται   . . . ἐς Ἴλιον
αὖλος δ' ἀδυμέλης . . .   . . . τ' ονεμίγνυτο
καὶ ψόφος κροτάλων -ως δ' ἄρα πάρθενοι
ἄειδον μέλος ἄγνον, ἴκανε δ' ἐς αἴθερα
ἄχω θεσπεσία . . .
πάντα δ' ἦς κὰτ ὄδο . . .
κράτηρες φίαλαί τ'
μύρρα καὶ κασία λίβανός τ' ονεμείχνυτο ·
γύναικες δ' ἐλέλυσδον ὄσαι προγενέστεραι,
πάντες δ' ἄνδρες ἐπήρατον ἴαχον ὄρθιον
Πάον' ὀνκαλέοντες ἐκάβολον εὐλύραν,
ὔμνην δ' Ἔκτορα κ Ἀνδρομάχαν θεοεικέλοις.

Cypro– . . .
The herald came . . .
Idaeus . . . swift messenger
    (one line missing)
"The rest of Asia . . . glory undying.
Hector and his companions are bringing a bright-eyed girl
From holy Thebes and Plakos . . .
The gentle Andromache in ships over the salty
Sea; and many bracelets of gold, and fragrant

Garments of purple, adornments skillfully wrought,
Silver drinking cups without number, and ivory."
Thus he spoke, and Hector's dear father rose quickly up . . .

Myrrh and casia and frankincense were mixed;
The women of elder years raised a cry of joy,
All the men shouted a lovely, high-pitched shout,
Calling upon the healer, the far-darter, the lyre-player,
And they sang of Hector and Andromache, who were like the
    gods.

The literary source of this story of the reception of Hector and
his bride Andromache as they arrive in Troy may be the lines
in *Iliad* 22. 468–72 where, in the description of Andromache's
grief at the death of Hector, mention is made of her marriage
and her bridal gifts. There is a strongly Homeric ring to the
poem: its verse is long and largely dactylic; it is narrative;
above all, there are numerous Homeric phrases, which give
the whole thing a totally different air from what we have seen
in Sappho before. Also, Attic correption occurs twice, and
while this license is not particularly Homeric, and is not unknown even in Sappho's poems of normal dialect, a double
occurrence of this rarity imparts an exotic, non-Lesbian flavor.
The closest relatives are the "abnormal" poems which may or
may not be epithalamian, Frs. 104–9.[69]

What kind of poem is this? How are we to account for it in
terms of the kinds of poetry that we know or suppose Sappho
to have written? There was a time when the poem was
regarded as spurious, and Page accepts it only "doubtfully."[70]
But other editors, Gallavotti, Treu, and Voigt, do not share
the doubts, and in view of the appended note in the papyrus
stating that this is the end of Sappho's second book, evidence
of authenticity must be regarded as excellent.[71] Those who
accept the poem as Sappho's have tended to regard it as an
epithalamian. The grounds for doing so are, first, a marriage
scene is described in the poem; secondly, the other fragments

of "abnormal" poetry have been regarded as marriage poems; and thirdly, these same fragments are long of line, like 44. This is not very strong evidence, and against it may be urged that the poem as we have it has absolutely nothing in it about a contemporary marriage. If the wedding of Hector and Andromache is being used to illustrate a wedding on Lesbos, it is strange that the poem ends without the slightest trace of the usual return to the immediate occasion. Moreover, no poem of Sappho's that has ever been taken to be epithalamian has just this meter. There is no lack of probability in the supposition that Sappho, poet of love and the world of women, would, in choosing a Homeric theme for treatment, be attracted to a story of marriage, even without using that story to illustrate or celebrate a particular and contemporary marriage.[72] Whatever may be believed about the theme of the poem, this feature of its form introduces a poetic style that we have not seen before in Sappho: mythical poetry without an ending (whether return or not) in the contemporary world.

There is one other fragment of Lesbian poetry that is strikingly like 44, the fragment printed by Lobel and Page as Alcaeus 304, column i, but assigned to Sappho in the edition of Max Treu and, more recently, in that of Eva-Maria Voigt.[73] Ascription to Sappho seems better justified. I am not convinced that there is evidence that both columns of the fragment are from the same poem; but poems in adjacent columns are likely to be by the same poet, and the poetry in column ii is more likely to be from a poem by Sappho than from a poem by Alcaeus.

There is no doubt about the subject and the general effect of eleven of the twelve lines of column i, even though only the second half of each line remains. The poem mentions that Apollo was borne by Coeus's daughter to "Cronus's son of the mighty name," and tells how Artemis (there seems to be little transition from brother to sister, nor is it needed in so familiar a story) declared that she would be a virgin and called upon

Zeus to grant her that favor; Zeus averred (the text continues) that she would be *Agrotera* (as she is in Homer and often in later literature and cult), and that Eros would never approach her. Reminiscences of the *Homeric Hymns* are obvious: in the *Hymn to Aphrodite* such a special license of virginity is issued to Themis in words very much like those of the present poem; and in the *Hymn to Apollo* the announcement of life-mission by the infant Apollo (131–32) is like line 5 of this poem in effect, though of course not in content.[74] Had we not Fr. 44 of Sappho, this affinity to the *Homeric Hymns* might be taken as evidence of Alcaeus's authorship, in view of his known tendency to imitate these and other poems. But in view of the second column of the fragment it seems better to suppose that Sappho was the author. Moreover, there is not the slightest trace of the moral intensity and dramatic contrast that characterize Alcaeus's known myth-poetry. The case for Alcaic authorship is very weak.

Here, once more, we find a piece of mythological poetry without a trace of contemporary frame, and we may tentatively think of these two fragments, one of them very important for our knowledge of the poetry of Sappho, as giving us a glimpse of yet another type of Sapphic poetry, mythological narrative displaying in its style much less of the native Lesbian essence, much more of the epic tradition, than most of Sappho's poems. On the basis of present evidence it is reasonable to call 44 a lyric narrative rather than an epithalamian, and to see in the Artemis poem a second example of the same kind of poetry. In the poems closest to the epic tradition in style, Sappho gives no deviant, local version, as she does in the prayer to Hera (17), but follows the standard "Homeric" story.

Stesichorus of Himera, a contemporary of Sappho's, was famous for mythological narrative poetry in lyric meters. Sappho, who by respectable ancient tradition is said to have visited Sicily, may very well have responded to his influence.[75] It can be added that ancient sources mention a substantial amount of mythical subject matter with which Sappho dealt. Prometheus, Selene and Endymion, and Medea all played some part in Sappho's poetry, though we have no knowledge of how she used these myths. If we can judge from 44 and the Artemis poem, this kind of composition was not Sappho's best, and it is hence the less surprising that we know little about it from the indirect tradition. But indirect tradition is an arbitrary as well as an incomplete witness. It would have us believe that Sappho's range of subjects was much more concerned with epithalamian poetry than the direct tradition has confirmed. It may be similarly misleading in its silence about Sappho's purely mythological poetry.[76]

We cannot claim for Sappho a range of subject or style comparable to that of Alcaeus.[77] But the picture of Sappho's art has changed vastly from that of the period before the papyrus discoveries. Then there were two brilliant and much admired poems, a scattering of short passages from, or assumed to be from, wedding songs, and a bevy of splendid and haunting lines and phrases characterized by John Addington Symonds as "diamonds, topazes, blazing rubies in which the fire of the soul is chrystalized forever." Now we have all of, or substantial parts of, six poems (1, 2, 16, 31, 44, and 96) from which we can judge Sappho's art; we also have important, though less complete, parts of four more poems (5, 17, 94, and 98). These ten poems give us a greatly increased knowledge of the form, style, content, and spirit of Sappho's poetry. A leading critic has expressed disappointment in the poetic level of the new fragments, finding them below the standard by which we were accustomed to judge Sappho.[78] Nearly all poetry is below the standard of Poems 1 and 31 of Sappho, but this ought not to prejudice our judgment about the rest. Moreover, there is inevitably a change in our attitude when a bevy of tantalizing "diamonds" is replaced by a group of poems of varying quality. If we had only the moon simile from 96, or only the phrases "lovely step" and "sparkling glance" from 16, these scraps would be treasured as jewels no less rare and exciting than the phrases that we have only in isolation.

Sappho's reputation as a poet has a broader and more stable basis than before the papyrological discoveries. We are now able, though still on slight evidence, to judge her critically instead of simply reacting to her romanticized place in the history of poetry. We now can see that Sappho's excellence as a poet consists far less of an outpouring of feelings than of the subtle artistry with which she binds a high degree of emotional intensity in a formal pattern.

The anger of Archilochus and Alcaeus in their poems of personal hatred is no less profoundly emotional than the passion and longing of Sappho. What is new in her poetry is the capacity to enlarge on emotion by myth or simile or description that replaces direct statement by illustration. The epode in which Archilochus curses the friend who betrayed him is un-forgettably expressive, but the hated one remains, throughout, the specific subject; the only way in which the poem moves from the immediate and personal level is through the re-sonances of Homeric evocations. In Alcaeus's poetry we find an artistically controlled expression of the poet's outlook almost only in the poet's dramatic mythological scenes, without specific linking to a contemporary topic. Only in Sappho, among these poets, do we repeatedly find the effective combination of a deeply felt current experience and an impression of that ex-perience conveyed by an inset scene that illuminates the im-mediate both by a complex relevance to it and a distanced reflection that enlarges and enhances the immediate. In 16, Helen's love of Paris illustrates a general truth about love, expresses the importance to Sappho of Sappho's love of Anactoria, and suggests by the combination that Sappho's emotion has a general significance. In 1, the picture and attitude of Aphrodite show us what love means in Sappho's life and what her current distress in love means for her and for the experience of love. In 96, the moonlit scene reflects the beauty of Atthis's absent beloved and suggests depths of beauty and significance in the phenomenon of love. This dynamism and comprehensive relevance of a part of a poem that is, relatively, at a remove from the immediate, is a significant step toward the complex relationships between contemporary experience and the myth-world of heroes that we find in the poetry of Pindar.

Perhaps we have lost some of the romantic excitement of "burning Sappho," the vehicle of passion, but we have gained much through coming to know better a poet of mature and energetic skill in composition.

CHAPTER FIVE

Anacreon

The second half of the sixth century was the period in which
the greatest development of the choral lyric forms took place.
The partheneion had already become an impressive art form
in the work of Alcman, in Sparta, in the seventh century. The
encomium, dirge, paean, dithyramb, and epinician were developed, and three great masters of choral lyric forms appear,
occupying the century from 540 to 440: Simonides, Pindar,
and Bacchylides. Monody had no such parallel growth. Sappho
and Alcaeus had no great successors. There are just two other
monodists whose extant poetry is significant in quantity,
Anacreon and Corinna, if indeed Corinna is a monodist. Both
are poets of substantial interest but relatively limited range.
Apart from them there is not much more than names, with
here and there a few interesting lines to arrest attention.
Anacreon has, of course, a great place in literary history:[1] he
was, for one thing, an important model for the odes of Horace.
In his years of maturity, Horace sympathized with the attitude
and spirit of the Greek poet, though his own range was much
wider. Of at least equal importance in literary history is the
fact that Anacreon's amatory and convivial poetry was imitated
in a collection of short lyrics composed in late antiquity and
called *Anacreontics*, which became in their turn a principal
model for light poetry of conviviality in the literature of
western Europe during the Renaissance.[2] Anacreon was an
extraordinarily imitable poet; much Attic poetry—the lyrics

of Aristophanes in particular—and Hellenistic poetry bears the
stamp of his style. There are grounds also, as our examination
of the fragments of Anacreon will suggest, for believing that
his manner of presentation contributed to the development of
epigrammatic poetry. It is therefore fitting that some of the
Anacreontics should have their way into the Palatine Anthology.

There is hardly anything, if there is anything at all, worth
saying about the course of monody between the time of Sappho
and Alcaeus and that of Anacreon, though a half-century or
more may have elapsed. It is conceivable that some of the
names we hear of in connection with the development of music
in the sixth century, such as Echembrotus, who won the first
victory in the flute-accompanied song at Delphi in 586, and
Sacadas, who in the same festival triumphed in flute-playing
and is said to have composed poems as well as tunes, had some
part in the history of lyric monody, but this is beyond recapture
and must in any case have been slight and peripheral; the
flute was more closely connected with elegy and with choral
lyric than with monody.

We arrive at Anacreon, then, directly from Sappho and
Alcaeus. He has affinities with both, but most of the affinities
are superficial. Like Sappho, he wrote poems of love; like
Alcaeus, he wrote drinking songs. Presently, a few examples
will show how vastly different he is from his predecessors in
both types. He is far closer in spirit, though not in form, to his
contemporary, the choral poet Ibycus, two brief fragments
(*PMG* 5 and 6) of whose poetry on love have a sophistication
of tone and a brilliance and complexity of metaphor which
Anacreon alone of the monodists approaches. This kinship
between a monodist and a choral poet demonstrates that the
two branches of lyric need not, at this stage, be very different.[3]
Nevertheless, the distinction is generally valid, and there is a
strong contrast between some of the very personal songs of
Anacreon and, a generation later, the elaborate choral poems

of Pindar, the performance of which seems to have been a major communal event.

Anacreon was an Ionian, as were most of the elegists, and this community of heritage may account for the community of attitude that is perceptible; Anacreon's own few elegiac fragments are significantly different in spirit neither from his other poetry nor from other contemporary elegy. His native state of Teos, a small city a little south and west of Smyrna, was close to the heart of Ionian civilization. In the era when Persian power supplanted Lydian in the cities of Asia Minor, about 545 B.C., Anacreon left Teos,[4] as did most of the populace, and settled in Abdera, on the Thracian coast northeast of Thasos. Of the rest of his life we know only that he lived for some time, probably a number of years, at the court of Polycrates, tyrant of Samos, and spent periods in Athens, first during the time of the Peisistratids, and then later when Aeschylus was already producing plays. We have not enough evidence about the circumstances of the writing of his poetry to link it with any particular period of his life (except for a few fragments attached to his sojourn at the court of Polycrates) and thus there is no useful purpose in trying to guess at the dates.[5] He is said by Eusebius to have flourished 532–529. To judge by his references to his gray hair and age, as well as by the chronological link with Aeschylus, he did not die young. We may place his life span at roughly 560-480.

Anacreon was not a prolific poet, if, as is recorded, his works in the Alexandrian edition consisted of only five books.[6] This is a little more than half of what Sappho left. His reputation in antiquity was as a writer of amatory and convivial poetry.[7] Cicero, indeed, declares that his poetry is *tota amatoria* but convivial poetry can well enough be amatory. Horace's imitations, drinking scenes and the half-humorous plight of the lover, usually the aging and unsuccessful lover, the objects of whose affections are oftener than not handsome boys, might be similarly described.

On the whole the extant fragments confirm this range of subject matter—a notably restricted range—provided that we accept, as Horace did, convivial poetry as embracing the kind of writing that informally urges a philosophy of life. The extant fragments tell us one further, fundamental fact about Anacreon's poetry that neither ancient comment nor ancient imitation gives much idea of: Anacreon was by temperament and habitual practice an ironist, and along with this a gifted satirist, often sharp, and once, at least, vehement; much of his extant verse is tinged if not permeated with the spirit of irony or ridicule, as likely to be directed against himself as another. If we do not perceive this characteristic it is not possible to understand the essential spirit of Anacreon's poetry. One more generalization: Anacreon was comparable with Archilochus as an ingenious, enterprising, and successful metrical experimenter.

Since Anacreon was regarded in antiquity as above all a poet of love, let us look first at what we have left of this type of poetry. In the broadest sense, most of the extant pieces can be so classified. Yet there is in his love poetry virtually none of the passion and earnestness that we find in Sappho and Catullus. Anacreon's most serious tone in amatory verse has an objectivity and reflectiveness foreign to erotic passion. Often, too, his love poetry has much of the sportiveness and whimsy of Horace's, with the lightness of tone modified by a note of irony or satire.

There are a few more than twenty pieces of Anacreon's poetry over two lines long, and most of these are not much longer. Of the longest pieces left, the majority are at least partly concerned with love. Papyrus discoveries have not as yet added much to the extant store of Anacreon's poetry, but of the two papyri that are reasonably, though not certainly, ascribed to him, both contain pieces of amatory verse that illustrate Anacreon's typical handling of this theme. POxy 2321 (which appears as Fr. 1 in Page's *Poetae Melici Graeci*, the

numbering of which is followed in this chapter except where
another edition is specified) contains two fragments of sufficient
length to provide substantial, though in one case bafflingly
ambiguous, information about the poetry of Anacreon. The
first and longer of these (1, fr. 1) is in three-line strophes of
predominantly choriambic and iambic units, each verse different. Thirteen lines are preserved, the first consisting only of
scattered letters. Then we read:

φοβερὰς δ' ἔχεις πρὸς ἄλλῳ
φρένας, ὦ καλλιπρόσωπε παίδων ·

καί σε δοκεῖ μὲν ἐν δόμοισι
πυκινῶς ἔχουσα μήτηρ
ἀτιτάλλειν · σὺ δέ . . .

τὰς ὑακινθίνας ἀρούρας
ἵνα Κύπρις ἐκ λεπάδνων
. . . ας κατέδησεν ἵππους

. . . δ' ἐν μέσῳ κατῆξας
. . . δι' ἄσσα πολλοὶ
πολιητέων φρένας ἐπτόεαται,

λεωφόρε λεωφόρ' Ἡροτίμη ·

Toward another your mind is timorous, O most fair-faced
of children;

(Your mother?) thinks that she tends you close (at home?),
but you . . .

The hyacinthine fields, where the Cyprian tethers her
mares, by their yoke straps . . .[8]

. . . in the midst you have shattered . . . at which the hearts
of many of the citizens were struck,

You are a thoroughfare, Herotime, a thoroughfare.

Much is unclear.[9] It is disputable whether the last line belongs with the rest or begins a new poem. If it begins a new poem, then the καλλιπρόσωπος παῖς ("fair-faced child") of the second line quoted may be a youth, and the belief that *pais* is more likely to refer to a youth than a girl is the principal reason for thinking that the last line does not belong with the rest. But it is by no means clear that *pais* must be a youth; in Fr. 3 *pai Dios* is Artemis, and in Fr. 28 there may be a use of *pais* for a girl.[10] There is no papyrological evidence to suggest that 13 begins another poem. The left margin is gone and with it evidence that the presence or absence of a *coronis* might have provided; but there is no extra space between 12 and 13, and there is no punctuation mark at the end of 12, whereas there is a high period after 13. This last fact is of questionable weight; other fragments of POxy 2321 have punctuation, and thus the mark after 13 is no isolated accident; on the other hand no other line of Fr. 1 has any punctuation, even though the ends of 2, 8, 10, 11, and 12 are visible. Of these only 12 seems to call for punctuation. There is one bit of intrinsic evidence to balance the uneasiness caused by the feminine use of *pais;* the horses of Aphrodite, in line 8, are apparently female, and there would be a point in their so being if a young woman is pictured as in some sense joining and thus becoming one of them. On the whole it is best to assume that the fragment is all of one poem, of which neither beginning nor end is preserved.

The point is crucial, and not only to the sociological question of Anacreon's taste in love partners, which we know, from other evidence, to have included both sexes. It makes a substantial difference also to the tone of the poem. Without line 13 we have, according to the restorations printed above,[11] a picture of a shy-seeming young person apparently still modestly at home under parental eye, but really in the flowering fields of Aphrodite, where the goddess's animals graze. The part played by the citizens is obscure, but it is worth noticing that the verb that describes their reaction (which may be the excitement of desire or of terror) is the same as that used by Sappho in describing her heart's response to the sight of her beloved (Fr. 31. 6).

There would be nothing in this to suggest that the poem is not in essence a genuine expression of love. The fancifulness of the imagery of Aphrodite's fields and mares, and the archness with which the contrast between the apparent and real behavior of the "child" is put, show a high degree of artistic objectivity and not necessarily a lack of sympathy. But if line 13 belongs to the poem, as I believe we must suppose, then a different note is sounded, a note which we shall see to be typical of Anacreon. The word λεώφορος, "thoroughfare," is meant to sting, and Anacreon repeats it. The bashful Herotime is not only called a devotee of Aphrodite, she is called a whore. Anacreon is not speaking simply as a lover. He may indeed be a suitor for the favors of Herotime, but if he is it is on the mocking terms of Fr. 44:

φίλη γάρ εἰς ξείνοισιν · ἔασον δέ με διψέοντα πιεῖν

You are kind to strangers; I too am thirsty; let me drink.

It comes closer to satire than to erotic verse; the ironical balance between the apparent decorum and real promiscuity of the girl ends with a brief, sharp slap. We shall see other examples of poetry that is in subject amatory but in tone something else.

The other substantial piece from POxy 2321 (1, fr. 4) is on the theme of the poet's fistfight with Eros. This theme was already familiar from a fragment quoted by Athenaeus (51):

φέρ' ὕδωρ φέρ' οἶνον ὦ παῖ φέρε δ' ἀνθεμόεντας ἡμὶν
στεφάνους ἔνεικον, ὡς δὴ πρὸς Ἔρωτα πυκταλίζω.

Bring water, bring wine, my boy, bring us wreaths
Bedecked with blossoms, for now I shall box with Eros.

In this mixture of Eros and the symposium the point seems to be that the poet's hope for a successful bout rests in the excellence, or the appropriateness, of his symposiac preparations. The new fragment, consisting of ten partly preserved lines, begins with the word πυκταλίζειν, which ends Fr. 51 and largely creates its tone, and ends with the words that begin 51:[12]

> . . . χαλεπῶς δ' ἐπυκτάλιζον
> . . . ἀνορέω τε κἀνακύπτω
> . . .   . . . πολλὴν ὀφείλω
> . . . χάριν ἐκφυγὼν ἔρωτα
> Δεύνυσε, παντάπασι, δεσμῶν
> . . . χαλεπῶν δι' Ἀφροδίτην.
> . . . φέροι μὲν οἶνον, ἄγγει
> . . . φέροι δ' ὕδωρ πάφλαζον
> . . .   . . . καλέοι
> . . . χάρις . . .

It was a hard fight . . . But now I look up and raise my head . . . I owe deep gratitude for my escape from Eros, O Dionysus, far from the harsh bondage imposed by Aphrodite . . . Let wine be brought in a bowl, let bubbling water be brought . . . let gracefulness . . .

If the papyrus lines are in fact all from one poem (and there is nothing to suggest otherwise)[13] then it is hard not to couple the poem with Fr. 51, as Gentili does,[14] and to suppose that there is in the two poems a counterpoint elaboration of the link between love and wine. The symposium is the preparation for love and it is equally the refreshment or consolation after the event. The question of Anacreon's success or failure in love is left open, perhaps because the poem is incomplete; but the uncertainty may have been deliberate. In any case, the reversal of the action (from symposium to bout, and the reverse), emphasized by strong verbal echoes, witnesses the highly stylized objectivity of the writer.

A passage from a second papyrus (2, fr. 1) illustrates one or

more kinds of Anacreontic love poetry, and raises a difficult
problem of interpretation. It consists of four trochaic strophes
preceded by the last two lines of a strophe, each strophe
consisting of three trochaic dimeters followed by a clausula
of the same colon catalectic. There appear to be two themes,
the connection between which is unclear. The first ten lines
have to do with the cutting of a boy's long hair; the rest with
the unhappiness of a woman. The preserved lines are easily
readable:

καί κόμης, ἥ τοι κατ' ἁβρὸν
ἐσκίαζεν αὐχένα ·

νῦν δὲ δὴ σὺ μὲν στολοκρός,
ἡ δ' ἐς αὐχμηρὰς πεσοῦσα
χεῖρας ἁθρόη μέλαιναν
ἐς κόνιν κατερρύη

τλημόνως τομῇ σιδήρου
περιπεσοῦσ' · ἐγὼ δ' ἄσῃσι
τείρομαι · τί γάρ τις ἔρξῃ
μηδ' ὑπὲρ Θρῄκης τυχών;

οἰκτρὰ δὴ φρονεῖν ἀκούω
τὴν ἀρίγνωτον γυναῖκα
πολλάκις δὲ δὴ τόδ' εἰπεῖν
δαίμον' αἰτιωμένην ·

ὡς ἂν εὖ πάθοιμι, μῆτερ,
εἴ μ' ἀμείλιχον φέρουσα
πόντον ἐσβάλοις θυίοντα
πορφυρέοισι κύμασι

. . .

. . . of the hair that used to shade
Your gentle neck;[15]

But now you are knob-headed
And the hair has fallen

Into rough hands and flowed in a heap
Down to the black dust,

Falling piteously before
The cut of the iron; and I am pierced
With sorrows. What is a man to do
Who has not succeeded for Thrace's sake?

Now I hear that this preeminent woman
Often thinks tearful thoughts,
Railing at her fate
And speaking thus:

"How well it would be for me
If you would take me, mother,
And throw me into the merciless sea
Boiling with purple waves.

The connective at line 11, δή, permits us to suppose that a new poem begins here, since δή can be incipient. There is no extra interlinear space in the papyrus; the margin is missing, hence no evidence is available from the presence or absence of a *coronis*.[16]

If we suppose that there are two poems we can make little of the second, but the first becomes generally clear. Anacreon expresses grief at the loss of the boy's beautiful hair. Perhaps the boy was Smerdies, since ancient writers mention the incident of the cutting of the hair of this favorite of Anacreon.[17] The mention of Thrace is rather puzzling. But since Smerdies was a Thracian, and since long hair was a Thracian characteristic, Anacreon may be saying that his efforts to maintain the honor of Thrace, by keeping the boy's hair uncut, have failed. The "cut of the iron" and the flow of the hair into the black dust are mock serious, echoing passages in Homer;[18] this would fit with the irony and exaggeration that run through the poem; Anacreon is pierced by sorrows, the word for "sorrows," the same as in Stanza 1 of Sappho's ode to Aphrodite (Fr. 1), clearly too intense a word to express sincere

feelings at such an incident; the "rough hands" of the barber[19]
are implicitly contrasted not only with the boy's smoothness—
no doubt his hands as well as his neck were ἀβραί ("tender")
—but with the poet's hands, much tenderer to the boy than
the barber's, and since αὐχμηρός is often used to refer to "coarse"
or "dry" hair, the contrast between the delicacy of the boy's
hair and the roughness of the barber's hands has a further
dimension of suggestion. The word στολοκρός, which I have
translated "knob-headed," is not found elsewhere except in
Hesychius, who gives two explanations of it. Under the word
itself he says that it means "shorn and rendered bald, either
a tree or a man." But under the word κόλον, which means
"without horns" and is regularly used of animals, he says that
οτολοκρός was also so used. Its use here suggests the soft young-
ness of the boy—he is not yet ready to be shorn—as well as
the deplorable baldness thus created. The implicit comparison
with a bullock or kid is certainly not a note of deadly earnest.[20]

If the whole fragment is one poem there is a substantial
difficulty of interpretation, though the tone of the first ten
lines is of course unaffected. Lobel's suggestion[21] that the "preeminent woman" is "Thrace personified" is far from satisfactory, but no better has been offered.[22] In the final stanza it
is by no means clear why a personified Thrace should "be
pictured as calling upon her mother." And if this stanza is a
continuation, then the desire for death, which must presumably
be induced by the incident of lines 1–10, is frigidly obvious
and excessive, and forms an inartistic anticlimax to the earlier
ironical expression of grief, an anticlimax that is hard to
attribute to a poet with as keen a sense of style as Anacreon
elsewhere shows.

It is fairer to Anacreon, in the absence of clear evidence, to
assume that line 11 begins a separate poem.[23] In this case there
is little hope of a convincing interpretation of the following
two stanzas. Gentili's notion[24] that the ἀρίγνωτος γυνή ("preeminent woman") is a well-known or "conspicuous" hetaira is

not improbable; if he is right, then the pathos of the last stanza
is presumably ironical and the poem may have been, like the
one addressed to Herotime, satirical. The dramatic technique
is somewhat reminiscent of Alcaeus Fr. 10, which is apparently
spoken by a female deer; a similar technique occurs in other
brief Anacreontic fragments (87, 40), spoken by women; 87 is
as follows:

κνυζή τις ἤδη καὶ πέπειρα γίνομαι
σὴν διὰ μαργοσύνην

I am becoming old and worn, because of your lust.

These words appear to strike a note of genuine pathos, but
they are in a satirical context.[25]

The papyrus fragments, in addition to demonstrating the
enigmatic nature of papyrus fragments, are a legitimate sample
of Anacreon's amatory verse: the themes are amatory, but
irony and satire predominate; the choice of words, images,
and poetic forms is imaginative and dramatic. It is sophisticated, intellectual verse, not without some depth of psychological understanding and sympathy, but objective rather than
passionate.

Other fragments of amatory poetry confirm and expand on
these characteristics. The conceit of the fistfight with love and
the irony of the poet's agony over his shorn favorite are
matched by other like sallies. Anacreon, in the spirit that later
tradition attached to Sappho, dives (31) "from the Leucadian
rock into the gray sea, drunk with love (μεθύων ἔρωτι)"; or else
he flies "to Olympus for the sake of Eros, since he does not
wish to sport with me" (33). Or, in a different mood, the poet
threatens to attack the Erotes for their indignities to him,
because (100) "They are violent and impudent and know not
against whom their darts should be hurled." In all these the
leitmotif is irony, the vehicle a whimsical conceit.

The play of fancy is a persistent feature of Anacreon's

amatory poetry. When the poet elaborates on the theme of
Eros fashioning and tempering him, as a metal-worker perfects
his material (68):

μεγάλῳ δηὖτέ μ' "Ερως ἔκοψεν ὥστε χαλκεὺς
πελέκει, χειμερίῃ δ' ἔλουσεν ἐν χαράδρῃ,

Eros, like a bronze-worker, has once again cut me with his
mighty ax, and dipped me in a wintry torrent,

the conceit is clearly dominant, and we feel that the poet as
craftsman keeps his distance from the suffering of his speaker.
But in another picture of Eros (53),

ἀστραγάλαι δ' "Ερωτός εἰσιν
μανίαι τε καὶ κυδοιμοί,

The dice that Eros rolls
Are madness and strife,

the imagery has a sharpness and power suggestive of genuine
distress. Of course we cannot know what emotions Anacreon
in fact felt, but his verses usually suggest detachment.

Not only Eros but his human manifestations are the subject
of the poet's fancy, and two of his most familiar fragments are
elaborations on the horsemanship of love. We have already
encountered the mares of Aphrodite; Anacreon's address to a
"Thracian filly" is the best-known of his poems and was made
more famous by Horace's imitation (72):[26]

πῶλε Θρῃκίη, τί δή με
λοξὸν ὄμμασι βλέπουσα
νηλέως φεύγεις, δοκεῖς δέ
μ' οὐδὲν εἰδέναι σοφόν;
ἴσθι τοι, καλῶς μὲν ἄν τοι
τὸν χαλινὸν ἐμβάλοιμι,
ἡνίας δ' ἔχων στρέφοιμί
σ' ἀμφὶ τέρματα δρόμου ·

νῦν δὲ λειμῶνάς τε βόσκεαι
κοῦφά τε σκιρτῶσα παίζεις,
δεξιὸν γὰρ ἱπποπείρην
οὐκ ἔχεις ἐπεμβάτην.

Thracian filly, why look at me
  With sidelong glance,
Why flee me ruthlessly
  And think that I have no wisdom?
Know this surely, I could well
  Throw a bridle on you,
Take the reins and turn you
  Around the circling track.
But now you crop the meadows,
  You lightly jump and play,
Because you have no rider
  Skilled in horsemanship.

The carefully sustained picture is given an air of lightness
by the simple, lilting, trochaic meter, and an air of irony by
the archness not only of the chief metaphor but of the "pitiless"
flight of the girl; νηλής as in νηλὴς χαλκός ("pitiless sword"),
found at *Iliad* 3. 292 and in many other passages of Homeric
sacrifice and battle, is generally a word of high emotional
content, and is clearly hyperbolic here. The idyllic naïveté of
these meadows, less exotic than the Cyprian's hyacinthine
fields of Fr. 1, is in contrast to the poet's urbane and experienced *sophia*. The *sophia* is not only the explicit point that
he is—though the girl does not know it—wise in the ways of
love.[27] It is also implicit in the whimsical cleverness of what
he says. The poet smiles, knowingly and patronizingly, on the
girl and at his own desires, so cleverly expressed.

In these light-toned artful pictures of love we see the model
for the prettiness and the arch conceits that give the *Anacreontics*
their mild charm. The other well-known metaphor of the
horsemanship of love will help to turn attention to a feature
of Anacreon's poetry that is not generally reflected in the

Anacreontics and that is one of the reasons why Anacreon's own
poetry has a vigor and solidity foreign to the *Anacreontics* (15):

> ὦ παῖ παρθένιον βλέπων
> δίζημαί σε, σὺ δ' οὐ κοεῖς
> οὐκ εἰδὼς ὅτι τῆς ἐμῆς
> ψυχῆς ἡνιοχεύεις.

Boy with the glance of a girl,
I seek you and you heed me not;
You do not know that you
Are my soul's charioteer.

Elaborate conceit is here replaced by brief metaphor that
comes at the end of a declaration, and makes an unexpected
and strong impact. The phrase τῆς ἐμῆς ψυχῆς ἡνιοχεύεις ("you
are my soul's charioteer") is striking not only for the metaphor
but for the meaning of the word ψυχή. In archaic usage ψυχή is
more likely to convey the mere notion of life than the suggestion
of personality which the metaphor gives.[28] On the strength of
the phrase παρθένιον βλέπων ("with the glance of a girl") and
the statement by Maximus of Tyre that Anacreon wrote about
"the eyes of Cleobulus," it has been supposed[29] that the
fragment is from the same poem as the following lines, which
illustrate again, though in what seems a distinctly different
tone, the poet's delight in emphasizing a final stylistic point
(14):

> Κλεοβούλου μὲν ἔγωγ' ἐρέω,
> Κλεοβούλῳ δ' ἐπιμαίνομαι,
> Κλεόβουλον δὲ διοσκέω.

Of Cleobulus I am enamored,
For Cleobulus I am mad,
At Cleobulus I stare and stare.

The rhetorical trick of *polyptosis*, a word in a series of different
cases, structurally dominates this fragment. We have seen

Archilochus using a similar rhetorical device for satire,[30] and indeed the artificiality of this kind of expression lends itself better to satire than to a tender emotion. But *polyptosis* is not Anacreon's only or, I think, main device here for achieving the effect he seeks. The last word, διοσκέω, is a *hapax*, and Hesychius, who tells us that it means "to look steadily at, constantly changing your viewpoint," may have only our passage in mind. It is an odd word, and it has been objected that after words picturing amorous passion it is a wretched anticlimax and must be a textual corruption.[31] But this misses the typically Anacreontic approach: like χάσκει at the end of Fr. 13 (which we shall examine presently) it is a deliberately odd and slightly absurd expression. The poet is laughing at himself. At the climax of the *polyptosis* erotic language is suddenly replaced by a word that suggests not the depth of the speaker's passion but the folly of his behavior.

Anacreon uses this device of sudden point, created by an unexpected final word or phrase, in a variety of ways. One of two short pieces that can be formally classed as hymns is in large part really this kind of rhetorically fashioned amatory verse (12):

ὦναξ, ᾧ δαμάλης Ἔρως
καὶ Νύμφαι κυανώπιδες
πορφυρῆ τ᾽ Ἀφροδίτη
συμπαίζουσιν, ἐπιστρέφεαι
δ᾽ ὑψηλὰς ὀρέων κορυφάς ·
γουνοῦμαί σε, σὺ δ᾽ εὐμενὴς
ἔλθ᾽ ἡμίν, κεχαρισμένης
δ᾽ εὐχωλῆς ἐπακούειν ·
Κλεοβούλῳ δ᾽ ἀγαθὸς γένευ
σύμβουλος, τὸν ἐμόν γ᾽ ἔρω —
τ᾽, ὦ Δεόνυσε, δέχεσθαι.

O lord, who join in play
With Eros the subduer,
And the dark-eyed nymphs,

And rosy Aphrodite,
You who roam
Over high mountain crests,
Come to us, I beseech you,
Hear with favor my prayer:
Be a good counsellor
To Cleobulus, O Dionysus,
Bid him accept my love.

To invoke Dionysus in an amatory cause is not really surprising
in a poet who repeatedly makes close connection between the
theme of conviviality and the theme of love. Like Sappho (Fr. 1),
Anacreon uses the traditional cletic form for a personal and
nonreligious theme. In this short poem—which gives every
evidence of being complete and has been so judged by most
editors[32]—the form of the cletic hymn is nearly complete: the
deity is invoked, praised, and asked a favor. All that is missing
is a description of past relations between deity and worshipper.
But the hymnic form is really only a preparation; the point is
to express the poet's love for Cleobulus, and the point is made
succinctly and suddenly at the end. Dignity is not thereby lost,
because here Anacreon uses no outlandish, mocking word at
the end. The stylish air created by the limpid and graceful
phraseology, the charm of the epithets, and the compressed
unity of the poem give it a stature that is far beyond the
pleasant triviality of Anacreon's imitators in the *Anacreontics*.

Anacreon uses his skill at achieving a sudden and unexpected final point for a sharply satirical effect in one of his
best-known fragments, which may be a complete poem, short
though it is (13):

σφαίρῃ δηὖτέ με πορφυρῇ
βάλλων χρυσοκόμης Ἔρως
νήνι ποικιλοσαμβάλῳ
συμπαίζειν προκαλεῖται ·

ἡ δ᾽, ἐστὶν γὰρ ἀπ᾽ εὐκτίτου
Λέσβου, τὴν μὲν ἐμὴν κόμην,

λευκὴ γάρ, καταμέμφεται,
πρὸς δ᾽ ἄλλην τινὰ χάσκει.

Once again with his crimson ball
Gold-haired Eros hits me,
And with a pretty-sandalled girl
Summons me to play.

But she is from stylish Lesbos
And my hair is gray.
She disdains it, and for another
Girl stands gaping.

There is more of Anacreon in this short piece than in any
other that we have:[33] handsome, succinct imagery, objective
treatment of an amatory theme, graceful self-mockery, and, at
the end, a sudden, sharp sting. The lively and colorful scene
of the first stanza is in contrast to the gray failure of the poet,
spurned by youth and smartness. Then, suddenly, the rejected
poet takes revenge. Some critics believe that the double revenge
indicated by the text as I have given it is more than the poet
intended, and that with the feminine word *allēn* ("other") we
should understand *komēn* ("hair").[34] In any case the indignity
inflicted by the last word is beyond question: smart though
she is when she rejects love, the sophisticated girl from Lesbos
is Eros's victim too; the word *chaskei* clearly implies naive,
open-mouthed wonder,[35] and so her passion is as foolish as
Anacreon's.

The compression and suddenness with which meaning is
realized in these short poems resemble the qualities of the epigrammatic verse which was at that time, in the hands of
Simonides, first achieving literary stature.

We have not yet found much amatory poetry of Anacreon
that is in the Sapphic or Catullan sense wholehearted and
unreserved poetry of love. Fr. 12, the hymn to Dionysus, is
the only poem we have examined that appears to be. There
are a few short fragments that may belong in such a category,

but, considering the mood of what can be judged with certainty,
it is hard not to suspect irony even where we cannot see it
clearly. When Anacreon says (62):

    ἀλλὰ πρόπινε
ῥαδινοὺς ὦ φίλε μηρούς,

Pledge those slender thighs, dear youth,

this may be purely erotic. But since the commentator who
quotes it in discussing the meaning of προπίνειν ("pledge") in
Pindar, *Olympian* 7. 5 cites at the same time a passage in which
Demosthenes uses the same word in bitter irony,[36] to indicate
political betrayal, there are some grounds for suspecting that
the tone of the Anacreontic passage too may be other than what
its surface shows. Without more context we cannot know.
Again the words (94):[37]

πλέξαντες μηροῖσι πέρι μηρούς

Entwining thighs with thighs,

are to all appearances ardently and graphically erotic, but
they are also strikingly like those of Archilochus 72, which, as
we have seen,[38] are almost certainly abusive. When Anacreon
says (83):

ἐρέω τε δηὖτε κοὐκ ἐρέω
καὶ μαίνομαι κοὐ μαίνομαι,

Once again I love and love not,
I am mad and yet not mad,

though the verbal analogy that comes to mind is Catullus's *odi
et amo*, it is far more likely that instead of the conflict of violent
emotions that tortured Catullus, the doubt that Anacreon expresses is of the reality of his feelings. He is torn not by conflicting passions but by a conflict between feelings and the
objective, sophisticated irony that colors so much of his poetry.

Just as in the poetry of Anacreon that can in a formal way be categorized as amatory there is a considerable mixture of tone and themes, so in those fragments that justify the designation convivial or symposiac there are admixtures of love, religion (of a sort), and, of course, irony. There is also a persistent note of moderation that Horace found congenial, and which is in keeping with the urbanity and reserve typical of Anacreon. A four-line elegiac piece, probably complete, gives a good example of this Anacreontic blend:[39]

οὐ φίλος ὃς κρητῆρι παρὰ πλέῳ οἰνοποτάζων
νείκεα καὶ πόλεμον δακρυόεντα λέγει,
ἀλλ᾽ ὅστις Μουσέων τε καὶ ἀγλαὰ δῶρ᾽ Ἀφροδίτης
συμμίσγων ἐρατῆς μνῄσκεται εὐφροσύνης.

He is not my friend, the man who at the well-filled
    mixing bowl
Tells, while he drinks, of strife and tearful war;
But he who recalls the bright gifts of the Muses and of
    Aphrodite
And mixes them with the charm of feasting.

The content needs no comment.[40] One point of style is worth emphasizing, because it gives evidence of a more sophisticated sense of form than we have seen in the earlier monodists. By the word συμμίσγων, in the last line, the poet makes the *kratêr*, the mixing bowl which is the symbol of the symposium, the symbol of his symposiac picture. Instead of enlarging upon the proper mixture in the bowl, he declares, as a cultural *magister vini*, what the proper spiritual components are that go with the gifts of Dionysus. This kind of composition goes beyond ring form (though it embraces it) and achieves a compression and intensity of statement that resemble Ibycus, Simonides, Pindar, and some of the odes of tragedy more than the earlier solo lyric.

The emphasis on the gifts of Aphrodite in connection with a symposium recalls the invocation, in Fr. 12, of Dionysus,

companion of Eros and Aphrodite, to counsel a youth to accept
the poet's love. Anacreon's interest in Dionysus is not, then,
separate from his emphasis on the erotic, but it adds a dimension
to his poetry. Gentili has called attention to the new importance, in the poetry of Anacreon, of "l'elemento dionisiaco."[41]
While of course Anacreon is preceded by Alcaeus as a composer of symposiac poetry, the emphasis on the person of
Dionysus is new, and has more in common with the pervasive
presence of Aphrodite in the poems of Sappho than with the
soldierly *camaraderie* of Alcaeus's symposiac poems. We have
already examined a hymn to Dionysus (12) that exemplifies
this new spirit; another fragment, very incomplete, suggests
the same atmosphere in the conduct of the symposium (65):

ἐπί δ' ὀφρύσιν σελίνων στεφανίσκους
θέμενοι θάλειαν ἑορτὴν ἀγάγωμεν
Διονύσῳ.

Let's put wreathlets of parsley on our brows
And hold a rich festival for Dionysus.

In this kind of poetry, whether it portrays a celebration in
honor of Dionysus, as here, or invokes his help in love, as in
Fr. 12, the question of the degree and quality of religious
feeling is hard to answer, harder than it is in Sappho's poems,
where even though we seldom if ever feel that we are dealing
with formal cult poetry, the figure of Aphrodite is a real
presence. Anacreon was an Ionian, and like other Ionians he
seems more readily than most Greeks to have secularized
traditional religious figures. His Dionysus is a symbol of the
symposium, though less archly so than his Eros is a symbol of
erotic experience. This quasi-religious symbolism is apparently
extended into the realm of political life in a cletic hymn to
Artemis, in glyconic meter (3):

γουνοῦμαί σ' ἐλαφηβόλε
ξανθὴ παῖ Διὸς ἀγρίων

δέσποιν' "Αρτεμι θηρῶν ·
ἦ κου νῦν ἐπὶ Ληθαίου
δίνῃσι θρασικαρδίων
ἀνδρῶν ἐσκατορᾷς πόλιν
χαίρουσ', οὐ γὰρ ἀνημέρους
ποιμαίνεις πολιήτας.

I call upon you, goddess of the hunt,
Light-haired child of Zeus, Artemis,
Mistress of beasts of the wild,
Who now upon the eddies of Lethaeus
Keep watch over a city
Of men with courageous hearts,
And rejoice that you are the shepherdess
Of citizens of no ungentle nature.

There are fewer of the formal characteristics of the cletic
hymn here than in the hymn to Dionysus, but in this case it
is almost certain that less than the whole poem is preserved.[42]
What remains is only an invocation, addressed to Artemis
Leukophryene, the Artemis of Magnesia, but there is as much
emphasis on the people whom the goddess watches over as on
the goddess herself. Whatever the historical connection or
significance of Anacreon's description of the Magnesians,[43]
neighbors of his native city, there can be no doubt that in
calling them both men of courage and men of civilized ways
the poet was concerned to pay them, in the guise of an invocation of their goddess, a compliment.

The theme of moderation in the symposium is a principal
vehicle of Anacreon's strong feeling for civilized behavior.
Athenaeus quotes two short passages (11), in Anacreontics,
which he indicates are from the same poem. The first calls
for the beginning of drinking:

ἄγε δὴ φέρ' ἡμὶν ὦ παῖ
κελέβην, ὅκως ἄμυστιν
προπίω, τὰ μὲν δέκ' ἐγχέας

ὕδατος, τὰ πέντε δ' οἴνου
κυάθους ὡς ἀνυβρίστως
ἀνὰ δηῦτε βασσαρήσω.

Come boy bring us a cup
That I may drink it off
In one breath; and mix
Ten measures of water
With five of wine, for I shall be
A Bassarid, but not a violent one.

The hilarity is to be restrained, just as Anacreon's amatory
passions are restrained. We remember Alcaeus's mixture of
two of wine to one of water. A Bassarid, a Thracian bacchant,
ought to be wild and hybristic; the ironic paradox is in
Anacreon's habitual manner. The other piece, which did not
follow the first directly in the poem, is like it in tone:

ἄγε, δηῦτε μηκέτ' οὕτω
πατάγῳ τε κἀλαλητῷ
Σκυθικὴν πόσιν παρ' οἴνῳ
μελετῶμεν, ἀλλὰ καλοῖς
ὑποπίνοντες ἐν ὕμνοις.

Come let us no more practice
Scythian manners at our wine,
With noise and tumult;
Rather let us have good songs
While we drink discreetly.

This is the civilized spirit that Horace imitated in his poetry
and no doubt shared in his outlook.

Anacreon's subdued and gentle tone, compounded of urbanity
and a strong feeling for the pleasures of living, produces in one
well-known poem, presumably written late in the poet's life,
a Mimnermian melancholy for the passing of youth and
pleasure (50):

πολιοὶ μὲν ἡμὶν ἤδη
κρόταφοι κάρη τε λευκόν,
χαρίεσσα δ᾽ οὐκέτ᾽ ἤβη
πάρα, γηραλέοι δ᾽ ὀδόντες,
γλυκεροῦ δ᾽ οὐκέτι πολλὸς
βιότου χρόνος λέλειπται ·

διὰ ταῦτ᾽ ἀνασταλύζω
θαμὰ Τάρταρον δεδοικώς ·
᾽Αΐδεω γάρ ἐστι δεινὸς
μυχός, ἀργαλῆ δ᾽ ἐς αὐτὸν
κάτοδος · καὶ γὰρ ἑτοῖμον
καταβάντι μὴ ἀναβῆναι.

My temples are already gray
And my head is white,
Sweet youth is no more mine,
My teeth are an old man's
And not much time
Of sweet life remains.

And so I often weep
Through fear of Tartarus;
The dark chamber of Hades
Is terrible, the road down
Is dreary and there is no ready way
For a man gone down to return.

The two strophes are in balance, each devoted to a different aspect of the poet's sorrow. The meter is the variant of Ionic dimeter that is called Anacreontic and is the commonest meter in the *Anacreontics*. The use of this rhythm, usually devoted to gay or ephemeral topics, gives a somewhat macabre air to the poem, as though Anacreon found the dark pessimism of it just next door to the sophisticated playfulness of his poetry of love and wine.[44]

The melancholy brooding and anxiety of this poem are unique, yet closely related to many of Anacreon's usual themes.

There is another unique poem of Anacreon's, the one principal
piece that we have not yet treated, which similarly deviates
from the general pattern and yet represents only an extreme
form of an integral, recurrent, and essential aspect of the art
and attitude of Anacreon. This is the one thoroughgoing and
unsparing satire that we have from Anacreon, and it is also
the longest extant poem of his (43):

πρὶν μὲν ἔχων βερβέριον, καλύμματ᾽ ἐσφηκωμένα,
καὶ ξυλίνους ἀστραγάλους ἐν ὠσὶ καὶ ψιλὸν περὶ
πλευρῇσι . . . βοός,

νήπλυτον εἴλυμα κακῆς ἀσπίδος, ἀρτοπώλισιν
κἀθελοπόρνοισιν ὁμιλέων ὁ πονηρὸς Ἀρτέμων,
κίβδηλον εὑρίσκων βίον,

πολλὰ μὲν ἐν δουρὶ τιθεὶς αὐχένα, πολλὰ δ᾽ ἐν τροχῷ,
πολλὰ δὲ νῶτον σκυτίνῃ μάστιγι θωμιχθείς, κόμην
πώγωνά τ᾽ ἐκτετιλμένος ·

νῦν δ᾽ ἐπιβαίνει σατινέων χρύσεα φορέων καθέρματα
παῖς Κύκης καὶ σκιαδίσκην ἐλεφαντίνην φορεῖ
γυναιξὶν αὔτως . . .

He used to wear a poor cloak, wasp-shaped head-gear,
Wooden ear-rings shaped like dice, and about his sides
The bare hide of an ox,

Unwashed cover of a cheap shield; with bread hawkers
And would-be prostitutes as his friends, the trickster Artemon
Found a dishonest living;

Many a time his neck was in the stocks and on the wheel,
Many a time his back felt the leather whip, and his hair
And beard were plucked.

But now he goes in carriages, wearing golden ear-rings,
Cyce's son, and carries an ivory sun shade,
With the women . . .

Artemon seems to have started his career not only at a low
level but, in garb and habits at least, as a mere barbarian, not

a Greek at all. The punishments of line 7 are not all identifiable in type, but are clearly degrading in nature; the plucking of beard and hair were for adultery. Artemon grown rich is only a dressed-up version of the old Artemon, still with the women.[45] At least one word is missing at the end, and possibly further stanzas, although a complete thought is certainly conveyed.

This satire is remarkable on many grounds. Above all, the use of precise, pictorial description, with long and often harsh epithets, gives a very different impression from the usual Anacreontic tunefulness. The poem is more akin to the epithet-laden epinician, or to the epic style, than to the usual short lines of monody. The sudden turn, in the last strophe, after a slow and careful build-up of the picture of what Artemon was, to what Artemon is now, is an extension of the technique that is apparent elsewhere in Anacreon's poetry; but in contrast with the usual rapidity of the final dagger thrust, there is a gravity here that is, in comparison, cumbersome yet at the same time forceful. The meter too is unusual, with its long lines of choriambics and iambics. The poem does not appeal to all readers; nevertheless, it contains powerful, vigorous, masculine composition. In the earnestness and harshness of its satire it is closer to Archilochus than to the Lesbian poets. Alcaeus can be as angry—angrier, in fact—but when he is he seems to lose the artistic deliberation that is apparent here and in Fr. 79 of Archilochus.

One other line remains from a poem that appears to have been like this one in tone and meter. Anacreon is sneering at someone for his effeminacy and refers (79) to the "chamber where he did not marry but was married." It seems also that Anacreon wrote some political poetry of a biting nature, to judge by one fragment (8) in which he refers to the faction which had seized power in Samos as "chatterers."[46]

Apart from this one Archilochian satire on Artemon, the poetry of Anacreon leaves the impression of being the work of an artist who had more originality and delight in expression than earnestness or profundity in what he said. In the words of an Italian critic, he is above all a "poet of courtliness, moved by no idealism . . . dedicated to pleasure: to love and wine, on such terms as to avoid inducing discomfort, to provide life with some lightness and ease."[47] If we had more of his poetry, the spirit of Fr. 43 might prove to be less atypical than it now appears. Moreover, the playful archness of manner should not blind us to the sharpness and firmness that Anacreon's amused irony and carefully moderated calls to pleasure reveal. Nevertheless, the main impact of Anacreon's poetry is in its craftsmanship, and the recent discoveries have reaffirmed this impression. The variety of his metrical forms is notable; the various Aeolic cola, the refinements and combinations of iambics, trochaics, choriambics, and Ionics, all attest to great skill and originality.

Though we seldom know the dimensions of a poem, it is hard to think of any of Anacreon's poems as being long. The delicate, lilting meters, the lightness of tone, and the rapidity with which a scene is painted and a point made are all marks of brevity. Some of Alcaeus's poems anticipate Anacreon's manner: in the brief and vivid pictures of conviviality as 38, with its somber allusion to Sisyphus, and 346, on the beginning of a drinking party, as well as in the mythological contrast between Helen and Andromache (42), we find the dramatic presentation that occurs again and again in Anacreon.

There is also a substantial debt to Archilochus, and it is probably Archilochus, of his precursors, whom Anacreon most resembles, not only in the biting satire of the Artemon poem or in the richness of metrical experimentation, but in that both poets have a degree of self-conscious irony of attitude that is foreign to Alcaeus and Sappho. The irony of Archilochus is expressed in a refusal to accept the superficial aspects of current standards of excellence: he will not put military decorum before enlightened self-preservation or confuse a general's appearance with his real worth. Anacreon's irony is different;

he too is a critic of society, but his tone is not that of anger or the desire for reform, but that of urbane recognition of the follies and weaknesses of mankind, including himself, which is often expressed with arch exaggeration: the poet is torn by anguish at the cutting of his favorite's hair; a prostitute is called ἀριγνώτη γυνή ("preeminent woman"); the poet will fling himself from the Leucadian cliffs or take up arms against Eros. Closely related to this habitual irony is Anacreon's delight in conceits (the horsemanship of love, Eros as blacksmith, and so on) and in the creation of meaning, often ironical meaning, by an unexpected ending, as in the poem concerning the girl from Lesbos and in the *polyptoton* on Cleobulus. These devices are a development in the same direction as the contemporary development of the art of the epigram, and both styles are moving away from the older lyric art to something closer to the scenic vividness of drama on the one hand and to the elaborations and rhetoric of prose on the other hand. The degree to which Anacreon makes lyric poetry a mannered and specialized craft may be a substantial cause for the failure, so far as we can tell, for monodic lyric to develop much after him.

CHAPTER SIX

Minor Voices

After Anacreon there are no monodists who have left substantial fragments except for Corinna, whose date is so doubtful that her poetry has a very isolated place. There are three poets whom, on the strength of the little we have, we could wish to know better: the doughty Telesilla of Argos, her near neighbor Praxilla of Sicyon, and the pugnacious Timocreon of Rhodes. Three others are mere shadows: Myrtis, Charixena, Cydias.[1]

Dating can be only approximate, but all six of these minor figures seem to belong to the late sixth and first half of the fifth centuries. Myrtis, whose home was the Boeotian village of Anthedon, was allegedly the teacher and a competitor of Pindar. That is the sum of our knowledge about her, except that Corinna thought that she had been ill-advised to enter, as a mere woman, into competition with Pindar. This tradition may conceivably mean that Myrtis, unlike Corinna and other poetesses, who adhered to local stories and a local dialect, used the themes and the style of the great choral lyricists, and in that sense was Pindar's competitor. But the one poem by Myrtis of known content (known by report; there are no fragments) is on a local theme, the sad story of Ochna and Eunostos, a Boeotian version of the story of Potiphar's wife, with an aetiological point. It answers the question, "Why are women barred from the shrine of Eunostos?"[2] (Answer: by falsely accusing Eunostos of raping her, Ochna caused him to be killed by her brothers.) In its obscurity and localism this is much the kind of subject that Corinna herself worked with.

This was an age of poetesses in the field of monody. Perhaps the growing dominance of choral lyric attracted the best poetic talents among men to it. Sappho wrote for marriage celebrations and Praxilla wrote a dithyramb, but it may be that generally the poetesses did not, and possibly could not, concern themselves with festivals and ritual occasions in which women did not participate and which they perhaps did not attend. Given that a number of women achieved success as poets, it is surprising that there is no trace of their having composed for so feminine a choral occasion as that of the partheneion. Whatever the reason, it was in the private, local, personal, relatively informal world of monody that the women of ancient Greece gained their place in the history of lyric poetry.

Telesilla of Argos was not only a poet of repute, but is said, in a story told by Herodotus, Plutarch, and Pausanias, to have saved her city from the Spartans. When the flower of the Argive army had been treacherously killed, she led the defense of the city and by the example of her bravery so inspired the Argives that they sustained a siege until the Spartans wearied and withdrew.[3] Of her poetry we have, apart from a few individual words, just two short lines, preserved by Hephaestion as an example of the meter named Telesillean for her, and consisting of a glyconic minus the first syllable ($-\cup\cup-\cup-$). The lines are (*PMG* 717):

ἁ δ᾽ Ἄρτεμις, ὦ κόραι,
φεύγοισα τὸν Ἀλφεόν

Artemis, O maidens, fleeing Alpheus . . .

They are probably the opening lines, since it is Hephaestion's practice to quote the beginning of a poem, and so we may guess that the subject was the story of Artemis and Alpheus. The address in the first line suggests the possibility of some

kind of *Mädchenkreis* like that of Sappho, but there is no
other evidence. We are informed that Telesilla wrote poems
about Apollo in which she referred to a temple of Apollo
Pythaeus, connected with the Argive town of Hermione; that
she mentioned also a temple of Artemis in Epidaurus; and that
she told the story of the slaying of the Niobids, which she might
well have done in poetry about Apollo and Artemis. The
emphasis on local stories is conspicuous. She may have written
a poem on the marriage of Zeus and Hera—the evidence is
in a scholium on a Theocritus papyrus—and this too could
have had local color, in view of the prominence of Hera in
Argos.[4]

Praxilla of Sicyon has left two famous fragments and a meter
named for her. The meter consists of three dactyls followed by
a trochaic metron. A two-line sample is preserved by
Hephaestion (*PMG* 754):

ὦ διὰ τῶν θυρίδων καλὸν ἐμβλέποισα
παρθένε τὰν κεφαλὰν τὰ δ' ἔνερθε νύμφα

You who glance sweetly in through the window
Maiden of face, bride below . . .

This intriguing start could lead almost anywhere. Is it praise?
Invective? A riddle poem?[5] We know no more. Of the two
well-known fragments, one is a couplet in greater Asclepiadeans
that was popular as a symposiac song (*PMG* 749):

Ἀδμήτου λόγον ὦ ἑταῖρε μαθὼν τοὺς ἀγαθοὺς φίλει,
τῶν δειλῶν δ' ἀπέχου γνοὺς ὅτι δειλῶν ὀλίγα χάρις.

Learn the story of Admetus, my friend, and love noble men,
Avoid the base; know that the base have little love.

Admetus is the example of the noble, of course, for his kindness
to Apollo; there is presumably not meant to be any suggestion
of the doubts and questions raised in Euripides'*Alcestis*. The

other principal fragment owes its preservation to the scorn with which its picture of Adonis was greeted. It consists of three hexameters, taken from a speech made by Adonis in answer to a question put to him by the Shades below, who, after his death, asked him what he thought was most beautiful in the world above. Adonis's answer was such that it gave rise to a saying, "Sillier than Praxilla's Adonis" (*PMG* 747):

κάλλιστον μὲν ἐγὼ λείπω φάος ἠελίοιο,
δεύτερον ἄστρα φαεινὰ σεληναίης τε πρόσωπον
ἠδὲ καὶ ὡραίους σικύους καὶ μῆλα καὶ ὄγχνας ·

The fairest thing that I left was the light of the sun,
Next, the shining stars and the face of the moon,
And then ripe figs and apples and pears.

The juxtaposition of the traditionally admired beauty of the firmament with the earthy and ordinary beauty of ripe fruit was too much for ancient critical taste. It is hard to know how to understand these lines. There may be a deliberate comic intent, but more likely the combination of discrepants arises from a naïveté something like that of Sappho, who ranges from traditional examples like the moon and dawn to such ordinary things as ribbons and hats, although not with such direct juxtaposition as there is in these lines. The sudden descent from heaven to ripe fruit is slightly bizarre, but it is not without appropriateness. Adonis, the spirit of growth, is thought of as longing above all for those things that symbolize the charms and abundance of nature. Is the silence about Aphrodite significant? We are barred from certain understanding by the absence of further evidence.

There is little more to say of Praxilla. She wrote a dithyramb called *Achilles*, from which a single hexameter remains. She was, then, in part a choral poet, though it is unlikely that all her poetry was choral. There are a few other traces of mythological subjects, and that is all.

Although Timocreon of Rhodes was best known as a writer
of comedies, he was also a lyric poet and a composer of invective poetry. He became the bitter enemy of Themistocles
who, when Timocreon had been sent into exile for Medizing,
declined to arrange for his recall in spite of their previous
friendship, and in spite of the fact that Themistocles was instrumental in the recall of several others in Timocreon's
position. The principal extant fragment of Timocreon is a
lively and abusive attack on Themistocles for his behavior
after the defeat of the Persians, when Themistocles did a good
deal of questionable political organizing, with financial under-
tones, among the island states. The poem is in dactylo-epitrites
and largely in the dialect of choral lyric.[6] Otherwise there is
no indication that the poem was choral, and it is of a type
unlikely to have been choral. The three extant strophes are
probably the entire poem (*PMG* 727):

ἀλλ' εἰ τύ γε Παυσανίαν ἢ καὶ τύ γε Ξάνθιππον αἰνεῖς,
ἢ τύ γε Λευτυχίδαν, ἐγὼ δ' Ἀριστείδαν ἐπαινέω
ἄνδρ' ἱερᾶν ἀπ' Ἀθανᾶν
ἐλθεῖν ἕνα λῷστον, ἐπεὶ Θεμιστοκλῆν ἤχθαρε Λατώ,

ψεύσταν ἄδικον προδόταν, ὃς Τιμοκρέοντα ξεῖνον ἐόντα
ἀργυρίοισι κοβαλικοῖσι πεισθεὶς οὐ κατᾶγεν
πατρίδ' Ἰαλυσὸν εἴσω,
λαβὼν δὲ τρί' ἀργυρίου τάλαντ' ἔβα πλέων εἰς ὄλεθρον,

τοὺς μὲν κατάγων ἀδίκως, τοὺς δ' ἐκδιώκων, τοὺς δὲ
    καίνων ·
ἀργυρίων δ' ὑπόπλεως Ἰσθμοῖ γελοίως πανδόκευε
ψυχρὰ τὰ κρεῖα παρίσχων ·
οἱ δ' ἤσθιον κηὔχοντο μὴ ὥραν Θεμιστοκλέος γενέσθαι.

You may praise Pausanias and you may praise Xanthippus,
And you Leotychides, but I praise Aristides
As the best man to come
From holy Athens since Leto has grown to hate Themistocles,

The liar, the cheat, the traitor, who was won
By knavish profit and did not restore Timocreon his friend
To his native city, Ialysus,
But took three talents of silver and sailed away to hell

Restoring some unjustly, expelling others, killing some.
Stuffed with silver he played the ridiculous innkeeper
At the Isthmus, serving cold meats.
And they ate and prayed that no heed be paid to Themistocles.

The allusion to Leto's hatred for Themistocles is probably a
sneer at his fall from power, when he was replaced by Aristides,
on the formation of the Delian League, with its center at Delos,
the island of Leto. The contrast between the honesty of
Aristides and the venality and ruthless injustice of Themistocles
is made the more bitter for Timocreon by the suggestion that
Themistocles was not always thus. The reference in the last
strophe is to the efforts of Themistocles to be awarded the
prize of honor for leadership, when the Greeks met, at the
Isthmus, to make the award. He bribed on a grand scale,
Timocreon implies, but unsuccessfully. Herodotus's version of
the story (8. 123–24), in which Themistocles wins by second
place votes but because of jealousy is awarded no prize, is a
good deal more flattering to Themistocles.

The composer of this poem has, clearly, more comic bent
than lyric. His style is animated but seldom dignified or
moving; the picture is vivid but exaggerated, the invective
against Themistocles strident. The technique is that of satire.
Anacreon's poem on Artemon is the lyric most akin to this,
but Anacreon's poem has far more grace and wit.

The opening lines of two more poems against Themistocles,
in lyric meters, are preserved, one of them written when
Themistocles, in his turn, was charged with Medizing (*PMG*
729):

οὐκ ἄρα Τιμοκρέων μόνος
Μήδοισιν ὁρκιατομεῖ ·

184 EARLY GREEK MONODY

ἀλλ' ἐντὶ κἄλλοι δὴ πονη-
ροὶ κοὐκ ἐγὼ μόνα κόλου-
ρις · ἐντὶ κἄλλαι 'λώπεκες.

So it was not only Timocreon
Who made terms with the Medes;
There are other rascals too.
I am not the only bushy tail;
There are other vixens too.

The meter is iambic, the tone satirical. The animal image is
a link with Archilochus, although the fox occurs also in Alcaeus
(LP 69) as a symbol of guile. A six-line passage inveighing
against wealth, the start of a drinking song according to the
scholium to Aristophanes where it is preserved, is in a different
vein (*PMG* 731):

ὤφελέν σ' ὦ τυφλὲ Πλοῦτε
μήτε γῇ μήτ' ἐν θαλάσσῃ
μήτ' ἐν ἠπείρῳ φανῆμεν,
ἀλλὰ Τάρταρόν τε ναίειν
κ'Ἀχέροντα · διὰ σὲ γὰρ πάντ'
αἰὲν ἀνθρώποις κακά.

Would that you, blind Plutus,
Had never appeared on earth
Or sea or on the continent,
But lived in Tartarus
And Acheron. Through you all
Man's evils come.

There are a few more scraps, one or two of which further
suggest that Timocreon had a predilection for fable in his
poetry. This feature is reminiscent of Archilochus, and so is
the general animated abusiveness of Timocreon's poetry. There
is, however, no trace of Archilochus's emotional power. While
more of the work of this lively and independent spirit would be
welcome,[7] on the whole it does not appear that by the loss of

Timocreon's poetry we have been robbed of a great treasure.
Two other minor names remain to be mentioned. Charixena,
who was a byword for old-fashioned style among the comic
poets of the late fifth century, was a composer of music and
may also have written poetry, but we have no definite trace of
it. Cydias of Hermione, whose dates are very uncertain but
probably fell in the late sixth or early fifth century, is once
quoted by Plato, in the *Charmides*, as a great authority on
matters of love. The fragment advises someone in love "not to
come like a fawn against a lion, to become a portion of his
meat" (*PMG* 714). The exact text is uncertain, and little can
be known except that it was on an erotic theme. One other
notice of Cydias exists (*PMG* 715) from which we know that
he wrote something about an eclipse, but there is not a word
of it left. It is uncertain whether the poem from which the
words, "the far sounding cry of the lyre," are quoted by
Aristophanes (*Clouds*, 967) was written by this poet or by one
Cedeides.

One of the most puzzling oddities in the history of ancient
Greek poetry is the small body of Boeotian poetry ascribed to
Corinna. The poetry itself is unusual in matter and unique in
linguistic appearance. The poet is so substantially unknown
that on present evidence it cannot be agreed whether she was
an older contemporary of Pindar, as ancient tradition has it,
or wrote as much as three hundred years later. She was not
one of the "Nine Lyric Poets," and this ought to mean, if we
accept Wilamowitz's canon,[8] that she was not edited as a
classic of a past age by the early Alexandrian editors. She was
at a later time added to the Nine,[9] which suggests that she
became known only then. Papyrus discoveries have added some
substantial passages to the brief quotations (mostly examples
of Boeotian forms) and references to content that were all that
the indirect tradition provided, but these new fragments do
not settle the problem of date.

Perhaps the oddest of all facts in this puzzle is how little

difference to Corinna's poetry the interval of 250–300 years
makes: she was so little influenced by and had so little influence
on Greek poetry that it does not matter much at which date
she wrote. The evidence for later date[10] is not sufficiently
strong and free of objections to override the persistent, if slight
and late, ancient tradition that she was Pindar's teacher,
adviser, and rival. There is great improbability in the supposition that a learned Boeotian like Plutarch could pass on
the story of Corinna's advice to Pindar on the proper poetic
use of myth if in fact the two poets' lives were spent centuries
apart. The story need not be accepted as true; Plutarch is not
that kind of witness. But since Corinna was sufficiently eminent
to achieve the stature of an edition Plutarch cannot have been
totally ignorant about her life, nor would he have deliberately
promulgated a manifest absurdity.[11]

Whatever her date, Corinna's place in Greek poetry is a
very solitary one. Our knowledge of her career, apart from
Plutarch's story and the information in Pausanias and others
that Corinna defeated Pindar in contests of poetry, consists
only of a notice in the *Suda:* "A Theban of Tanagra, pupil of
Myrtis; nicknamed Fly; lyric poetess; said to have defeated
Pindar five times; wrote five books and epigrams and lyric
nomes." Her works, then, were not very extensive, about
equal to Anacreon's. What is now extant consists of: Berlin
Papyrus 284, which has four fragmentary columns of poetry,
including two sections where a number of consecutive whole
lines are left, of twenty-two and forty lines respectively,
seemingly from two different poems; POxy 2370, the only
papyrus fragment that is unquestionably Corinna's work,
containing lines elsewhere quoted and ascribed to her, and
consisting of about twenty lines that appear to be from an
introduction to a poem or poems, in which Corinna speaks of
mythological subjects she has treated in her poetry; PSI 1174
and POxy 2371–74, which cannot confidently be assigned to
Corinna (though they are Boeotian), and in any case are so

slight in content and dubious in meaning that they would add
almost nothing to our knowledge of Corinna; and, finally,
about twelve brief quotations of a line or two, as many more
of less than a single line, and again as many references to
things that Corinna wrote about.

Essentially, our picture of Corinna comes from the two
passages in P. Berol. 284, which constitute *PMG* 654. Their
similarity to POxy 2370 in dialect, meter, style, and material
is such that ascription to Corinna is fully justified. The first
passage begins with eleven very fragmentary lines and then
becomes readable in the course of a song sung by either
Cithaeron or Helicon, probably Cithaeron:[12]

Κώρει–
τες ἔκρουψαν δάθιον θιᾶς
βρέφος ἄντροι, λαθράδαν ἀγ–
κουλομείταο Κρόνω, τα–
νίκά νιν κλέψε μάκηρα 'Ρεία

μεγάλαν τ' ἀθανάτων ἔσ–
ς ἔλε τιμάν · τάδ' ἔμελψεμ ·
μάκαρας δ' αὐτίκα Μώσῃ
φερέμεν ψᾶφον ἔταττον
κρουφίαν κάλπιδας ἐν χρου–
σοφαῖς · τὺ δ' ἄμα πάντες ὦρθεν ·

πλίονας δ' εἷλε Κιθηρών ·
τάχα δ' 'Ερμᾶς ἀνέφανέν
νιν ἀούσας ἐρατὰν ὡς
ἔλε νίκαν στεφάννυσιν
. . . ατώ. ανεκόσμιον
μάκαρες · τῶ δὲ νόος γεγάθι ·

ὁ δὲ λούπῃσι κάθεκτος
χαλεπῆσιν Fελικὼν ἐ–
. . . λιττάδα πέτραν
. . . κεν δ' ὄρος · ὐκτρῶς
. . . ων οὐψόθεν εἴρι–
σέ νιν ἐμ μουριάδεσσι λάυς ·

"The Curetes hid (?) the sacred infant of the goddess in a cave, secretly from crooked-counselling Cronus since the blessed Rhea had spirited him away

and so won great honor from the immortals." Thus he sang, and the Muses bade the blessed ones bring their secret ballot immediately to the urns shining with gold, and they all rose together.

Cithaeron got the majority, and quickly Hermes proclaimed him, shouting that he had won lovely victory. The blessed gods crowned him with wreaths, and his spirit was glad.

But Helicon, overtaken by sharp grief . . . bare rock . . . and groaning heavily he dashed it in ten thousand boulders.

Here the legible passage ends. How much preceded is unknown. There is a *coronis* between lines 11 and 12 of col. ii, marking the end of a poem, probably of this poem, since the stanzas are still of six lines. That would mean that twenty-nine more lines followed those quoted. Presumably there should be thirty, completing five more strophes; perhaps a line is missing, either through a fault of the copying or a loss from the papyrus.

It is a singing contest between Cithaeron and Helicon, with the Muses, appropriate to the contest and to the region, presiding. The "blessed" who vote must be the Olympians, but only Hermes is named. Corinna is doing what she seems nearly always to have done in her poems; she is telling a local Boeotian myth. The story (an aetiological myth about the eponyms of the two principal mountains of the region) is told with simplicity and clarity, though the appropriateness of the story of the infant Zeus is not apparent. Neither is it clear why the vote goes against the mountain of the presiding Muses. Perhaps Cithaeron over Helicon is meant to symbolize local over national poetry; this would give a sort of analogy to part of the explanation offered by Pausanias for Corinna's victories over Pindar (9. 22. 3): "It seems to me that she won because of her dialect, because she sang, not in Dorian dialect like

Pindar, but in dialect that Aeolians would understand; also because she was the most beautiful woman of her day, to judge by her statue." In fact, the language is very much the standard language of lyric poetry (perhaps more than usually dependent on epic diction) but with a strong overlay of Boeotian spelling that gives the whole the appearance of a quaint and local dialect, reminiscent of Sappho's Lesbian, though perhaps, as Lobel and Maas maintain, less fundamentally vernacular. A good deal of this orthographic quaintness may be the contribution of a Hellenistic editor, since it is third century Boeotian, not fifth. The style is plain, with just a few rather tame epithets (crooked-counselling Cronus, blessed Rhea) and one fairly rare color word, *chrousophaês* "gold-shining." The metrical pattern consists of stanzas of five Ionic dimeters followed by a clausula of the form ∪∪– –∪∪–∪– –. This is not a naive metrical system.

The effectiveness of the poem depends, in essence, on its narrative power. In the elemental and gigantic emotions of the mountainous contestants, especially in the sorrow of Helicon, there is some resemblance to Ovid. The detailed elaboration of the lumbering unreality of these figures is a little like the picture of Mount Tmolus as judge in a musical contest in *Metamorphoses* 11, or of some of Ovid's detailed and bizarre transformations: Arachne becoming a spider, or Baucis and Philemon trees. But there is no break in the earnest naïveté of Corinna's scene, while Ovid is seldom able to maintain such an atmosphere for long without some trace of self-conscious irony. On the whole, the narrative tends to divide with the stanza divisions: 17–22 describe the preparations for voting, 23–28 the effect on the winner, 29–35 the effect on the loser. It may be, as Bolling suggests, that lines 17–18 are not the end of Cithaeron's song but descriptive of the gods' reaction to it.[13] Then the sense division by stanzas would be even more regular. But the scene would develop less dramatically: the result of the vote would be anticipated and the impact of the later stanzas lessened. Also, the following words would come in less naturally. Bolling's word-division, τὰ δ' ἔμελψεμ (τά relative), does not really overcome the awkwardness.

The passage in col. iii consists of eight five-line strophes; these were preceded by ten similar strophes and followed by ten more and two lines of another with no *coronis* visible; in other words, the passage is apparently from a poem of more than 142 lines. The metrical pattern is fairly similar to that of the preceding poem.

The content is another myth, again Boeotian, unfamiliar, and rich in dialogue. As the passage begins, the prophet Acraephen is telling the river god Asopus the whereabouts of nine of Asopus's daughters. He explains that Zeus has three of them, Poseidon three, Apollo two, Hermes one. The poem continues (18–24):

> οὔτω γὰρ "Ερως
> κὴ Κούπρις πιθέταν, τιὼς
> ἐν δόμως βάντας κρουφάδαν
> κώρας ἐννί᾽ ἐλέσθη ·
>
> τή ποκ᾽ εἰρώων γενέθλαν
> ἐσγεννάσονθ᾽ εἰμιθίων,
> κάσσονθη πολουσπερίες.

For thus did Eros and the Cyprian persuade them to go secretly to your house and take nine daughters.

Sometime they will beget a race of heroic demigods, and will be fruitful.

Acraephen then describes how the prerogative of being the prophet of Apollo (at the shrine Ptoon) came to him after Euonymus, Hyricus, and Acraephen's father, Orion.[14] It is not clear how, or even whether, the two topics of the poem were related. At line 46 of col. iii the speech ends, and the final strophe preserved is (47–51):

> ὣς ἔφα μάντις περάγεις ·
> τὸν δ᾽ 'Ασωπὸς ἀσπασίως

δεξιᾶς ἐφαψάμενος
δάκρού τ' ὀκτάλλων προβαλὼν
ὦδ' ἀμώψατο φωνῇ ·

Thus spoke the prophet most holy, and Asopus
gladly grasped his right hand and shed a tear
from his eyes and spoke thus in answer . . .

As in the first story, there is dramatized narrative, with little
adornment. Zeus (in line 13) is, conventionally, "king and
father of all"; Poseidon (line 14) is "sea-ruling" (the standard
Homeric epithet, *pontomedôn*, in tmesis); Hermes (lines 17–18)
is simply "good son of Maia"; Eros, in the first line quoted, is
without epithet. This bareness is alleviated by the vividness
and rapidity that mark Corinna's narrative style. There is a
good deal that is Homeric, as in the two epithets linked by
τε . . . τε (23–24), and the formulas of conversation, ὡς ἔφα
("thus he spoke," 47) and ὦδ' ἀμώψατο ("thus he replied,"
51).

Almost everything else that remains or can be inferred
suggests that these two passages are typical of what Corinna
did, in style and in content. From the indirect tradition we
know some of her other subjects: Orion, Boiotos (son of
Poseidon and eponym of Boeotia), the Seven against Thebes,
Iolaus, the daughters of Euonymus (the first prophet of the
Ptoon), the daughters of Minyas, a battle between Hermes
and Ares. In short, nearly the whole range of Corinna's
mythology is Boeotian, and where there is evidence of her
handling such non-Boeotian themes as the shield of Athena
and the story of Orestes (which occur only in PSI 1174, and
may not be Corinna's) it is not difficult to imagine a Boeotian
connection.

A few fragments reveal poems or parts of poems on personal,
not mythological, subjects. Thus Fr. 664 *PMG*, "For my part
I blame even sweet-voiced Myrtis for entering, woman as she
is, into rivalry with Pindar." The passage was quoted to

illustrate a grammatical form, and no hint of context is given. It need not be more than an introductory personal section, possibly justifying Corinna's own adherence to the local scene for her material and her audience. Such a personal introduction seems to be preserved in POxy 2370 (*PMG* 655), where Corinna declares that "Terpsichore (comes to) me as I sing the fair deeds of heroes[15] for the women of Tanagra, with their white gowns, and greatly the city rejoices in my sweetly flattering voice." The rest of the fragment goes on to mention some themes that she has "adorned with words," including the stories of Cephisus and Orion.

Corinna was, then, a provincial poet, specializing in Boeotian narratives and addressing herself to the woman of her native town of Tanagra. It is not certain whether Corinna's poetry was meant for choral or for solo performance. Solo is more probable, since there is no indication that her poetry was of any known choral type, and it is difficult to see what choral occasion it would have served.[16] The slight evidence we have suggests that her poems were longer than most monody, but the short cola and strophes she uses and the metrical patterns are akin to monody rather than choral lyric. Moreover, the longest known poems of Sappho (44) and Alcaeus (*LGS* 138) are poems entirely or largely on mythological topics, just as these poems of Corinna are.

Corinna is a curious cross between the highly personal and localized Sappho and the practitioners of narrative lyric such as Stesichorus and Bacchylides. If we had more of Sappho's narrative poetry, like Fr. 44, we might have something closer in spirit to Corinna. But the comparison with Sappho does not go far. Corinna's was a much less powerful and expressive lyric voice than Sappho's. We find in her work nothing of the striking impact of individual personality that gives the monodic poetry of Archilochus, Alcaeus, and Sappho its special charm and excitement. Corinna's fame seems to have rested on her treatment of Boeotian myths in lyric form. She did this with narrative and dramatic liveliness, but with a rather barren simplicity of style, little elegance, and no perceptible warmth of personal participation. In her very different way she is as distant as Anacreon from the earlier personal poetry.

CHAPTER SEVEN

Monody and Epigram

Monodic lyric had only a brief formal history. The genre had scarcely achieved its proper nature when it yielded to and was incorporated into other forms of poetry. In its brevity, the history of monody is like that of Greek tragedy as we know it. But whereas tragedy developed into an undistinguished continuation of itself in the fourth century B.C., monody died both a more clearcut and a more fruitful death. While there was, in later centuries, a continuing trickle of poems that are formally to be classified as lyric monody, this poetry is quantitatively as well as in quality a negligible body. The real continuation of solo lyric was in other forms of poetry. We can therefore more appropriately speak of a transition to related forms, which experienced a lively and interesting literary flowering, than of a conclusion to the record of monody.

Monody begins with a strong dependence on epic, its language and style reflecting those of epic. Throughout monodic lyric, in fact, as in all the genres of Greek poetry, the Homeric and epic background continues as an active and profound influence in stories, diction, and outlook. The links are strongest in Archilochus, where Homeric phrases abound, often in applications or contexts that contrast strikingly with their originals. There is already present in Archilochus, however, the metrical independence from Homer that constitutes a fundamental distinction between the markedly innovative poetry of the lyric tradition and such poems as the *Homeric Hymns* and the

Hesiodic corpus. Hesiod is, of course, very conscious of a difference between his purposes and concerns and those of Homer, and it would be wrong to suggest that his poetry is without significant innovations. Yet because the metrical and dictional similarities are so close to Homer, one can more readily describe the Hesiodic poetry as an extension of epic to new territory than as a distinctly new kind of poetry.

Metrical freedom from epic and metrical variety are evidently important in the achievement of new departures in poetry. They are so not only because of the intrinsic novelty of their rhythm and music but because they helped to break the hold of the traditional patterns of style imposed by hexameter verse. The *Homeric Hymns* to Demeter and Hermes are superior and delightful works of literature, but they are stylistically almost indistinguishable from such narratives within the epic corpus as the story of Ares and Aphrodite in *Odyssey* 8. They maintain the relative impersonality of the epic poet. As we noticed in Chapter Two, the further Archilochus departs metrically from epic, the more completely does his poetry free itself from the epic style in other respects as well. The epodes and the asynartetic fragments provide the most dramatic, the most personal, and the most emotional of his poetry. But almost everywhere in Archilochus's poetry we are aware of the presence of the poet; and we are aware, in a personal way, of his addressee. Someone is nearly always being challenged, advised, satirized, or cursed. The voice of Archilochus replaces the impersonal voice of the epic poet, and a specific, concerned addressee replaces the undesignated audience of epic, which is presumably the community. Personal experience and exemplifying fable replace myth and saga.

While there are present in the poetry of Archilochus the factors essential to the development of personal poetry, they are still, in some important ways, only nascent. With the Lesbian poets the monodic genre reaches its maturity, both in the stanzas which by their use of them became the typical monodic form, and in the conspicuous localism of the language and content. It is doubtful that Archilochus had any direct influence on the development of their stanza form, which probably came from a separate tradition of cult hymnody. But in effect his epodes and asynartetic verses are transitional from stichic to stanzaic poetry, far more so than the elegiac couplet, because of their much closer affinity of rhythms.

While no poet could be more personal in his expression of emotions than Archilochus, in the poetry of Alcaeus and Sappho the sense of personal presence is broadened and more individualized. The dialect of Alcaeus and Sappho, with its many Lesbian idioms, is much further removed from the language of epic than is Archilochus's Ionic. Also, their mythological and religious references are often peculiarly Lesbian, as in the case of the divine trinity of Hera, Zeus, and Dionysus, invoked by both poets. Their frequent use of myth rarely brings them close to epic. Sappho's juxtaposition of myth and immediate situation, and Alcaeus's succinct and dramatic moral illustrations are more akin to the fables of Archilochus than to epic saga. Only in such rare instances as the narrative myth of Sappho 44 is there anything approaching the epic manner. Similarly, the hymns of Sappho and Alcaeus bear little resemblance, apart from specific borrowings by Alcaeus, to the *Homeric Hymns*, which carry on the diction and style of epic along with its meter.

The individual personality of the poet and his exact location in time and place are further emphasized by the nature of the audience. When Archilochus addresses someone like Glaucus or Pericles we usually have no indication of the relationship between poet and addressee. We assume that they are fellow soldiers or fellow citizens. In the case of Glaucus we now know, from epigraphical evidence, that he was the leader of the Parians fighting on Thasos; elsewhere we assume those addressed to be members of the community at large. But the people to whom Alcaeus and Sappho address their poems are members of a special and private audience, a group of political conspirators or a circle of women bound together in an emotional union.

This address to a private audience, separate from the polis as a whole, was probably momentous for the history of Greek lyric. Both Alcaeus and Sappho were strongly individualistic and independent, and their personal statements, their interpretations of myth and of contemporary society, and their refinements of poetic form and language accentuated and perhaps even created distinct cultural groups within the community. Their poetry could not in any full sense be the expression of the whole community. We do not feel this separation in the poetry of Archilochus, even though we are conscious of his intensely personal outlook. He speaks as a member of the citizenry, and even when he addresses someone on very personal matters, as he does Lycambes, the impression remains that the audience is also the community. With Anacreon, finally, we shall arrive at purely personal as opposed to communal poetry. The transition is in process with the Lesbian poets.

The poets' retreat (if this is not too strong a designation) from the polis left a role to be filled. Epic had already lost it, in all likelihood, or was by the beginning of the sixth century fast losing it, with the increasing unreality of its heroic style of life in relation to contemporary society. The earliest elegy had, indeed, a communal role, with its political and military advice and exhortations. Later, under influences which we shall examine presently, the elegiac form became the vehicle for a wide range of styles and emotions, including amatory, convivial, memorial, and dedicatory verse. But in the middle of the sixth century it was not elegy, but, above all, choral lyric which expanded its range to occupy the communal preeminence which was alien to the increasingly private nature of monody.

There may have been other monodists in the first half of the sixth century, perhaps using the lyric forms in much the same

way as Sappho and Alcaeus did. But we know nothing of
them. The one successor whom we really do know hastens the
retreat into privacy that the Lesbian poets began. Anacreon,
though his poetry continues the stanzaic tradition of the
Lesbians, was by natural bent far more of an ironist than
Sappho or Alcaeus, and his bent strongly influenced his use of
the genre. There is apparent in his poetry a high degree of self-
consciousness in the use of forms and themes, an increase in
wit, whimsy, and epigrammatic thrust. These characteristics
combine to produce a great division between the outlook, the
attachments, and the adventures of the poet in his private
world and the public, political world of the state.

At the risk of over-simplifying, one could say in summary
that monody begins its history as the poetic response of a
society that has grown away from monarchy and feudalism
and has come to value the exploits and the opinions of the
citizen; that it reaches the high point of its development with
two contemporary poets the intensity of whose emotional and
social attachments can only be satisfied by the loyalties and
excitement of special groups within the state; and that it has,
in another generation, moved away from its original role as
the expression of the citizen, the *politês*, and has taken on the
private voice of the artist as observer and craftsman.

The sixth and early fifth centuries were a time of increasing
brilliance and fame for choral lyric. The growing prevalence
of great public festivals engaged and rewarded the efforts of
poets whose extant works clearly indicate their proficiency and
interest in poetry much like that of Sappho and Alcaeus. Thus
not only are Simonides, Pindar, and Bacchylides writing choral
poetry instead of monody, they are, often, writing choral
poetry that embraces the spirit, the function, and in a partial
way, the material of monody. Simonides' lines on Danae and
Perseus afloat λάρνακι ἐν δαιδαλέᾳ ("in a colorful chest," *PMG*
543) have in sentiment, matter, and treatment much in common with poetry of Sappho and Alcaeus; the two erotic

fragments of Ibycus (*PMG* 286, 287) have a quality of passion and personal concern that seems more appropriate to monody than to choral lyric.[1]

In the same period, in Attica, the festivals of Dionysus with their performances of dithyramb, tragedy, and comedy came to occupy Athenian literary talent. In turn, the fully developed tragic form deeply influenced the contemporary and subsequent lyric practices, as the extant poetry of Bacchylides and Timotheus, among others, reveals. In the course of the fifth century—whether or not as a result of the influence of tragedy —the element of music came to play a vastly increased role, as we can clearly gather from the adverse comments thereon in various plays of Aristophanes and in the one extant choral fragment of Pratinas (*PMG* 708). The growing dominance of music meant, for good or ill, a diminution of the importance of words in lyric poetry, and this may have had an especially inhibiting effect on monody, which by the simplicity of its form was the less amenable to such embellishments. Solo singing, moreover, depends more than choral on the intelligibility of what is sung.

Choral poetry and tragedy, then, became the chief lyric expression of the community. But monody had, ultimately, another successor, the epigram. In the chapter on Anacreon attention was called to the specialization of his use of the monodic form of short stanzaic poems in Aeolic meters, his strong tendency toward brevity, wit, and rhetorical point, often with a sudden revelation, at the very end, of the full meaning of the poem or of the sympathy of the poet. These are some of the characteristics of epigram, and it is surely not entirely a coincidence that the Anacreontic lyric and the general decline of monody coincided chronologically with the first rise to prominence of the Greek epigram.

The epigram is the most prevalent and persistent form of poetry through centuries of late Greek antiquity, beginning with the Hellenistic age. While the narrative role that had

earlier been played in turn by epic, choral lyric, and tragedy
is in the Hellenistic period largely taken over by elegy and
hexameter forms, including the type of poem sometimes called
the epyllion, the poetry of personal emotion becomes, apart
from a meager continuation of formal personal lyric, epigram.[2]
Callimachus's epigram (Pfeiffer 2) memoralizing his dead
friend Heraclitus is far closer to the old monody than is any
of the seven formal lyric fragments we have from Callimachus.
Can we see in the early development of epigram, as well as in
the late history of archaic monody, the seed of this succession?

Few if any of the Hellenistic and later Greek epigrams of
the Greek Anthology originated as epigrammata in the original
sense of inscriptions on a tomb or a monument, and the earliest
inscription-epigrams that are known are much more prosaic
and businesslike, much less lyric, than the epigram later
became.[3] Conversely, some of the epigrams in the Anthology
which are ascribed to early poets—Archilochus, Sappho,
Anacreon, and Simonides—almost certainly never appeared
as inscriptions, but represent rather "monodic elegy," perhaps
only parts of the original[4] in the brief, epigrammatic form in
which they are preserved in the Anthology. The inscription-
epigrams are by no means all in the elegiac couplets that
became universal; dactylic hexameter is about as common in
the earliest surviving examples. Why elegiac couplet soon
achieved complete domination is not certain; Paul Friedländer suggests that the hexameter inscriptions represent a
Homeric tradition, and "when men ceased to feel themselves
akin to the heroes of Homer the inscriptions in epic style
became obsolete."[5] This may be, but another suggestion of
Friedländer's seems to me more certainly cogent, and it is
germane to our concern with the link between epigram and
lyric: "[Elegiac couplet] had . . . the artistic advantage of a
closed form, while the hexameter, essentially, admitted of in-
finite repetition."[6] The effect of completion is not, however,
inevitably present in elegiac, as the verses of Tyrtaeus reveal;

there must also be brevity and rhetorical organization to create epigrammatic form from elegy. The need to say something appropriate and emotionally satisfying, and to say it briefly, no doubt had its influence on the development of this style. In the poetry of Anacreon, which is generally brief and rhetorically pointed, we see another manifestation of the same tendency, and it seems likely that the influence proceeded from Anacreon—who inherited established lyric forms largely suitable for his purposes—to epigram rather than the reverse.

Inscriptional poetry is anonymous. The epigrams ascribed to the famous poets of the early period may be later forgeries, as is the case with the three under Sappho's name; they may be contemporary with the poet to whom they are attributed but of unverifiable authorship, as with some of the many that pass as Simonides'; or they may be not epigrams in the proper sense, but fragments of elegies. A striking example of this last class, showing very well the emotional and lyric force of the genre, is the two-line sepulchral epigram that has found its way into the Anthology (*AP* 7. 441) and is numbered as Fr. 16 of Archilochus[7] in Diehl, *ALG:*

ὑψηλοὺς Μεγάτιμον ᾽Αριστοφόωντά τε Νάξου
κίονας, ὦ μεγάλη γαῖ᾽, ὑπένερθεν ἔχεις.

Tall pillars of Naxos, Megatimus and Aristophon,
O mighty earth, you hold beneath you.

In their trenchancy, their sense of completeness, their simple but strong imagery, and their suppressed but evident emotional force, these lines belong to a kind of poetry that both prefigures the later epigram and is closely related to lyric style and spirit.

Simonides, to whom many epigrams are ascribed, must surely in fact have composed many; but to determine which of the extant poems are actually his would be difficult, for the information is inconclusive. Even on the famous ὦ ξεῖν᾽ ἀγγέλλειν ("Stranger, tell them at Sparta . . ." 92 D) the evidence is conflicting.[8] But it is clear that a great increase in the composition of epigrams of literary quality took place in Simonides' day and was much associated with him. *AP* 7. 511 (84 D), not a real sepulchral epigram[9] but verses of condolence for Callias, is ascribed to Simonides. It provides a good example of the dignity and emotional reserve of epigrams of this period:

σῆμα καταφθιμένοιο Μεγακλέος εὖτ' ἂν ἴδωμαι,
οἰκτίρω σε τάλαν Καλλία οἷ' ἔπαθες.

Whenever I look upon the tomb of Megacles, who has perished,
    I pity you, poor Callias, for what you have suffered.

To Anacreon too are ascribed a number of epigrams, and again the problem of determining authenticity is insoluble. Whether Anacreon's or not, the following, ascribed to him, is especially strong and succinct (101 D):

κάρτερος ἐν πολέμοις Τιμόκριτος, οὗ τόδε σῆμα ·
"Ἄρης δ' οὐκ ἀγαθῶν φείδεται, ἀλλὰ κακῶν.

Brave in war was Timocritus, whose tomb this is;
    Ares spares not the brave men but the cowards.

Comparison with an anonymous Attic epigram that was certainly inscribed (it is preserved only epigraphically) shows how close in spirit the Anacreontic lines are to the best of the true epigrams (Friedländer-Hoffleit 71):

Σῆμα πατὴρ Κλείβουλος ἀποφθιμένῳ Ξενοφάντῳ
θῆκε τόδ' ἀντ' ἀρετῆς ἠδὲ σαοφροσύνης.

The father, Cleobulus, set this up for Xenophantus, who is
    dead,
    As a monument to his courage and excellence of spirit.

A poem of two elegiac couplets which is ascribed to Anacreon and classed as an epigram, though perhaps it is not literally one, provides an interesting link between this type of poem and earlier poetry (*AP* 7. 263, 102 D):

καὶ σὲ Κλεηνορίδη, πόθος ὤλεσε πατρίδος αἴης
θαρσήσαντα νότου λαίλαπι χειμερίη
ὥρη γάρ σε πέδησεν ἀνέγγυος · ὑγρὰ δὲ τὴν σήν
κύματ' ἀφ' ἱμερτὴν ἔκλυσεν ἡλικίην.

You too, Cleanorides, were destroyed by longing for your
native land,
Entrusting yourself to the wintry gale of Notus;
The weather, faithless, constrained you, and the flowing
Waves washed away your lovely youth.

The phrase at the end is similar to a phrase in another poem attributed to Anacreon, a trochaic memorial fragment (90 D):

'Αλκίμων σ', ὠριστοκλείδη, πρῶτον οἰκτίρω φίλων ·
ὤλεσας δ' ἥβην ἀμύνων πατρίδος δουληίην.

You first of all my friends I mourn, Alcimon, son of Aristocles;
You lost your youth keeping slavery from your country.

In an epigram ascribed to Simonides (115 D) the phrase ἀγλαὸν ὤλεσαν ἥβην ("They lost their splendid youth") occurs. That the phrase concerning the destruction of youth became an epigrammatic formula is shown by its occurrence in two epigrams of this period preserved epigraphically. One of these, Friedländer-Hoffleit 135, is a four-line poem to Tettichus; the pertinent phrase is in line 3:

ἐν πολέμῳ φθίμενον, νεαρὰν ἥβην ὀλέσαντα.

(Tettichus) who died in war, and lost his tender youth.

In IG I² 943 a single hexameter line has a phrase, ἀπώλεσαν ἀγλαὸν ἥβαν, identical in wording to the phrase in Simonides 115 D. We have, then, four forms of the same basic phrase, in metrically different lines: hexameter, pentameter, and trochaic.

Are the poets adapting to elegiac poetry a formula used in epigrams, or is it a matter of poetic influence on the inscriptions? There is good reason to believe that the direction was from literary tradition to epigram. An earlier, close literary analogy occurs not in earlier elegy or in Homer (though the loss of youth is of course a basic general theme in the *Iliad*) but specifically in iambics of Archilochus (Treu, *Archilochos* 10), in which, despite their very fragmentary condition, the phrases κῦμ' ἁλὸς κατέκλυσεν ("the wave of the sea washed . . . away"), and two lines below, ἥβην ἀγλαὴν ἀπώλεσας ("you lost your lovely youth") are clearly visible.[10] The relationship is thus not limited to general similarities of form and content between epigram and the lyrical tradition. There is also the same closeness of diction that we have seen elsewhere, between Homer and Archilochus, Hesiod and Alcaeus, Archilochus and Alcaeus, and Archilochus and Anacreon.[11]

Only slightly later in time, if at all later, than the lyrics of Anacreon are a group of short lyrics preserved by Athenaeus and called Attic Scolia. The name σκόλιον for a convivial song, may have come from the practice of calling, at a symposium, on one member of the group after another, in irregular (the adjective σκόλιος means "bent," "crooked") order, to sing a song, the irregularity of order increasing the impromptu and informal nature of the procedure. The twenty-five songs preserved by Athenaeus, all of four lines or fewer, in a variety of lyric meters, include invocations of several deities and lyric versions of gnomic *sententiae*, of which the following is an example (7 D):

Ὑγιαίνειν μὲν ἄριστον ἀνδρὶ θνατῷ,
δεύτερον δὲ φυὰν καλὸν γενέσθαι,
τὸ τρίτον δὲ πλουτεῖν ἀδόλως
καὶ τὸ τέταρτον ἡβᾶν μετὰ τῶν φίλων.

Best of all a mortal man's possessions is health,
And second is to be handsome of form;

Third comes wealth, honestly got,
And fourth, to be young with your friends.

In general the emotional intensity is much less than in the
epigrams, but these poems share with epigram brevity and a
strong sense of concise but complete statement. Another and
more specific point of contact is in subject matter. Four of
the Attic Scolia are in praise of the tyrannicides, Harmodius
and Aristogeiton. One of these is as follows (13 D):

Αἰεὶ σφῷν κλέος ἔσσεται κατ' αἶαν,
φίλταθ' ῾Αρμόδιε καὶ ᾿Αριστόγειτον,
ὅτι τὸν τύραννον κτανέτην
ἰσονόμους τ' ᾿Αθήνας ἐποιησάτην.

Your glory will last forever on earth,
Beloved Harmodius and Aristogeiton,
Because you killed the tyrant
And brought equality to Athens.

An epigram on the same subject is preserved by Hephaestion
(Friedländer-Hoffleit 150):

῾Η μέγ' ᾿Αθηναίοισι φόως γένεθ' ἡνίκ' ᾿Αριστο-
γείτων ῞Ιππαρχον κτεῖνε καὶ ῾Αρμόδιος.

Truly a great light came to the Athenians, when
Aristogeiton and Harmodius killed Hipparchus.

Wilamowitz calls this a "Trinkspruch in elegischer Form";[12]
it is very close to the Attic Scolia, and if, as may be the case,
a second couplet, known to have existed later, was part of the
original poem, then the content of the epigram may have been
even closer to that of the Scolia.[13]

Enough has been said to give support to the thought that,
just as the later epigram continued many aspects of monody
and replaced it as a poetic vehicle for personal expression, so
in the years when monody was in the hands of its last archaic

exponents, epigram was already being used for similar topics. There is good evidence that monody had direct influence upon epigram. At a later time the scope of epigram's subject matter was greatly enlarged. While early epigram was inscriptionally functional, and thus almost exclusively sepulchral and dedicatory, in the Hellenistic period epigram became an accepted poetic form with a literary tradition and no longer necessarily or usually had a practical function. It was then extended to many kinds of content and styles of utterance, convivial, declamatory, satirical, amatory. In other words, it came to occupy the field that earlier was held, though never exclusively, by monodic lyric. To compare the persistent flourishing, the variety, and the animation of the Hellenistic epigram with the pallor, derivativeness, and limitedness of material in such late lyric forms as the cult hymns and the *Anacreontics* is to become aware of how complete the transformation was. The similarities that we have observed between the style of Anacreon's lyrics and that of the epigram contemporary with him show the beginning of this succession.

The monodic form that Anacreon practiced was, of course, not the first stage in the development toward epigram. The earlier monodists modified the λέξις εἰρομένη, the strung-out, paratactic style, that is characteristic of most early Greek literary compositions, notably the early elegy, by their penchant for ring form. Anacreon's fondness for brevity and rhetorical point only hastened the process that had already begun. The increasingly epigrammatic monodic form was ultimately replaced by the epigram, which in turn lent itself more and more to the range of subjects, tones, and attitudes that had been characteristic of monody. Thus epigram gave centuries of continuous, lively existence to Greek personal poetry.

As a specific genre of lyric poetry, however, Greek monody virtually ends with Corinna's provincial voice of doubtful age and with the trickle of obscure names and talents that were recorded at the beginning of Chapter Six. There are a few examples from the Hellenistic period—some short fragments of lyrics by Callimachus, a few hexameter lines of Erinna, lyric in tone and subject, and a very few anonymous pieces, for the most part of undistinguished quality. The riddle poems and pattern poems of the third and second centuries use some lyric meters, but are essentially a different genre. The so-called meliambics of the Cynic-inspired Cercidas of Megalopolis have flashes of lyric brilliance,[14] and it would be pedantic to draw a firm line between lyric poetry and the idylls of Theocritus. But neither in the intervening time of almost two centuries between the late archaic monodists and the Hellenistic age, nor in Hellenistic poetry, is there a substantial body of work that can be formally classified as lyric monody.

Notes

Chapter One: *Introduction*

1. In W. B. Yeats's Introduction to the *Oxford Book of Modern Verse* the use of "lyric" and "lyric poetry" on pp. ix, xii, xv, xvi, and xvii is not discernibly different from that of "verse" on p. xiv and either is fully interchangeable with "poetry" or "poem." T. S. Eliot has some good comments on the loose and unsatisfactory nature of the term "lyric" in "The Three Voices of Poetry," *On Poetry and Poets* (New York 1957) 105–6.

2. In *PLG* Bergk made his *terminus ante quem* for inclusion the age of Alexander (*PLG*[1] I. xix); in subsequent editions he lowered it to 300; in the *Anthologia* later poetry was included (some had already been in *PLG*, as Appendixes). In other respects, the rationale stated by Bergk, *PLG*[1] I. xviii has been generally maintained by the successive editors of *ALG*. For some modifications see Diehl's comments, *ALG*[3] I. iii.

3. The earliest meaning of *melos* is "limb," and how it came to designate a kind of poetry is not clear. Perhaps there is a connection between the meaning "limb" and the articulation of lyric poems, which are divided into clearly defined metrical "parts" such as cola and stanzas. But the verses of hexameter, elegiac, and iambic poetry are no less limb-like.

Full references and discussion are to be found in Hans Färber's *Die Lyrik in der Kunsttheorie der Antike*; see especially I, pp. 7–16, where evidence is analyzed indicating that the use of *lurikos* and *lurikê* developed late (probably not before the first century B.C.) and principally in connection with the biographical tradition of the "Nine Lyric Poets" and in reference to music, while *melikos* and *melikê* were earlier and continued to be generally used in discussions of literary theory, especially in the classification of poetry. In Latin the use of *lyricus*, *lyrica* appears as early as that of *melicus*, *melica* and soon became dominant, perhaps, as Färber suggests, because *lyra* became a "Lehnwort" while *melos* remained a "Fremdwort." The Latin usage no doubt determined ours. See also Schmid-Stählin, *Griechische Literaturgeschichte* 1. 1. 13 and 325. ᾠδή seems always to have been used to mean song quite generally, while μέλος was specifically accompanied song. For references see Färber II, pp. 10, 11, and 16.

4. On the Alexandrian canons see J. E. Sandys, *A History of Classical Scholarship*[3] 1. 130-31, U. von Wilamowitz, *Textgeschichte*, 5-11, 63-71, and R. Pfeiffer, *History of Classical Scholarship* (Oxford 1968) 205-9.

5. Just as Corinna's membership in the group is in some doubt, so is her date. There may be a connection between the two uncertainties. See below, ch. 6.

6. Wilamowitz op. cit., 5-11; for a different view, see Pfeiffer, op. cit. 205-6.

7. Wilamowitz, op. cit., 7: "Das ist ein litterarischen Urteil, die Absonderung einer classischen Litteratur von allem späteren."

8. It was not that the nomes and dithyrambs had fallen into neglect and been lost. Timotheus achieved great popularity, despite the critics. Originally unpopular, he achieved success, according to tradition, with the *Persians* (Satyrus, *Life of Euripides*, POxy 1176); in 320 B.C., a generation after Timotheus's death, a song of his was sung by a victorious boys' chorus (*IG* 3. 1246). Polybius (4. 20. 8) says that the nomes of Philoxenus and Timotheus were in his day (mid-second century B.C.) learned and annually performed as a part of the education of Arcadian children.

9. For the Grenfell papyrus see *New Chapters in the History of Greek Literature*, edited by J. U. Powell and A. E. Barber (Oxford 1921) 54, and J. U. Powell, *Collectanea Alexandrina* (Oxford 1925) 177-80; for the late poem on contentment see Powell, *Collectanea Alexandrina*, 199-200. The *Anacreontics* and other late poems are in Bergk *PLG*[4] 3. 296-375.

10. Ancient literary criticism usually ascribes invention (εὕρησις

or the like) to the earliest known exponent of a poetic form or meter; thus Clement of Alexandria (*Stromata* 1. 79) tells us that Archilochus thought up (ἐπενόησεν) the iamb, and Plutarch, *De musica* 28, that Terpander was the inventor (εὑρετής) of the scolium. Since most of our informants are late and were not, so far as we know, equipped with full knowledge of the crucial early period, such ascriptions are likely to be based on no more than assumptions or the mere urge for some concrete statement.

11. For an edition of the *Chrestomathy* with translation and exhaustive commentary, see Albert Severyns, *Recherches sur la Chrestomathie de Proclos*, Tome 2 ("Bibliothèque de la Faculté de Philosophie et Lettres de l'Université de Liège," Fasc. 79), Liège and Paris 1938. A useful summary of the melic types, largely based on Proclus, is given in the Introduction to H. Weir Smyth's *Greek Melic Poets*. Edmonds's long essay on lyric poetry at the end of Volume 3 of *Lyra Graeca* is a repository of information on this subject; chapter 1 of Bowra's *GLP*² is an expert and succinct account. Färber gives the main ancient references. A sensible appraisal of what value this information about types has for the study of the poetry is given by A. E. Harvey, "The Classification of Greek Lyric Poetry," *CQ* 49 (1955) 157–75.

What degree of authority should be granted to the *Chrestomathy* (to which we owe also our knowledge of the contents of the epics of the Trojan Cycle, apart from the *Iliad* and the *Odyssey*) is most uncertain. Its date is unknown. Almost certainly it was not the product of the fifth century Neoplatonist Proclus, and it is generally supposed to have been the work of a scholar of the second century after Christ. His sources are unknown, except that one small section, on the derivation and meaning of *hymnos*, is known from parallel authorities who give their sources to derive from the work *On the Lyric Poets* by the industrious Didymus Chalkenteros, of the first century B.C. Since Proclus often gives a variety of views, it is apparent that he did not follow Didymus or any other one authority throughout, and Severyns believes that Proclus is sometimes presenting original views.

12. Or "those who are superior." The text reads ὑπηρέτας, which is obviously wrong. Severyns emends to ὑπερόντας. Kaibel's ὑπερέχοντας is better. Orion, a lexicographer and excerpter of the fifth

century, says, in discussing the hymn, πάντα γὰρ εἰς τοὺς ὑπερέχοντας γραφόμενα ἀποφαινόμεθα ὕμνους, and ascribes the statement, along with others on the hymn which to some degree correspond to what Proclus says, to Didymus. For the quotation from Orion and discussion, see Severyns 117–19.

13. Powell, *Collectanea Alexandrina* 162–64.

14. Cf. Harvey, op. cit. (n. 11, above).

15. It is hard to contest Harvey's conclusion (175) that the results, for our knowledge of poetic forms, are "depressingly negative."

16. The point is made by Färber (16). Plato, *Laws* 6. 764d, distinguishes between monodic and choral *mousikê*, but since he is concerned with the judging of solo and choral performances in contests, and groups several instrumental performances with monody, the passage has little bearing on the distinction of types of composition.

17. *GLP*² 3; cf. Edmonds, *Lyra Graeca* 3. 592.

18. Op. cit. 159.

19. This question with regard to Corinna is discussed briefly in Ch. 6. Ibycus is regularly classed as a choral poet, but Richmond Lattimore, *Greek Lyrics*² (Chicago 1960) holds that the fragments of love poetry, *PMG* 286–87, are monody, and I know of no specific evidence to contradict this opinion.

20. The organization of Sappho's poems is discussed in ch. 4, of Alcaeus's in ch. 3.

21. Iambic trimeters and trochaic tetrameters are used stichically in separate poems as well as in drama.

22. The nome, in some stages at least of its development, was a solo performance including dance. Such seems clearly implied by Aristotle, *Problems* 19. 15 (918b). But it is likely that the solo element came only with the late history of the nome, in the fifth century, and that the performance was part solo and part choral.

The choreography for all lyric poetry is lost without trace, probably because the library collections, not concerned with performance, only with text, did not preserve choreographed copies. Cf. Jean Irigoin, *Histoire du Texte de Pindare* (Paris 1952) 8.

23. Many treatments of the subject of ancient Greek music are so obscured in technical discussion that they are useless except,

perhaps, to experts. The following two authorities are informative and intelligible: the article on Greek Music in the *OCD*, by J. F. Mountford and R. P. Winnington-Ingram; Donald Jay Grout, *A History of Western Music* (New York 1960) chapter 1.

24. These testimonia are given in the "Life" sections of Edmonds, *Lyra Graeca*.

25. The *Suda* ascribes to her *plêktron*, "quill". Probably both references are to the same invention, whichever it was, *pêktis* or *plêktron*.

26. As A. M. Dale points out in "Stichos and Stanza," *CQ* N.S. 13 (1963) 46–50, it is not necessary to assume a long history of gradual development of the individual metrical forms. "Precision and regulation are . . . [the] very essence [of Greek quantitative rhythms], and the career of each of its metrical types starts with the first poet of genius who gave precise definition to a syllabic sequence of that particular kind" (49).

27. *Odyssey* 8. 262 ff. has been taken to indicate that the youths at the court of Alcinous dance while Demodocus sings, in hexameters, the story of Ares and Aphrodite. The assumption is unwarranted. The youths dance (262–65) and then Demodocus begins his song (ἀνεβάλλετο, 266); again after the song two youths danced while the rest clapped their hands in time, and "a mighty din arose" (370–79). This noise would be an astonishing accompaniment to solo singing by Demodocus.

28. Extant folksongs customarily form a section, entitled *Carmina Popularia*, in modern collections of Greek lyric; cf. Bergk *PLG* 3. 654–88, Page *PMG* 449–70; Edmonds, *Lyra Graeca* 3. 488–596 (quoting ancient comments about such songs).

29. A number of the Attic Scolia quoted by Athenaeus (*PMG* 884–909) are four-line poems (with each line a colon), apparently complete, and this suggests that the four-line stanza was by the time of these songs (fifth century B.C.) a recognized form. The four-line stanzas of the monodists may have been the models.

30. The evidence, drawn mostly from the geographer and antiquarian Pausanias, of the second century A.D., is assembled on pp. 583–611 of Volume 3 of Edmonds, *Lyra Graeca*, and in Schmid-Stählin, *Geschichte der Griechischen Literatur* 1. 1. 325–38.

31. But it is worth noticing that according to Callimachus a

hymn associated with Olen (not necessarily composed by him) was danced to by maidens; hence it was probably not hexameter. Cf. *Lyra Graeca* 3. 488.

32. For Olympus see *RE* 18. 1. 321–24.

33. See, for example, Plate 86 of *Crete in Colour*, by Olivier Reverdin, London 1961.

Chapter Two: *Archilochus*

1. More will be said on Terpander in ch. 3.

2. David A. Campbell, "Flutes and Elegiac Couplets," *JHS* 84 (1964) 63–68, raises some doubts as to how universal flute accompaniment was, in view of the informal and personal nature of some elegiacs, notably of Archilochus. But there is no doubt that some early elegy was accompanied by the flute. Campbell's article presents the evidence.

3. On the varying features of the archaic states see N. G. L. Hammond, *A History of Greece to 320 B.C.* (Oxford 1967) 82–88, 97–108.

4. POxy 2389 fr. 9 col. i and POxy 2506 fr. 1, both fragments of commentaries on the lyric poets, give evidence that there was in antiquity debate whether Alcman was Lydian or Laconian; the evidence of the papyrus, which is fragmentary, is hard to interpret. In my opinion POxy 2506 argues for Lydian birth. Cf. *Ox. Pap.* 24 (1957) 28, 40–41; 29 (1963) 2–3; Campbell, *GLPS* 192–93; Page, *PMG* 29–30.

5. See Chester G. Starr, *The Origins of Greek Civilization* (New York 1961) 111: "The tendency of tradition . . . was to set the major movement from Greece in the twelfth and eleventh centuries. . . . At any later date extensive colonization of Asia Minor is virtually inexplicable. In the Dark Ages the mainland was primarily engaged in rebuilding its social and political structure . . . and had neither any serious surplus of population nor a strong enough organization to launch out overseas."

6. Archilochus composed in iambic trimeter, elegiac couplet, trochaic tetrameter, various kinds of epodes, more than one hymn form (in addition to the traditional hymn to Heracles and Iolaus

sung for victors at Olympia and ascribed to Archilochus [120], new epigraphical fragments from Paros, concerning which more will be said later in this chapter, give evidence of a hymn to Dionysus [cf. Treu, *Archilochos* 46 and 209]), and one or more verse types called *asynarteton*, consisting of two different juxtaposed cola and thus akin to epodic form.

7. The grammarian Marius Victorinus describes Archilochus as "singularis artificii in excogitandis ac formandis novis metris" (*Grammatici Latini* 6. 1. 104 Keil; quoted by Edmonds, *Elegy and Iambus* 2. 90). Testimony to a specific link between Archilochus and lyric is given by a tradition about Thaletas of Crete, one of the reputedly influential lyric inventors of the seventh century; according to Plutarch, *De musica* 10, "he imitated the *melê* of Archilochus, but lengthened them and added the paeonic and cretic meters, which Archilochus had not used." Cf. Edmonds, *Lyra Graeca* 1. 36.

8. On the question of the relationship between the historical life of Archilochus and the attitude and actions of the "I" of the poems, see below, n. 62.

9. Cf. Lasserre-Bonnard (ix-xii). It may be, as they suggest, that the contretemps with Lycambes and his daughter was connected in some way with Archilochus's illegitimacy, but this is unknown. Treu, *Archilochos* 162, thinks that Fr. 74 gives evidence that Lycambes found a son-in-law with more money and prestige.

10. Fr. 149 B; cf. Fr. 53 D.

11. The sources of the biographical material are for the most part assembled in the editions of Treu (116–41) and Lasserre-Bonnard (ciii–xii), and, most completely except for the recent evidence (on which see p. 27), by Edmonds, *Elegy and Iambus* 2. 82–97.

Scepticism is still appropriate as to the suicide of Lycambes and his daughters. Like the Sappho-Phaon stories, it has the air of a *märchen*. The theme of "satire that kills" is recurrent in at least one early literature: see Stith Thompson, *Motif-Index of Folk Literature* M402. For the Lycambes-Neobule story there is a relevant papyrus fragment (Treu, *Archilochos* 130–31) giving parts of some lines purporting to be an epitaph for the daughters of Lycambes, uttered by them. The fragment is edited with commentary by G. W. Bond,

"Archilochus and the Lycambides: A New Literary Fragment," *Hermathena* 80 (1952) 3–11. Bond judges it to be Hellenistic, but observes that it provides the earliest reference to the fact of suicide and to the plurality of daughters, and insists that the burden of proof now rests on those who disbelieve. We can, however, say that there is some evidence that the story was not current in Athens at the end of the fifth century, since Critias gives no hint of it in his list of the bad things known about Archilochus from the poet's writings. The comic poets of the fourth century were fertile in creating legends. It was probably then that the story of Sappho and Phaon took shape; the Lycambes story is similar enough in tone to give it the air of a comic invention.

J. Pouilloux, "Archiloque et Thasos: Histoire et Poésie," *Archi-loque: Entretiens* 10, 3–27, undertakes an assessment of the reflection of Archilochus's experience on Thasos and against the Thracians in the extant fragments. His resulting picture is probably quite close to the general spirit of the poet's activities and the expedition, but it is often only a guess that any specific fragment belongs in the picture.

12. On the dating see Alan Blakeway, "The Date of Archilochus," *Greek Poetry and Life* (Oxford 1936) 34–55, urging the earlier date, and F. Jacoby, "The Date of Archilochus," *CQ* 35 (1941) 97–109, championing the later. Lasserre-Bonnard (xxiii-xxvi) point out that it need not be assumed that the eclipse referred to was witnessed by the poet himself; that of 711 would still be a vivid memory during his childhood. They argue also that "the father," who, according to Aristotle (who quotes the first line) is the speaker, may be Archilochus's father rather than Lycambes as is generally thought and as seems probable from Aristotle's words. Much against the supposition that it is the poet's father is POxy 2313 fr. 1a, which continues the poem and clearly has something about a marriage; this sounds like Lycambes. The problem remains, however, of how it is that this poem, which if it refers to the eclipse of 648 must have been written near the end of Archilochus's life, is on a theme that presumably belongs to his youth. Was the poet still fulminating, years after his rejection? Or did the rejection come in fact late in his life? Or is our dating of Archilochus still too early? Peter Green, *The Shadow of the Parthenon* (London 1972) 268-75, professes to solve

all the problems by providing an eclipse in 689, 96 per cent total on Thasos, 92 on Paros. But if Archilochus's lines are evidence at all, they are evidence of a total eclipse: "Zeus . . . brought night from midday." This is not likely to have been said of a 92 per cent eclipse, nor even of one of 96 per cent, according to experts; anyway, there are no grounds for putting Archilochus on Thasos in 689. Furthermore, the other biographical evidence does not, in spite of Green's assertions, favor 689.

13. The Mnesiepes inscription was first published by N. M. Kontoleon, *Archaiologikê Ephêmeris* 1952, 32–95. There is a useful description of it by Eugene Vanderpool, "New Inscriptions Concerning Archilochus," *AJP* 76 (1955) 186–88. Treu, *Archilochos* 40–62, has text and translation of both inscriptions, and on pp. 152–55 and (especially) 205–15, analysis and suggestions for interpretation of the fragments of poetry.

14. Epigram xxi of Theocritus (Treu, *Archilochos* 128) suggests a threefold division, into iambic, elegiac (so Treu reasonably interprets ἔπεα, which normally means hexameter, in which Archilochus did not so far as is known write), and lyric, which would presumably include the epodes.

15. Anton Scherer, "Die Sprache des Archilochos," *Archiloque: Entretiens* 10, 89–106, sees a greater departure from epic style in the iambic than in the elegiac poetry. This is a natural concomitant of the greater departure from epic meter. In the same volume, Denys Page, "Archilochus and the Oral Tradition," 119–63, while insisting on the very close adherence to epic style in most of Archilochus's poetry (I am inclined to believe that Page overemphasizes the adherence, and sometimes fails to see how differently the epic formulas can be used), nevertheless notes (162) that "when the metres depart wholly from the dactylic, the language begins to move away from the traditional formulas." He too sees less—but still very strong—epic tradition in the iambic poetry (154).

16. The Lasserre-Bonnard text, following Lasserre's book, *Les Épodes d'Archiloque* (Paris 1950), tends to assign a great many fragments to epodes when there is no evidence for doing so. Lasserre argues (*Les Épodes d'Archiloque* 13–27) that in later antiquity Archilochus was primarily famed as an epodist and that consequently most quotations from him are likely to be from epodes.

Frail at best, the case has been seriously undermined by the fact that the one extensive papyrus fragment of Archilochus's poetry so far discovered, POxy 2310, is iambic, not epodic. Neither the epigram of Theocritus (see n. 14) nor Plutarch, *De musica,* suggests any predominance of epodes, nor does the epigraphical evidence found on Paros.

17. Fr. 74. See below, ch. 5. For other similar phrases cf. *Ox. Pap.* 22. 8.

18. Treu, *Archilochos* 177–85 gives a full analytical account of suggestions and possibilities, which Gerber's bibliography, *CW* 61 (1968) 275–76, supplements. See also M. L. West, *Iambi et Elegi Graeci* 1 (Oxford 1971) 10–11.

19. Two poems: Werner Peek, *Philologus* 99 (1955) 196–202, J. H. Mette, *Philologus* 88 (1960) 493–94, West, op. cit. (n. 18). Three poems: Davide Giordano, *Aegyptus* 37 (1957) 211–18. *Myrmex* as a man: Peek, *ibid.,* Giordano, *ibid.,* G. Schiassi, *RFIC* 35 (1957) 151–66. Lines 17–21 as an oracle, the woman as Neobule: Lasserre-Bonnard 11–12. Γύναι as a man: Denys Page, *PCPS* 187 (1961) 68–69.

20. So Treu, *Archilochos* 182. Cf. the Aesopian story of the ant and the dove (296, Halm).

21. *On the Sublime* 13. 3. Dio Chrysostom (*or.* 33.11) declares that Homer and Archilochus are beyond compare; and that just as nearly everything draws the praise of Homer so everything draws the censure of Archilochus, "because he saw that men were in need of this." Velleius Paterculus 1.5 pairs Homer and Archilochus as the only writers who innovated and were perfect in what they innovated. (Both *testimonia* are quoted by Treu, *Archilochos* 136, 138.)

22. *Hibeh Papyri* 2 (1955) 8–9. The editor, E. G. Turner, in his note accompanying the text, refers to evidence of other similar collections. Cf. Treu, *Archilochos* 174–76.

23. On the text and interpretation see Treu, *Archilochos* 189–90 and Richard Harder, *Hermes* 80 (1952) 381–84.

24. The tradition that Archilochus was a mercenary is probably based mainly on Fr. 40:

καὶ δὴ 'πίκουρος ὥστε Κὰρ κεκλήσομαι.

I shall, like a Carian, be called a mercenary.

It is not certain that the word ἐπίκουρος would yet have the clear connotation of "paid ally." In the *Iliad* (2. 815, etc.) it means only "ally," and we have no way of knowing the point of Archilochus's reference. It is easier, given the resourcelessness of ancient biography, to see how this line could, in later times, produce such a tradition than to see how it confirms it. Cf. Lasserre-Bonnard (xxi-xxii).

25. C. M. Bowra, "A Couplet of Archilochus," *AFC* 6 (1953-4) 37-43, maintains that ἐν δορί is wrong for "reclining on my spear," the dative alone being correct. But the grammatical objection is insubstantial, as Bruno Gentili, *RFIC* 93 (1965) 130, shows. Victor Ehrenberg, "Archilochus Frag. 2D," *CP* 57 (1962) 239-40, gives a good analogy for ἐν δορί meaning "at warfare," from an unknown comedy *(adesp.* 451 K), ἀνὴρ ἄριστος τἄλλα πλὴν ἐν ἀσπίδι.

26. Fr. 3 is particularly strong in epic language and spirit. See Page, "Archilochus and the Oral Tradition," *Archiloque: Entretiens* 10, 132: "Nothing but the metre distinguishes these lines from any five average lines of the Iliad." This is correct; but Page often overstates Archilochus's closeness to Homer, emphasizing too much the verbal echoes and too little the sometimes profound differences in spirit. His assessment of Fr. 1 is just: "A social revolution is epitomized in this couplet: yet the language remains as traditional as anything in Homer."

27. There is no indication, either in Archilochus's description of his abandonment of his shield, or in Herodotus's report (5. 95) of Alcaeus's similar misadventure, of the note of shame that is prominent in Horace's "relicta non bene parmula / cum fracta virtus et minaces / turpe solum tetigere mento" *(Odes* 2. 7. 10-12). Horace apparently borrowed also from another poem by Archilochus: the words "sed me per hostes Mercurius celer / denso paventem sustulit aere" can reasonably be associated with a fragment preserved in the Sosthenes monument (51). In one of several quotations from poems of Archilochus there occur, in what is apparently a battle description, the words πῇ μ' ἔσωσε 'Ερμ . . . , "Where Hermes [a very probable restoration] saved me." But there are no grounds for restoring τρέμοντα in this fragment, as is done in D³. The occasion (not the poem) may have been the same as that of Fr. 6, since the Saioi of Fr. 6 are probably the same

Thracian tribe as the Sapai, whose name occurs in a prose passage of Fr. 51 just before the mention of Archilochus's rescue by Hermes. Cf. *RE* Suppl. 6. 647–48 for late references to the Sapai and citation of Strabo 12. 549, who says that the Sapai (Sapaioi) were earlier called Saioi.

Anacreon's incident (*PMG* 36) is the first to suggest a lack of martial spirit, in that he says that he threw (ῥίψας) his shield away. The Herodotean report of what Alcaeus said in his poem about the loss of his shield seems almost a reversal of the recurrent Homeric description of the saving of a slain warrior's armor. In the case of Alcaeus, Herodotus reports, αὐτὸς μὲν φεύγων ἐκφεύγει, τὰ δέ οἱ ὅπλα ἴσχουσι Ἀθηναῖοι. This reversal seems to be the same kind of assertion —whether conscious or not—of a new standard of values that is to be seen in the Archilochus passage that concerns us. The earliest passage in which Archilochus is reproached for his action is from Critias, of the Thirty Tyrants, who is quoted by Aelian (*Var. Hist.* 10. 13); the pejorative connotation of ῥίψασπις is clear in Aristophanes' references (e.g. *Clouds* 353) and in the Spartan dictum, "With your shield or on it," but neither Archilochus nor Alcaeus was or thought he was a ῥίψασπις.

Some fragmentary lines in POxy 2313 (fr. 5) containing the words ἀσπίδα and ἔντος are conjectured by Lasserre-Bonnard (113) to refer to another incident in which the poet gave up his shield, but there is not enough context to make this more than a guess. Treu, *Archilochos* 186, with at least as much justification, tentatively likens the passage to the military elegies of Callinus and Tyrtaeus.

28. What Jaeger says (*Paideia* 1. 119–20) about the contrast in values made explicit by the poem is well worth reading, but he is wrong in calling Archilochus a "runaway" and misleading in suggesting that Archilochus thinks of his conduct as "inadequacy." The designation of the tone of this poem as "flippant" (Dover, *Archiloque: Entretiens* 10, 184, 196) leaves out a great deal.

29. Page, *Archiloque: Entretiens* 10, 132: "All the words are Homeric." As Page points out, the epic word ἀμώμητον is used "in a significant manner," and this use contradicts Page's assertion (133) that "the poet neither intends nor achieves any special effect by the contrast between contemporary theme and traditional

phrasing. He composes in this manner because he has no choice; his technique is wholly that of the oral Epic." To use epic language and to use an epic epithet with significantly different effect from its epic use is *ipso facto* to achieve (whether or not by intention) a special effect.

30. Cf. also μικρός ... δέμας, ἀλλὰ μαχητής (*Iliad* 5. 801) describing Tydeus. This parallel is mentioned by Page, *Archiloque: Entretiens* 10, 159. In the language of this poem Page finds more than the usual departure from Homeric diction: "The need to describe a particular aspect of the contemporary scene compels Archilochus to seek his phraseology outside the traditional patterns." Cf. also Page's comments (159) concerning the relationship of the content of the poem to epic tradition. (Page recognizes but tends to minimize the difference.)

31. Max Treu, *Von Homer Zur Lyrik*, 265–67, has perceptive comments on this topic.

32. Frs. 7, 10, 11, and 12 are similar enough in tone and apparent reference to permit the conjecture that all are from the poem ἐπὶ τοῦ ναυαγίου referred to by "Longinus," *Subl.* 10. 7. Fr. 12 is identified by Plutarch, *aud. poet.* 6. 23a, as from a poem lamenting the death of Archilochus's sister's husband, lost at sea. It is only conjecture that Longinus and Plutarch refer to the same event, and that 7, 11, and 12 are connected with either reference.

33. This transferred use of *euplokamos* was too strong for some nineteenth-century critics, and various emendations were proposed. Cf. Bergk, *PLG*⁴ 2. 386.

34. Hermann Fränkel, *DuP* 183–85, discusses these passages.

35. Hermann Fränkel's article, "Man's 'Ephemeros' Nature," *TAPA* 77 (1946) 131–45, is most illuminating on the whole subject of the archaic concept of the mutability of human fortunes.

36. The letters τειθει cannot be right, since there is no syntactical justification for τ' here. Conjectures have been numerous. It is hard to see how so clear and obvious a phrase as, e.g., τοῖς θεοῖσι ῥεῖα πάντα (which I translate) got displaced by the existing unintelligible letters.

37. Cf. *Ajax* 678, 1361.

38. Cf. *Antigone* 522–23.

39. In *Iphigenia at Aulis*, Iphigenia in a speech of self-sacrifice

(1368–1401) bids her mother give up her anger against Agamemnon even though that anger is justified. There is no suggestion that Agamemnon is not guilty. Iphigenia is willing to rise above personal emotions to achieve a common good by her self-sacrifice. Socrates' declaration, *Crito* 49b–c, that it is wrong to requite injustice with injustice is the first explicit rejection of the traditional outlook.

40. Recent editors have mostly adopted Herzog's δέννοις ("with insults") for δεινοῖς. This suits the idea, important in the Lycambes story and expressed in Frs. 88 and 103, of the terrible power of Archilochus's weapon of satire. On the other hand, the broad menace suggested by the general word, δεινόν, is a very effective threat. It seems best not to emend. Cf. the note *ad loc.* in Campbell, *GLPS*.

41. Ascription to Archilochus has been questioned and cannot be considered certain; but the grounds for denying the poem to Archilochus and ascribing it to the later iambist Hipponax are not strong. I have argued for attribution to Archilochus in "The Authorship of the Strasbourg Epodes," *TAPA* 92 (1961) 267–82. References to the principal articles on the controversy are given there.

42. The papyrus has επιχοι. A number of recent editors have emended to ἐπέχοι rather than ἐπιχέοι. In the context ἐπιχέοι seems to me more probable and infinitely more expressive. Ἐπέχοι, "may . . . be upon," "hold," with φυκία as subject, is rather feebly general and lacking in the graphic quality of ἐπιχέοι, "may seaweed pour over him." Admittedly, the middle would be expected for this intransitive meaning and I know of no parallel use of ἐπιχέω or χέω. But still there is no great improbability in an intransitive meaning here.

43. Fr. 39, τρώγων . . . δούλιον χόρτον.

44. κύμασι πλαζόμενος recalls *Odyssey* 5. 388–89, κύματι . . . πλάζετο, of Odysseus, in the storm sent by Poseidon. The χνόος of line 6 recalls ἐκ κεφαλῆς δ᾽ ἔσμηχεν ἁλὸς χνόον, 6. 226, when Odysseus, having been cast up, like Archilochus's victim, cleans off the traces of his sea disaster. Line 3 is a Homeric echo; Θρήϊκες ἀκρόκομοι are the first words of *Iliad* 4. 533.

45. Max Treu translates in accordance with the first alternative, without comment. Lasserre-Bonnard follow the second, with an explanatory note. The problem is χεῖρα θιγεῖν, which ought not to

mean "to touch" somebody's "hand," since the genitive is proper for that (cf. 88a). The grammatical argument, though strong, is not decisive; but since a dubious meekness of expression is achieved by the assumption of dubious grammar, the case for the first interpretation is doubly weak. The idiom of ἐμοὶ γένοιτο χεῖρα . . . θιγεῖν, "May it be mine that my hand touch," is not beyond reproach; it is correct but cumbersome.

46. Cf. Otto von Weber, *Die Beziehungen zwischen Homer und den Alteren Griechischen Lyrikern* (Bonn 1955) 31.

Even Fr. 72 is strikingly Homeric in style, as Treu, *Archilochos* 222, observes. It is based on a battle scene, *Iliad* 13. 130–31, δόρυ δουρί, σάκος σάκεϊ . . . ἀσπὶς ἄρ' ἀσπίδ' ἔρειδε. The scene recurs in the *Certamen Homeri et Hesiodi* 188–89 and is imitated in Tyrtaeus, Fr. 8. 31–32.

47. Cf. n. 16, above.

48. For analysis of epodic and asynartetic forms see James Halporn, Martin Ostwald, and Thomas Rosenmeyer, *The Meters of Greek and Latin Poetry* (Indianapolis 1963) 26–27. We know nothing about lyric stanzas before the extant poets, but must allow for the likelihood that they existed in some form.

49. The line between *asynarteton* and epode can be variously drawn. In Diehl, Fr. 112 is called the former, in Lasserre-Bonnard and Halporn-Ostwald-Rosenmeyer the latter. Lasserre-Bonnard find some evidence for other kinds of epode; but the evidence is inevitably ambiguous, when the fragments are so short and when uits used in epodes and units used in other kinds of poetry can be identical.

50. Cf. n. 7, above.

51. Fr. 79a is not included in Lasserre-Bonnard, being regarded by them, as by many critics, as not Archilochus's. See n. 41, above.

52. A good, brief account of Archilochus's use of fables and of the early use of fables in Greece is given by Treu, *Archilochos* 230–35; an analysis of the story of the fox and the eagle is included.

53. No. 5 in Halm's edition of Aesop.

54. Discussion: Treu, *Archilochos* 230–35, Lasserre, *Les Épodes* ch. 2.

55. The σκυτάλη, properly a staff or club, was at Sparta used as a means of conveying messages in code. A strip of leather was wound,

at a slant, onto the σκυτάλη, the message was inscribed, unrolled, and sent to its recipient who, equipped with an identical σκυτάλη, wound the strip onto it to read the message.

56. Cf. Treu, *Archilochos* 237. The exact form of the original is also quite doubtful.

57. The fox thus occurs in three Archilochian fables, twice as a figure of craft. Perhaps Alcaeus's use of the fox for his hated enemy Pittacus was taken from this. Alcaeus in other respects shows Archilochian influence. (Cf., e.g., the phrase in Fr. 81, ἀλώπηξ . . . πυκνὸν ἔχουσα νόον, with Alcaeus, Fr. 130. 24.) See ch. 3.

58. The context in which Aristotle gives us this information (*Rhetoric* 1418b. 30–33) is a discussion of the technique of rhetorical attack by putting objectionable statements in the mouth of a third person.

59. F. H. Sandbach, *CR* 56 (1942) 63–65, identifies the Gyrean heights as the ridge of the island of Tenos, just north of Paros.

60. See Treu, *Archilochos* 116 and 249.

61. Ivan Boserup, "Archiloque ou Epigone Alexandrin?" *C & M* 27 (1966) 28–38, considers the second alternative of his title the more likely, and in any case doubts, on various grounds including metrical, the connection with 56. The question needs further study.

62. Dover, *Archiloque: Entretiens* 10, 200–212, asks whether we can assume that the poetry of Archilochus represents the "personality and views of the poet himself." After giving a number of examples of "preliterate song," from various cultures, designed to illustrate characteristic topics and attitudes of Archilochus, Dover speculates as to how much of the poetry that is written as if in the *persona* of the poet and about his own experiences exemplifies in fact "the assumed personality and the imaginary situation."

There is no doubt that some dramatic lyric poetry was written by Archilochus, Alcaeus, and Anacreon; fictitious *personae* occur in their poems. But when, as in the shield poem, for example, or in the poem about the general, the poet provides no evidence of a *persona* other than that of the poet, are these attitudes to be taken as Archilochus's or not? Dover seems about to assert that they are not: "My approach . . . is agnostic to the point of nihilism, and . . . implies that we no longer know about Archilochus many things which, in common with the Greeks themselves from the

Classical period onwards, we have always believed that we knew."
But in the end Dover's position is fairly conventional: "The
fragments may tell us less of Archilochus's own life than we thought
they did; but they tell us no less than before what standpoints he
preferred to adopt, what emotions he preferred to express, and what
topics he preferred to develop; and these are the elements which
compose his personality as an artist." If the reservations are only
about the actuality of events, not of outlook, they are only of
secondary interest. Perhaps Archilochus in fact did not lose his
shield, but only wrote a poem developing the topic of the loss of a
shield, and adopting a point of view and expressing emotions that
he regarded as appropriate. For the biography of Archilochus the
question of fact is important; for the poetry it does not, as Dover
says, matter much. Most of Archilochus's poetry is devoted to
adopting attitudes and expressing emotions: his views on generals,
on the proper way to meet disaster, on friends who betray, on how
to endure a night watch aboard ship, and so on. The reporting of
events, the narrative element, is less important, and so the question
of biographical precision does not much arise. Would it really
matter to us if we found it necessary to believe that 79a actually
concerned somebody else who had been betrayed by a friend? We
would have evidence of astonishing empathy on the part of the
poet, but I do not see that our judgment of the poem would be
affected. In the discussion following his paper, Dover agrees with
Max Treu that 79a "most certainly expresses the emotions of the
poet himself" (220). To go this far leaves little of poetic significance
in the distinction between actual and imagined.

The problem of the *persona* in poetry becomes important when a
poet creates a first-person *persona* whose views and emotions are in
some contrast with those of the poet, and when the poet maintains
distance from the speaker whom he has created. Theocritus,
Horace, Virgil in the *Eclogues*, and the Roman elegiac poets are
conspicuous ancient examples. How early can it be found? There
are traces of it in Anacreon, in some of whose poems one can feel
the presence of a consistent, constructed "character" speaking, a
character whose attitudes are sufficiently naive and stereotyped to
suggest artificiality; the poet then is behind rather than in his
poetic *persona*. I cannot detect any such implicit split in the poetry

of Archilochus, Sappho, or Alcaeus. On this technique in Theocritus cf. Edward W. Spofford, "Theocritus and Polyphemus," *AJP* 99 (1969) 22–35. See Robert Bagg on a difference in this respect between Archilochus and Sappho, *Arion* 3 (1964) 44–46.

63. Page, *Archiloque: Entretiens* 10, 129–31, discusses these lines and concludes that "part of the phrasing is certainly traditional, readymade, all of it may be." But some of Page's bases for judgment are questionable. Speaking of κοίλων . . . κάδων he says that "the epithet 'hollow' is added not because it is specially appropriate here, but . . . because it is *not* specially appropriate." And hence, according to Page, it is a matter of traditional formula-making. I do not suppose that we can know why Archilochus chose the word κοῖλος here, but I can—and so can any reader who cares to look— see ways in which the word *is* specially appropriate here. The strong alliteration adds to the sense of urgency and energy in the passage; there is an intriguing prolepsis (the caskets are certainly *going* to be hollow when Archilochus and his friends are through); the transfer from the Homeric phrase "hollow ships" to an unfamiliar phrase, describing caskets aboard a ship, gives the kind of epic/non-epic combination that is typical of Archilochus's style, and that individualizes the scene.

Page says, of this fragment, that (133) "the poet neither intends nor achieves any special effect by the contrast between contemporary theme and traditional phrasing. He composes in this manner because he has no choice; his technique is wholly that of the oral Epic." This judgment is presumptuous. To say that the poet did not "intend" this effect and had "no choice" is an unprovable hypothesis. Similarly, in discussing Fr. 112 Page sees only the Homeric words, and concludes that (139) "actuality of theme (if indeed it is actual) makes no discernible difference either to the manner or to the matter of what is said." As to the striking transfer of use of ἐλυσθείς and other words, with its consequences for the effect of the poetry (see p. 42, above), Page says nothing. In the report of the discussion following Page's paper, Snell (169) and Treu (167) briefly criticize this narrowness of view. Anton Scherer's position, in his lecture in the same volume, "Die Sprache des Archilochos," is quite different (96–97): "Die epischen Elemente bei Archilochos dienen aber nur dazu, das Ionische, das die Grundlage seiner Iambendichtung bildet, zu stilisieren. Die Sprache ist nicht etwa episch mit stärkerer Einmischung von Ionischen, sondern ionische Umgangsprache, gehoben durch bewusst ausgewählte Bestandteile der epischen Kunstsprache, die durch Ihre altertümliche Patina wirken sollen, aber nicht die Stileinheit der Sprache aufheben dürfen" (106): ... Wir haben ... mit einer neuen Kunstsprache zu tun, die der Epos an Einheitlichkeit klar überlegen ist." These comments apply principally, but not solely, to the iambic poetry. (See Page, p. 154.)

64. The fragment provides still another example of Archilochus's relationship to the epic tradition. The line quoted is strongly reminiscent of *Odyssey* 14.228:

$$\text{ἄλλος γὰρ τ' ἄλλοισιν ἀνὴρ ἐπιτέρπεται ἔργοις.}$$

Different men delight in different deeds.

The context of the generalization in Homer is a list of heroic, warrior activities; Archilochus's examples are earthily unheroic.

65. For comments on this poem see Dover, *Archiloque: Entretiens* 10, 186, and Gerber, *Euterpe* 18–19.

66. It is only a guess that the two parts are from one poem. Cf. B. Marzullo, *RhM* 100 (1957) 68–82. Marzullo points out that the second part of the fragment is much influenced by traditional epic descriptions of a warrior (*Iliad* 16.791, etc.).

Chapter Three: *Alcaeus*

1. As A. M. Dale points out, in "Stichos and Stanza," *CQ* N.S. 13 (1963) 46–50, the trochaic tetrameter, as used by Archilochus (who is the earliest user of it), is a two-line stanza; the part of the verse after the diaeresis has a clausular effect. But it seems most likely that there were other models for the stanzas of the Lesbian poets, with their concentration on Aeolic cola.

2. A fragment of choral poetry (Page, *PMG* 939) traditionally ascribed to Arion, a contemporary of Stesichorus, is obviously from a much later time.

3. B. A. van Groningen, "A propos de Terpandre," *Mnemosyne*

4. 8 (1955) 177–91, maintains that of the four brief fragments traditionally ascribed to Terpander, two are authentic, one the opening lines of a nome, the other probably the beginning of a hymn to Zeus. Page, *PMG*, prints these two fragments under Terpander's name but comments (362), "Terpandri fragmenta melica extant me iudice nulla." Wilamowitz, *Textgeschichte*, likewise considers all spurious. In Bergk, *PLG*, six short fragments are ascribed to him.

    4. *Mar. Par.* 34, Eusebius, *Chron.*, Migne 19 , Col. 455.

    5. Athenaeus 14. 37, Timotheus, *Persae* 225–28.

    6. Aristotle, *Probl.* 19. 32, Plutarch, *De musica* 12.

    7. Van Groningen, op. cit., argues that the Terpandrian nome was relatively simple, with only *archa, omphalos,* and *sphragis.*

    8. *Suda,* μετὰ Λέσβιον ᾠδόν, Sappho 106. Van Groningen, op. cit., believes that the Terpandrian nome was entirely in hexameters, and that the essential difference between it and the *Homeric Hymns* was that it was sung, while they were recited.

    9. *Suda, ibid.,* Aelian, *Varia Hist.* 12.50.

    10. Alcaeus 283 may, but need not, show its author's consciousness of Sappho 16; for a comparison of the two poems see ch. 4. Alcaeus 115 has phrases strongly reminiscent of Sappho's poetry, expecially of Fr. 2. Fr. 137 of Sappho preserves a tradition of Alcaeus as suitor of Sappho and Sappho's rejection of his suit. There is a good deal of uncertainty about the nature of the fragment; and if Aristotle, to whom we owe the tradition, is correct in saying that the poetry of this fragment reflects such a relationship, it is more likely to be evidence of a fairly casual and probably largely literary acquaintance than of intimacy. It is almost inconceivable, given two poets who spoke mainly about themselves and their experiences, that we would have no more evidence than this if the relationship had been close. If the fragment does in fact give evidence of a relationship between the two poets it does not add any information as to literary influence; but it lends strength to the probability of it, and the fact that it is Alcaeus who makes the approach, which Sappho rejects, says something about the direction that such influence is likely to have taken. On the fragment, see Page, *SA* 104–9. The one other reference to Sappho in Alcaeus, a single line preserved by Hephaestion (Fr. 384), is in the same meter and may be from the same poem. In it, the epithet ἄγνα

suggests a relationship of admiration rather than anything erotic. On the line and the problems of its authenticity cf. especially Alessandra Rome, "L'Uso degli Epiteti in Saffo e Alceo," *SCO* 14 (1965) 210-46. The article is a valuable examination of the epithets of the two poets, especially those inherited from the epic tradition. See also Bruno Gentili, "La Veneranda Saffo," *Quaderni Urbinati* 2 (1966) 37-62.

11. Alcaeus (130) refers to his loss, by exile, of "what his father and his grandfather possessed." Since this directly follows a mention of the council and the assembly, the reference might be thought to suggest that the oligarchy had existed through much of the seventh century. This need not be so; the council and the assembly would very likely have existed, in Homeric fashion, under the monarchy.

12. He is called αἴδως ἄξιος, which would most naturally mean "worthy of respect." Treu translates "dieser Ehrenmann," with the note "muss ironisch gemeint sein" (37, 145). Perhaps it means "worthy of shame," since αἰδώς can designate what calls for ashamedness as well as what calls for respect, as in *Iliad* 16. 422, 17. 336. There may be a deliberate, ironic ambiguity. The word occurs only here in Alcaeus.

13. Strabo 13. 617.

14. LP have πέρ for πρός, thus eliminating Attic correption (mute plus liquid not giving metrical length). There is nothing else amiss with πρός here; the phrase need not, as Lobel thinks (Σάπφους Μέλη xlv) mean "against one's will," since Euripides' *Andromache* 730 provides a clear case to the contrary. Πρὸς τὸ βίαιον, Aeschylus, *Agamemnon* 130, is analogous; Fränkel's translation, "with violence," is correct; Moira, who performs the act of violence, is not under duress. Attic correption occurs elsewhere in Lesbian poetry; it should not be removed here.

15. *Suda*, s.v. Πιττακός.

16. *Politics* 1285a31: αἱρετὴ τυραννίς.

17. *Life of Pittacus* 1.

18. Page, *SA* 151-52.

19. POxy 2506 fr. 98.

20. *Politics* 1285a31-38.

21. Diogenes Laertius, *Life of Pittacus* 3.

22. POxy 2506 fr. 98 refers to "the third return." Since we have no evidence for a fourth exile (only two are attested, but a third is

implied by this fragment), there is some reason to suppose that
Alcaeus ended up in Mytilene.

23. Cf. Treu, *Alkaios* 122–23 and Jaeger, *Paideia* 1. 182 ff.

24. *SA* 243.

25. A. Andrewes, *The Greek Tyrants* (London 1956) 96.

26. There is perhaps some slight further evidence in a new
papyrus fragment tending toward the rehabilitation of Alcaeus's
reputation. In fr. 77 of POxy 2506 a commentary containing biographical information on a number of the lyric poets, there is
apparently a refutation of allegations that Alcaeus had been guilty
of a murder.

27. The length of eleven of Alcaeus's poems is known or can be
fairly confidently guessed within a few lines: Fr. 6 (28 lines; 1–28),
33a (8 lines; 3–10), 34 (fr. a and lines 1 and 2 of b; the poem had
24 lines), 38a (12 lines; 1–12), 42 (16 lines), 43 (8 lines), 44 (8
lines), 129 (32 lines), 130 (24 lines; 16–39), 283 (probably about
24 lines), 296a (8 lines; 1–8).

28. Fr. 130 if, as is probable (cf. Page, *SA* 200–201), a new poem
begins at 16, is almost all extant; but the last stanza is virtually
blank.

29. Cf. *Ox. Pap.* 18 (1941) 2166c. Page, *SA* 326, lists this as
complete in eight lines, but on page 226 says that "the first two
stanzas are preserved." POxy 2307 fr. 1 (LP 306 fr. 1) has the
opening words as a lemma in a commentary. There is some marginal
evidence confirming that this is the beginning of a poem.

30. The Ship of State appears in several poems: 6, 73, 208a–366,
and 249. A beached and neglected ship represents an aging and
spent prostitute, 306 fr. 14, col. ii (see also pp. 79–80). Fr. 119 contains
what is almost certainly an allegory of the growth and ripening of
crops and vines, but its context is so unreadable that the reference
of the allegory is doubtful; it may be a poem of love (Treu, *Alkaios*
166–68) or it may apply to politics and Pittacus (Page, *SA*, and
Carl Theander, *Aegyptus* 32 [1952] 179–90). On Alcaic allegory
generally see G. Perrotta, "Alceo," *A & R* 4 (1936) 221–41.

31. Cf. Page, *SA* 273.

32. On the nature of this incident and the question of his
throwing his shield away see above, ch. 2 n. 27.

33. Line 23 of Fr. 129 echoes line 12 of Archilochus 79.

34. Cf. n. 10, above.

35. Fr. 368 bids someone call τὸν χαρίεντα Μένωνα, if Alcaeus is to have pleasure in a symposium; the two lines of the fragment take us no further. The reference may or may not be erotic. The fragment is not certainly by Alcaeus.

36. Page, *SA* 297–98, so takes it. Barner, *Neuere Alkaios-Papyri* 16–30, calls it a "Frühlingslied," and, following earlier suggestions, believes that it may refer to a festival in a grove of Aphrodite. Lobel, whom Barner quotes, sees in it reference to "some alfresco festivity." Such a setting neither ensures erotic content nor renders it improbable.

37. It is probable that these three fragments represent only two poems. 380 is in the same Ionic meter as 10, a meter not much used by Alcaeus.

38. *SA* 289–90. Barner, *Neuere Alkaios-Papyri* 11–16, thinks that the poem was a *propemptikon*, sung at a symposium for a friend about to embark on a sea voyage at the beginning of spring. The evidence is meager. More cogently, Barner calls attention (13) to the feeling for the seasonal changes of nature that the fragment reveals.

39. Several words and passages are doubtful of meaning. εὔδειλον is a *hapax* and can only be guessed at; the customary assumption is that it is a variant of the Homeric εὐδείελος, "far-seen," or "sunny." Gentili, "Note ad Alceo," *Maia* 3 (1950) 255–60, relates it to Homeric δείλη, "afternoon," and translates "che s' illumina al tramonto"; this would still be related to εὐδείελος; see Chantraine, *Dictionnaire Etymologique de la Langue Grecque*, s. v. δείελος. The place of the sanctuary, according to L. Robert, *REA* 62 (1960) 304–5, was not a high place (as has often been assumed, from εὔδειλον) but a conspicuous sea-side plain at Messon, modern Mesa, near ancient Pyrrha, which would make either meaning of εὐδείελον feasible. Appropriate ruins have been discovered at Mesa. Jerome D. Quinn, "Cape Phokas, Lesbos—Site of an Ancient Sanctuary," *AJA* 65 (1961) 391–93, proposes Cape Phokas, on the south coast of Lesbos, and is endorsed by Picard, "L'Asyle Temporaire du Poète Alcée," *RA* 1962, 2. 43–69.

Page, *SA* 164, urges that ἐπωνύμασσαν be translated "named." But the verb can mean "invoke," "call upon as" as Beattie, "A Note on

Alcaeus Fr. 129," *CR* 6 (1956) 189–91, argues; nor is it likely that
the Lesbians invented all these titles, since Antiaeus was probably
a traditional title equivalent to ἱκέσιος, cf. Picard, *BCH* 70 (1946)
457–58. The point of the epithets is to designate which of the many
aspects of these deities were emphasized in their worship at this
shrine. The epithet of Dionysus, κεμήλιος, is an enigma, and two
suggestions about it are of roughly equal merit: a) that it is a
variant of κειμήλιος, which is proposed by the *editor princeps* and
followed by a number of critics; b) that it is related to κεμάς and
means "god of the fawn," an idea put forward by Picard, *BCH* 70
(1946) 463–65 and *RA* 1962.2.54, and by Gentili, *Maia* 3 (1950)
256–57. Beattie, op. cit., suggests Σεμελήϊον for δεκεμηλιον.

The phrase κήνων οὐ διαλέξατο πρὸς θῦμον, 21–22, has been much
disputed. I am convinced that the interpretation followed by Page,
Treu, and Bowra is wrong. If it means "these matters," as they
believe, it ought to be accusative, not genitive. Kamerbeek,
Mnemosyne 13 (1947) 108, is essentially right, if the text is sound:
"eorum voluntatis rationem non habens," with διαλέξατο used as
in *Iliad* 11. 407. Perhaps the text should be emended to κῆν' ὦν.
Then the pronoun would mean what Page, Treu, and Bowra want
it to mean, and a connective would be provided. The asyndeton is
not a serious objection to the papyrus reading, though it would be
in a poem by Sappho. If the text is right, κήνων will refer to the
betrayed men. This interpretation is grammatically sound, Anacreon
providing an excellent parallel for πρὸς θῦμον (95 Bergk, 55 Gentili,
who comments, *ad. loc.*, on the analogy of usage); and it is stylistically far superior for two reasons: it justifies the asyndeton,
because it is a dramatic breaking away from the immediate thought
back to the dead men; and it fits with Alcaeus's use of demonstrative pronouns in an emphatic way, where a name might be
expected, as τωνδέων 130. 21, κῆνος 70. 6 and 72. 7, ὁ δέ 69. 6.

40. Cf. Picard, "La Triade Zeus-Hera-Dionysus dans l'Orient
Hellenique," *BCH* 70 (1946) 455–73, Edouard Will, "Autour des
Fragments d'Alcée," *RA* 6.39 (1952) 156–69, Stella, "Gli dei di
Lesbo in Alceo 129 LP," *PP* 11 (1956) 321–34, and especially
Robert, *REA* 62 (1960) 285–94. Stella and Robert maintain that
the goddess is not Hera; on the basis of inscriptions Robert believes
that she is simply Αἰολήϊα κυδαλίμα θέος, πάντων γενέθλα, related to

the later θεὰ Αἰολὶς καρποφόρος, with whom the Agrippinas are honorifically identified on inscriptions.

41. Cf. Page, *SA* 200–1.

42. The fragment has its share of lacunae and doubtful words. The term ἐσχάτιαι (24), according to Robert, op. cit., 304–5, refers to "the edges of the *polis*, the frontier region between *poleis*." λυκαιμίαις (25) is very doubtful; for discussion, reporting many suggestions, see Page, *SA* 205. Lines 26–27 are particularly disputable; the text is incomplete and almost certainly corrupt, and yet there is enough to hint at the original meaning and to suggest that that meaning is of importance for the outlook of Alcaeus. I follow in part the restoration and interpretation of Bolling, *AJP* 82 (1961) 151 ff., which takes στάσις in its meaning of "faction" or "party". Bolling makes ·a tempting further suggestion, to restore πρὸς κρέσσονος instead of the usual πρὸς κρέσσονας, and translate "to destroy our faction at the bidding of him who has power . . ." This would give a good Alcaic sentiment, but it demands too much of πρός with the genitive; I do not believe that the Greek can mean this. Beattie, *JHS* 77 (1957) 320, offers the interesting suggestion οὐκ ἄρμενον, to patch the meter without changing the sense. Page, *SA* 206–7, doubtingly translates: "For it is ignoble (?) to renounce rebellion against . . ." and Bowra, *GLP* 146, suggests, "For it is not good (?) to give up rebellion against the . . ." Neither is adequate for ἄμεινον or for ὀννέλην, which, as Bolling insists, means "destroy," not "renounce." Others have changed ὀννέλην; thus Kamerbeek, "De novis carminibus Alcaei," *Mnemosyne* 13 (1947) 94–120, reads ὀννέχην "take up," or "maintain." Another approach is to take the negative with the infinitive; thus Latte, *MH* 4 (1947) 142: "Besser den Kampf mit der Übermacht nicht aufzunehmen." As Treu shows, *Alkaios Lieder* 135, this thought can be found in Hesiod (*WD* 210 is a very close parallel), Herodotus, and Pindar, and may well reflect a maxim. Antonino Luppino, "Sul Carme di Alceo in l'Esilio," *RFIC* 90 (1962) 34–38, adds further instances of the proverb but maintains that Alcaeus is contradicting it: "It is *not* better . . ." In any case the problem of the wrong meaning of ὀννέλην remains. Kamerbeek, *Mnemosyne* 4. 6 (1953) 92, argues that the metrical anomaly of ἄμεινον ὀνν- (∪–∪– for –∪∪–) is paralleled in Alcaeus 167, where line 17 has ∪–∪–, lines 3 and 19 –∪∪–.

While there is no assurance that these lines are all in the same poem, it is probable, and the parallel metrical usage seems to me to justify ἄμεινον here.

To interpret *stasis* as "faction," as I follow Bolling in doing, is possible also in the one other Alcaic use of the word, which admits of the same ambiguity: in 326 τῶν ἀνέμων στάσιν, στάσις can be either the "strife" or the "set" of the winds. Information about other early uses of the word does not determine which is more likely in Alcaeus. Solon was already using it in the sense of "strife" (4. 19), but "faction," implying as it does "position" or "stand," is actually closer to the literal meaning of the word, and the meaning "strife" seems necessarily to imply it. This interpretation of the passage assumes that Alcaeus was in the same mind as in Fr. 70. 7–8: "Let Myrsilus snap at the city until Ares is pleased to turn us to our weapons." Alcaeus does not want to destroy the *hetairia* by premature, improperly-planned action against a stronger opponent. He is willing to wait and plan.

43. Luppino, op. cit., argues that Alcaeus is complaining that Pittacus has done away with the council and assembly, not that they continue while he, in exile, is barred from them. This interpretation goes against the wording and the spirit. The verb ἀπελήλαμαι would have far less point, and the entire picture of exile, including the reminiscence of Achilles in the *Iliad*, would be less effective. His longing must be for something that exists but is beyond his reach when in exile.

44. Cf. Page, *SA* 160, n. 4.

45. For the location of the shrine see n.39, above. According to Robert, the shrine was a federal sanctuary shared by several neighboring *poleis*.

46. The sentence occurs in the *Life of Pittacus* and is quoted as LP Fr. 429 of Alcaeus.

47. Cf. *Suda*, s. v. Πιττακός, and Diogenes Laertius, *Life of Pittacus* 1.

48. Cf. Anacreon, Fr. 11, and Horace, *Odes* 1. 27. 1, 2: Natis in usum laetitiae scyphis/pugnare Thracum est.

49. For discussion, see Page, *SA* 171–74. Bowra, *GLP* 148–49, calls attention to the improbabilities of Page's analysis and offers an unsatisfactory alternative interpretation, suggesting that "you"

may be either Pittacus or a friend of Alcaeus. In the latter case the question may imply good family, not lowly; Alcaeus wonders why his friend is dishonoring his family by his conduct. But this does not explain why Alcaeus has seen fit to refer to his friend's family by referring to his mother. Many critics take τεαύτης as though it referred to "stock" or "family," but, as Page insists, this is a mere evasion of the problem; τεαύτης ἐκγεγόνων can only naturally mean "from such a mother." Benedetto, "Pittaco e Alceo," *PP* 41 (1955) 97–118, and Gomme, "Interpretations of Some Poems of Sappho and Alcaeus," *JHS* 77 (1957) 255–66, think that κῆνος is Pittacus's mother's father. I find it incredible that Alcaeus would have had so lively an interest in Pittacus's maternal grandfather. It is conceivable that κῆνος may be Myrsilus. The fact that Pittacus's connection with him was through a woman may have induced the poet more readily to make reference to Pittacus's mother.

50. It is not certain that the participle εὐωχήμενος modifies βάρμος, but the following stanza certainly has a new subject in κῆνος.

51. 'Επὶ τεύχεσι (ἐπί in tmesis with τρόπην) is proposed by Kamerbeek, *Mnemosyne* 4. 6 (1953) 89; the papyrus has επιτ.ύχε .. [.

52. Barner, *Neuere Alkaios-Papyri* 105, n. 1, takes αὐάτην as "madness," and thinks that it refers to the election of Pittacus, comparing 348, βαρυδαίμονος πόλιος. But αὐάτη here is the result of the strife and battle, and as such is paired with Pittacus's glory. The pre-Aeschylean usage of ἄτη is analysed in a Cornell doctoral thesis, "The Use and Meaning of ATH in the Seven Extant Plays of Aeschylus," by Richard E. Doyle, S. J. Doyle's analysis of types of usage indicates that "ruin" is more likely here. This passage is discussed on p. 30 of Doyle's thesis.

53. The two basic meanings of *stasis*, "strife" and "stand," are both possible in the only two places where Alcaeus uses the word, here and in 130. 26 (cf. n. 42, above). Here the ambiguity helps the metaphor: Alcaeus is concerned by both the direction and the conflict of the winds.

54. The word for "anchors," ἄγκυραι, has been questioned and replaced by some editors; Reinach in the Budé text has ἄγκυλαι, "cables," Page, *SA* ἄγκονναι, "wooldings," for which Barner, *Neuere Alkaios-Papyri* 129, thinks that the marginal gloss to line 2 of Fr. 208a, col. ii, provides support. The grounds for doubt are that the

ship is in motion, not at anchor. The difficulty has been exaggerated: the meaning may be that the ship is in unintended motion, the anchor failing to hold to the bottom. We may suppose the ship to have hove to in a storm; then, as can happen in a bad storm, the anchors are unable to hold.

Fr. 208a probably belongs to the same poem, according to the indication of the fragments of a commentary (305, col. ii), which seems to be about 326 and 208a; see lines 20 and 29. This does not prove that they are from the same poem, but it strongly suggests it. 208a adds this much: "Both feet (?) (remain) in the sheets, and this alone (saves) me; the cargo . . . (lost)." See also n. 55, below.

55. Cf. Page, *SA* 189. Just as the appropriateness of the details of a Homeric simile to the situation that gives rise to the simile is subject to great differences of opinion, so it is with the words of 208a quoted at the end of note 54. Though Page (188) holds that "one might think that there must be some limits to allegory and that the detail here has passed beyond them," it is easy to see an allegorical meaning for these words: "It is only my stubborn personal concern that keeps me from giving in, engulfed in the storm of political disasters, even as the prosperity of the state has vanished." Kamerbeek, *Mnemosyne* 4. 6 (1953) 90–91, takes πόδες as the bottoms of the sails, which still remain, held by the sheets, and may yet save the ship. This would be a little simpler to interpret allegorically, but would not materially change the meaning. As Barner, *Neuere Alkaios-Papyri* 130, points out, ἀμφότεροι suggests that Alcaeus means his feet; if sails or ropes, why the emphasis on "both"?

56. For discussion, see ch. 4.

57. It is generally assumed that the poet writes from exile; the occasion is probably the exile at Pyrrha.

Fr. 306 gives a number of pieces of a commentary on several poems, possibly including 73, and specifically speaks of allegory twice (fr. 14, col. i and col. ii). Fr. 14, col. i, may refer to 73 (cf. Page, *SA* 192) but this is far from certain. That col. ii refers to 73 seems most unlikely. G. L. Koniaris, "Some Thoughts on Alcaeus's Frs. D15, X14m, X16," *Hermes* 94 (1966) 385–97, undermines quite effectively the supposed connections between 306, fr. 14, col. ii, and 73.

58. It has been suggested with not much probability that 73 and 326 are parts of the same poem. The grounds are common meter and allegory. But the tone and circumstance are entirely different.

59. The best MS support is for νέμω; one MS has νόμω, which, as Page suggests, could be from νόμῳ "in the manner of." I accept this not very probable emendation to give a text to translate. Other suggestions include A. Y. Campbell's (CR 7 [1957] 4) 'ν σχερώ, "following close," and J. Taillardat's (RPh 39 [1965] 80–83) λαμπροτέρῳ 'νέμω, "of a stronger wind."

60. Heraclitus, Quaest. Hom. 1. 8, says specifically that 1–3, all that he quotes, are allegorical.

61. For a thorough and responsible exploitation of these fragments cf. Barner, Neuere Alkaios-Papyri. Among further hints of the life and politics of Alcaeus are: 69, on the contrast between the Lydians' treatment of "us" and Pittacus's (see pp. 61–62, above); 296a, on somebody's "thought" which was followed by disaster to the city and death, by the will of Zeus (Page's reconstruction, SA 299, is extremely speculative); 305, col. i, a commentary on at least two poems, one of which has the phrase "drawing from the salt sea," which the commentator explains as meaning unremitting war, the other the phrase "let there not be war" (see p. 59, above); 306, fr. 9, a commentary on two poems, one suggesting a moment of success over Pittacus, the other containing a lemma with the name Zeus and referring to the oath broken by Pittacus. In the small and scattered fragments that probably contain political poetry there is recurrent mention of Pittacus, of Zeus, and of oaths, further testimony to the searing and lasting effect on Alcaeus's spirit, as well as on his political fortunes, of Pittacus's defection from the hetairoi. Among these scraps are 112 (but the elaborate restoration by Diels, which appears in Treu's edition, p. 38, is not to be taken seriously as historical evidence), 114, 75, 106, 67, 348, and (perhaps) 200.

62. Fr. 114, with its mention of the "revealing" of the plot against Myrsilus, may be a reference to Pittacus's betrayal of the hetairoi. If it is, the distinction between a period of defeat but spirited resistance and one of despair is weakened. Fr. 249, with its prudent advice about planning a voyage before entrusting one's

ship to the waves, may be early, as I have suggested, or it may, as Barner thinks (*Neuere Alkaios-Papyri* 124), indicate an experienced and reflective mood and hence a later stage in Alcaeus's political life. To such a period could be accomodated the note of biding one's time that perhaps is to be seen in 130. 26–27, 70. 10–11, and possibly the reconciliatory suggestions of 305. 14–21.

63. On the question of which is allegory see Page *SA* 194–96. Page decides, uncertainly, that the ship is the real subject, even though the explanation, in the commentary, that "sand" in the poem signifies impurity seems to suggest that the ship is the allegory. Page thinks that even "if the ship is the real subject" Alcaeus "may still try to relate 'sand' to the allegorical subject." I do not see why Alcaeus would talk about sand in an allegorical description of an aging courtesan. See further on this topic Koniaris, op. cit.

64. The allegory of Fr. 119 (cf. above, n. 30), intractable though it is, gives clear further evidence of Alcaeus's extensive and complex use of this mode of expression.

65. Cf. Gennaro Perrotta, "Alceo," *A & R* 3. 4 (1936) 221–41, on allegory, especially 229–31; "Non è una figura rettorica composta a freddo, dove ogni elemento è simbolo di qualche cosa, dove a ogni simbolo corrisponde la cosa simboleggiata. Non è un enimma, insomme, que abbia bisogno di una spiegazione. . . . È un' immagine che parla alla fantasia del poeta. . . Poichè nei poeti, sopratutto nei grandi poeti antichi, non domina la logica, domina la fantasia" (230).

66. Page, *SA* 189.

67. The manuscripts of Athenaeus have in line 2 αιτα, which is probably corrupt, though some editors defend it as a vocative. Cf. *SA* 307. I suggest οὔατα as the likeliest word in the context. There are Homeric antecedents for the use of this word, "ears," for "handles." The probability of decorated handles on *cylices* in Mytilene at this period may be doubted, but it is not a far-fetched idea; and Alcaeus may be in exile. Being an unfamiliar form, οὔατα would be easily miscopied and corrupted in late antiquity.

68. See Page, *SA* 308, for an excellent note on the ancient Greek mixtures of wine and water. Two of water to one of wine was usual. In the phrase giving the proportion of water to wine, the amount of water is usually put first.

69. For a description of the game and references to ancient sources see Page, *SA* 314.

70. For discussion of what themes may be touched on see Barner, *Neuere Alkaios-Papyri* 99–102.

71. See above, pp. 64–65.

72. So Page, *SA* 301. As often, the crucial left margin is missing, and thus the possibility of a *coronis*; there is no extra space, but neither is there before line 1, where the *coronis* confirms what sense and style would suggest, the beginning of a poem.

73. I follow Page's text in *SA*; the restorations are by various editors.

74. Barner (11–12) instances this poem, with others, to exemplify the prominence of the inescapable power of Zeus in the thought of Alcaeus. There is support elsewhere for this view; but in this poem Zeus is mythologically appropriate for the story of Sisyphus, and what the poem illustrates more strikingly is the typical archaic resignation to the power of deity. Moreover, the son of Cronus may in this context be Hades, not Zeus.

75. *Odes* 1. 10; the scholiast Porphyrio is our informant about the Alcaic model.

76. Page thinks otherwise, *SA* 255: "These are conventional formulas, which none needs to borrow from another." Yet Horace's ode to Hermes has a very different opening. Had Alcaeus not wanted to reflect the Homeric tradition he could have avoided the traditional phrases.

77. *Orat.* 14.

78. On the cletic hymn generally, see the discussion of Sappho, Fr. 1, in ch. 4.

79. I follow Treu's text, *Alkaios* 24.

80. As Page points out, *SA* 267.

81. The hymns too were probably short poems. The hymn to the Dioscuri was, according to the indications of the papyrus, of twenty-four lines; the lengths of other hymns are unknown. Horace's ode to Hermes, a short poem, is some slight evidence that its model was short. Himerius's paraphrase could, as Page observes, *SA* 246, be of quite a short poem. Edmonds, in *Lyra Graeca*, gets it all into a composition of twenty-four lines.

82. I follow the supplements printed by Page, *SA* 278–79.

83. Thus there is ring composition. But the verbal echo in Page's text, ὤλεσε (3), ἀπώλοντ' (15) is only conjectural, ὤλεσε being a restoration.

84. Page's supplements (*SA* 275) are followed. The only supplements that make a substantial conjecture about meaning are, a) to take θῦμος as subject of πείθ' (line 9) (though the word θῦμος is certain its ending is missing; it may be object, and something else, possibly Aphrodite, subject); and b) the introduction of Aphrodite in lines 9–10; there is probably a reference to "the child of Zeus and . . . ," but the mother is uncertain; it may, e.g., be Leda (so some editors).

85. The word is probably ἐπτόαισε; cf. Sappho 31. 6.

86. Page, *SA* 280–81, suggests specifically that 42, with its attack on Helen, may reflect Stesichorus.

87. This feature of archaic literary style has been convincingly described and illustrated by Hermann Fränkel, "Eine Stileigenheit der Frühgriechischen Literatur."

88. Reinhold Merkelbach, *Zeitschrift für Papyrologie und Epigraphik* 1 (1967) 81–95. The poem has been further studied in the light of the new papyrus by Hugh Lloyd-Jones, "The Cologne Fragment of Alcaeus," *GRBS* 9 (1968) 125–39, and is Fr. 138 in Page, *Lyrica Graeca Selecta*, Oxford 1968.

89. Ὕρραδον (ωυρραδον = ὦ Ὕρραδον) is not an acceptable patronymic for Pittacus, yet it is hard to believe that it is not connected with him. The patronymic Ὕρραος is attested by Fr. 129. 13, Ὕρραον. The statement by Dionysius Thrax (*Grammatici Graeci* 3. 221) that there are three types of patronymics, those in -δης, those in -ιων, and a special Lesbian form in -διος, as an example of which Dionysius gives Ὑρράδιος, both provides a second form of patronymic for Pittacus and excludes the papyrus form, which could, if vocative, be only a masculine in -ων or a neuter. Lloyd-Jones (135–36) reasonably suggests that the form in the papyrus is a mistake for ὠυρράδιον, in "some such phrase as Ὑρράδιον γένεθλον." The papyrus indicates that the ω and the υ are separate syllables; this would of course create a metrical problem, but since there is obviously synizesis the papyrus indication must be wrong. Voigt, *SetA*, adopts Snell's suggestion, ὦ Ὕρρα (vocative of Hyrrhas) δον-.

In spite of the imperfections of assuming that the letters are some form of address to Pittacus there seems to be nothing else that can reasonably be done with them. No other known word is probable, and the resemblances to other references to Pittacus cannot be ignored.

90. Lloyd-Jones observes (136) that the letters κεληто in the line after ωυρραδον are reminiscent of the passage in the *Odyssey* (5. 371) in which Odysseus, shipwrecked by Poseidon, bestrides a plank, "as if riding a race horse" (κέληθ' ὡς ἵππον). It is more likely that the shipwrecked Ajax, in the myth, is in a similar situation than that the κέλης here has a connection with Pittacus. Does the poet then return to the myth after mentioning Pittacus? Or has he after all never left the myth?

91. As is inevitable in so fragmentary a text, there is much that is in doubt. I have reproduced, for the most part, the text of Page, *LGS*. Lines 25–31 are obelized in the papyrus; probably 24 was too, since it begins the stanza which 25–27 continue. Page suggests that what this signifies is not that the lines are spurious but that they are out of place, and that 32–39 ought to have preceded them.

92. It is possible that Poseidon comes into the story in the fragmentary lines of the second column. The agency of Athena in the incident of the storm is reminiscent of the brief mention of the general troubles of the returning Achaeans in *Odyssey* 5. 108–9.

93. This survey of Alcaeus's poetry has given attention to most but not all of the principal fragments. One conspicuous omission is 357, an eight-line (or sixteen-line if we follow Page in dividing the long lines into two metrical units each) fragment, which may be a complete poem except for an opening line, describing weapons and armor, piece by piece, as they stand in the hall, ready for use in "the task," no doubt the task of civil strife. Its contents are analyzed at length by Page, *SA* 209–23. As Barner, *Neuere Alkaios-Papyri* 52–62, points out, Fr. 179, col. ii appears to be another description of weapons.

Chapter Four: *Sappho*

1. *Mar. Par.* 36.
2. Cf. Alcaeus, Fr. 112. 23 and marginal note.
3. Cf. Alcaeus, Fr. 112. 24, and Page, *SA* 174–75.

4. For elaborate reconstruction of Fr. 98 and accompanying historical speculations of more ingenuity than probability, see Carlo Gallavotti, "Rilievo storici sulla nuova ode di Saffo," *SIFC* 18 (1942) 161–74. P. Odo Bauer, "Sapphos Verbannung," *Gymnasium* 70 (1963) 1–10, in equal but opposite speculation, holds that Sappho was in a party hostile to Alcaeus, was exiled by his group during a period of ascendancy which it enjoyed, and was in fact, like Pittacus, an outsider because of her foreign or partly foreign origin. Bauer's case for Sappho's foreign extraction depends in part on a learned study by Günther Zuntz, "On the Etymology of Sappho's Name," *MH* 8 (1951) 12–35, in which Zuntz argues with much probability that Sappho's name is Asian. The rest of Bauer's case is, however, fragile and filled with reckless assumptions.

5. Athenaeus 10. 424e. Since in the next sentence Athenaeus refers to such service by Sappho's brother in the Prytaneion of the Mytileneians, the inference of his high birth seems clear. Gomme, *JHS* 77 (1957) 259, expresses doubt: one of Sappho's brothers was a trader and aristocrats do not engage in trade. But the distinction between aristocracy and trade may be more a phenomenon of fifth century Athens and nineteenth century England than of Lesbos at any period.

6. On this complex, difficult, and endlessly discussed subject the following modern critics provide the best help: Page, who throughout *SA* and especially in the section entitled "On the Content and Character of Sappho's Poetry," gives an eminently sensible analysis; Manuel Fernandez-Galiano, whose *Safo* (Madrid 1958) is primarily a biographical study of Sappho; Reinhold Merkelbach, whose "Sappho und ihr Kreis," *Philologus* 101 (1957) 1–29 gives a good picture of the probable nature and spirit of the "Kreis," though it is far more precise about the activities of Sappho's group than the evidence warrants, and contains much on Fr. 31 that is in my opinion wrong (discussion later in this chapter); and J. M. Edmonds, whose section "The Life of Sappho" in *Lyra Graeca* 2 conveniently assembles the ancient evidence. M. L. West, "Burning Sappho," *Maia* 22 (1970) 307-30, has cogent observations on the relationship between Sappho's poetry and her life, as well as notes on several fragments, especially Frs. 1, 2, and 31.

7. The Ovidian letter of Sappho to Phaon, *Heroides* 15, nicely

illustrates the opinion and the disagreement. In a passage where Sappho is represented as expressing her dissatisfaction, now that she pines for Phaon, with various girls who have had her affection, these words occur (line 19): (*puellae*) *quas hic* (or *non*) *sine crimine amavi*. The MSS are divided between *hic* and *non*, between assertion and denial of a homosexual relationship. For a "clinical scrutiny" bearing upon Sappho's sex life, written by a psychiatrist, see George Devereux, "The Nature of Sappho's Seizure in Fr. 31LP as Evidence of her Inversion," *CQ* 64 (1970) 17–31. Devereux diagnoses the symptoms described in Fr. 31 as being exactly those of an anxiety crisis and consequently "proof positive of her lesbianism." But reservations are surely permissible as to the scientific authority of an analysis of a passage of poetry. M. Marcovich, "Sappho Fr. 31: Anxiety Attack or Love Declaration?", *CQ* 66 (1972) 19–32 shows the weaknesses of Devereux's arguments on philological grounds and makes a number of valuable observations on the interpretation of the poem. Devereux, incidentally, does not believe that the Phaon story is necessarily at odds with homosexuality; see p. 23 of his article.

8. Fr. 30 gives this number in a subscription to the Book.

9. POxy 1232 has Fr. 43 marked off in two-line stanzas, Fr. 44 stichic.

10. It is mentioned by Photius (cf. Edmonds, *Lyra Graeca* 2. 180) in a context which might suggest that the Book 8 he is referring to consisted of poems arranged by subject; but the evidence is slight. Page's deduction about it (*SA* 116–19) from the bibliographical fragment, 103 (that the ten poems whose opening lines are given constituted Book 8), is too conjectural to be taken seriously. Treu, *Sappho* 167–69, is just as likely to be right in supposing that the ten poems form an anthology. The evidence of the fragment seems to me most naturally to suggest that nine of the ten poems of the fragment are epithalamians.

11. Servius, *Georgics* 1. 31; Page, *SA* 116.

12. Page suggests, on some good grounds, that metrically appropriate epithalamians were assigned to the various metrically determined books, and placed at the end of them (*SA* 125–26). Thus (in Book 1) 30, which is known to be the last poem of the book, is certainly epithalamian, and 27 seems to be; in the inter-

vening scraps, several words would suit epithalamians well and
none would be out of place. But I am doubtful about Book 2; see
the discussion of Fr. 44 later in this chapter.

13. While there is for most of this poem what can be regarded
as an accepted text, which I follow, there are several important
points of doubt or disagreement. περσκεθοισα, line 6, though usually
accepted, is very uncertain, since only one of the dotted letters
deserves to be called probable (the θ seems, judging from the plate
in *Ox. Pap.* 10, to be likely). In lines 12–13 there was probably a
mention of whoever "misled" Helen, whether Paris or Eros or
Aphrodite. From the αμπτον of line 13 most critics have assumed
some such meaning as "a woman in love is easily persuaded." In
line 19, LP dagger κἀνόπλοισι and Page, *SA*, emends to καὶ πανόπλοις,
because of the Attic correption of the papyrus text. But Attic
correption is inadequate grounds for textual emendation in the
early poets. I have argued this case and given examples of the
sporadic appearance of Attic correption, in "The Authorship of the
Strasbourg Epodes," *TAPA* 92 (1961) 267–82. Voigt, *SetA*, keeps
the papyrus reading.

14. We have the following evidence about the length of Sappho's
poems: fifteen poems either certainly or very probably of 20 or
fewer lines (certain: 17, 62, 63, and ten poems from an unspecified
book [Fr. 103]; probable: 2,5), three poems longer than 20 lines
(1 is 28 lines, 44 is more than 34 lines, 94 is at least 33 lines). In
other words, out of eighteen instances, sixteen are shorter than 32
lines. Fr. 99, cols. i and ii, gives evidence of a poem of 18 lines and
one of at least 22 lines, but the authorship of these scraps is very
doubtful; they are as likely to be Alcaeus's as Sappho's; cf. *Ox.
Pap.* 21. 10–11, Treu, *Sappho* 165, Snell, *Hermes* 81 (1953) 118–19,
Gomme, *JHS* 77 (1957) 255–66; Snell and Gomme ascribe them
to Alcaeus. Milne is much too dogmatic in his comments on length
and form in Book 1 of Sappho, *Aegyptus* 13 (1933) 176–78 and
Hermes 71 (1936) 126–28, when he declares that five stanzas is "the
norm." He also repeats, with more confidence than evidence, the
notion first put forward by Hunt, *Ox. Pap.* 10. 21, that the poems
were organized in alphabetical order of opening letters. The only
impressive evidence is o, π, and perhaps π in 16, 17, 18. This is
not enough to generalize from, as Hunt realized.

15. Sense can be made of the poem only if it is accepted that "whatever you love" is universally "the fairest thing." Bowra, *GLP*² 180–81, and Merkelbach, *Philologus* 101 (1957) 16, would have it that it is a female preference, deliberately contrasted with the masculine interests of war. Page, *SA* 55–56, and George Koniaris, *Hermes* 95 (1967) 257–61, are right; Koniaris's rigorously logical analysis leaves the question in no doubt. Robert Bagg, in a brief analysis of the poem, *Arion* 3 (1964) 67–69, insists that κάλλιστον means something less bland than "most beautiful," and would like to translate "most thrilling." But he translates by "fairest," and I think that we must be so restrained. Of course more is implied. Sappho's language remains simple even when, as here, we sense a power and excitement of feelings that far transcend the linguistic simplicity.

Garry Wills, "The Sapphic 'Umwertung aller Werte,' (Fr. 16)," *AJP* 88 (1967) 434–42, persuasively argues that in the Priamel Sappho enunciates a principle of entirely subjective judgment, negating the traditional values of society, going even beyond the "Protagorean homo-mensura" to "a vision of a beautiful and destructive anarchy." But his conclusion, based on the mention of Helen's conduct and the analogies between what Sappho loves and the opening military scenes, that "Sappho wants her flesh and movement of beauty to be full of danger" and values her contemporary world "precisely for its imperiled atmosphere," seems to be purely fanciful, supported neither by this poem nor by any other poetry of Sappho's nor by anything known about Sappho.

16. There appears to be no authority for using the English word "preamble" in this meaning, sensible though it would be; we may either keep the original Latin or borrow the German. On the use of this convention in Greek literature see Ulrich Schmid, *Die Priamel der Werte im Griechischen* (Wiesbaden 1964).

17. Page (*SA* 55–57) finds little but censure to express on this poem, but his adverse comments seem to be based only on subjective impressions. As my comments on the poem will suggest, I question the cogency of Merkelbach's notion that Helen's desertion is a mythical model of Anactoria's desertion of Sappho and the *Mädchenkreis* (*Philologus* 101 [1957] 15). Against this view, see

Herbert Eisinger, "Zur Interpretation von Sappho fr. 16 LP,"
Philologus 103 (1959) 130–35, and George Koniaris, "On Sappho,
Fr. 16 (L. P.)," *Hermes* 95 (1967) 257–68.

18. The perception of personal characteristics, of what distinguishes one persons's way from that of anyone else, is among the
new features introduced by archaic lyric. There is little trace of it
in Homer or in early elegy. Archilochus has it in his description of
a general (60); he and Sappho are the first to show it. Cf. Max
Treu, *Von Homer zur Lyrik* (Munich 1955) 170–203.

19. The phrase κωὐκ ἐθέλοισα, Fr. 1. 24, has the same effect,
though in a lighter mood.

20. The text is found in Dionysius of Halicarnassus *Comp.* 173–79
and, partially, on a thin horizontal strip of papyrus (POxy 2288)
that is especially significant at line 19. The text is generally sound
except for line 19, where in the MSS of Dionysius the line begins
with καισαγην or μαισαγην. POxy 2288 gives what Lobel believes
can only reasonably have come from ἄψ σ᾽ ἄγην. All interpretations
based on Dionysius are thus made more improbable; none was
satisfactory anyway. No entirely convincing interpretation of the
sentence has been proposed. The idea of taking πείθω as Πείθω
(accusative case) is surely wrong; Bolling, *AJP* 82 (1961) 153–54,
shows that it is a most improbable accusative. My translation takes
σ᾽ as dative and ἄγην as a result infinitive, literally "whom am I to
persuade so as to bring (her) back for you to your friendship?"
I presume that Bolling so takes the sentence; he is satisfied with
the reading ("crystal clear") but does not bother to translate. Page
finds the reading intolerable and in his translation uses his emendation, τάγην, which is too stylistically awkward to be persuasive.
Koniaris, "On Sappho, Fr. 1 (Lobel-Page)," *Philologus* 109 (1965)
30–38, objects to the notion of bringing *back*, on the grounds that
"the notion of reappointment—of leading back—rather than the
general notion of appointment seems . . . somewhat strange in this
poem" (36). He has in mind the fact that this love is clearly one of
a series (δηῦτε). But the suffering of Sappho that is a feature of the
poem and the mention of "injustice" (20) fit as well with a broken-
off affection as with a hitherto unsuccessful suit. Ernst Heitsch,
Hermes 95 (1967) 385–86, maintains that the letter before ς may
be ι and proposes εἰσάγην, thus approximating the text of Dionysius.

He interprets the verb intransitively ("whom shall I persuade to bring herself to your love"), thus meeting Koniaris's objection. For the intransitive meaning he finds support in Homeric scholia which interpret ἐξαγαγόντες, *Iliad* 7. 336, and ἐσάγουσα, 6. 252, as intransitive. The suggestion is interesting but the support is frail, since neither Homeric example need or reasonably can be taken as intransitive. The most recent suggestion, made by R. Van Bennekom, *Mnemosyne* 4. 25 (1972) 113–22, is to read Πείθων / αἶσ' ἄγην ἐς σάν . . . , meaning "Whose turn is it this time to be led by Peitho to your love?" I am not persuaded by the author's explanation of the use of αἶσα nor does the introduction of Peitho seem right for the context.

André Rivier, "Observations sur Sappho 1. 19 sq.," *REG* 80 (1967) 84–92, believes that the word ἀδικεῖν must at this period suggest infidelity to a formal obligation, not just amorous infidelity, and that the obligation was that undertaken when a girl entered Sappho's circle. The "injustice" is a girl's defection to a rival group. Sappho, as leader, takes the infidelity personally. Thus Page's τάγην is right, and the sentence means "Qui, encore, vais-je persuader de reprendre place au circle de ton amour?" I am unable to accept so strong a phrase as μαινόλᾳ θύμῳ as being part of a formal and impersonal reaction. And since δίκη could be used metaphorically, nonlegally, by Anaximander, it seems reasonable to suppose that Sappho could similarly use ἀδικεῖν.

Κωὐκ ἐθέλοισα (24) has been repeatedly questioned, on the grounds that only θέλω, not ἐθέλω, occurs in Sappho and Alcaeus. Gomme's defense, *JHS* 77 (1957) 261–66, is persuasive: we have too narrow a basis for decision to be prepared to emend away this reading, and there is even some likelihood that other forms of ἐθέλω did occur in Sappho, in view of ἐθέλ[in Alcaeus 66. Much ingenuity has been spent on emending the phrase. The simplest remedy, κωὐκὶ θέλοισα, merely replaces one unattested form with another. Κωὔ σε θέλοισαν raises severe problems of interpretation; if we are to suppose that Sappho willingly envisages the prospect that soon she will not want the girl's affection we are negating the *rapport* between Sappho and Aphrodite that the rest of the poem creates (cf. Gomme, op. cit. 264). A. J. Beattie, "A Note on Sappho, Fr. 1," *CQ* 51 (1957) 180–83, proposes κὼς σὺ θέλοισα, construed with the following line, and preceded by a full stop. Sappho is speaking, θέλοισα

modifies Aphrodite, the understood subject of ἔλθε. Along with this
reading, Beattie offers the suggestion that it is a man whom Sappho
loves. Arguing, as others have, that what Sappho asks is a reversal
—not only is the beloved to love her but she is to flee the beloved—
he compares Catullus's "Miser Catulle, desinas ineptire." But is it
thinkable that this poem of Catullus should invoke Venus? To
imagine it is to emphasize how impossible this interpretation of
Sappho's poem is. Κωὖκ ἀέκοισα is supported by several critics,
among them Bolling, *AJP* 82 (1961) 151–63: ἐθέλοισα came in as
a gloss on the whole phrase οὐκ ἀέκοισα. While κωὖκ ἀέκοισα is
palaeographically attractive, "not unwillingly" is tame and pointless,
a feeble and anticlimactic repetition of φιλήσει.

   The view that ποικιλόθρονος refers not to a throne but to θρόνα,
decorations on the garment of the goddess, has been put forward
repeatedly; cf. Lillian B. Lawler, *PQ* 27 (1948) 80–84, Bolling,
AJP 79 (1958) 275–82, and Michael J. C. Putnam, *CJ* 56 (1960–
61) 79–83. But the analogy with χρυσόθρονος, etc., is enough to
justify taking -θρονος as throne. The ποικιλο - certainly suggests the
deviousness of Aphrodite, fitting well with δολόπλοκε, and -θρονος
as throne seems right as emphasizing her divine quality.

   As Treu points out (*Sappho* 176), POxy 2288, which has a punctuation dot between χρύσιον and ἦλθε, supports taking χρύσιον with
δόμον. It has more often been taken with ἄρμα, and Wilamowitz's
crisp argument is cogent (*SuS* 45): "Natürlich ist der Wagen
golden, nicht das Haus, denn das ist uns hier einerlei." The naïveté
of having sparrows draw the weight of a gold chariot would not be
out of place in this fantasy. Yet the indication of the papyrus
seems to me to take priority, and there is another consideration of
form: nowhere else does Sappho split an epithet-noun group
between stanzas.

   21. The markings on POxy 2288 confirm that what Dionysius
quotes is the whole poem.

   22. On the hymnal aspect of the poem there is an important
study by A. Cameron, "Sappho's Prayer to Aphrodite," *HTR* 32
(1934) 1–17. Though he finds that the customary formulas of
prayer are not rigidly or completely followed, Cameron declares
that "all is appropriate to the traditional structure of prayer" (4).
The opening section omits some traditional aspects, and the authen-

tication of the appeal, by reminding the deity of earlier response to prayer, is unusually long (Sophocles [*OT* 162] gives an example of the usual form), "akin to epic technique," but such "exemplary narrative" is a legitimate prayer formula, perhaps derived from "a primitive form of spell" (4). The language, though Homeric influence is strong, is partly in "conventional sacral style." Against the notion that Sappho is describing a veritable epiphany (espoused since by Bowra, *GLP*² 202–3) Cameron is firm: "The description of Aphrodite's flight has none of the accuracy of observation and truth to nature" usual in an epiphany; "it is rather Homeric and conventional" (13). "We are on the solid ground of ancient religious belief and practice, and the relationship to the divinity to which the passage points is very different from visionary mysticism or divine exaltation." Apart from a tendency to strain some of the verbal similarities to prayer and spell formulas, Cameron's analysis is judicious and persuasive.

23. Cf. Page, *SA* 12. Δηῦτε occurs elsewhere in Sappho five times (22, 83, 99, 127, and 130). Two passages are too fragmentary for the context to be determinable; in two the context is love, in one it is not. The word is found in Alcman, Anacreon, and Ibycus in connection with the onset of love. To attach great interpretative importance to the repetition of what appears to have been a thoroughly conventional word is very risky. Page's interpretation of the whole poem, featuring the idea that Sappho is laughing at her love problems, is largely based on the repetition of δηῦτε and on the conviction that διώξει (21) necessarily implies that Sappho will tomorrow flee the love she so earnestly seeks today. Page's interpretation is sharply and convincingly rebutted by Gomme, *JHS* 77 (1957) 264; George Koniaris, *Philologus* 109 (1965) 30–38, has patiently and effectively destroyed Page's argument from διώξει. On this last point see also A. Cameron, "Sappho and Aphrodite Again," *HTR* 57 (1964) 237–39.

24. Page, *SA* 18.

25. Nobody, presumably, would be disposed to deny the ring form of this poem. Milne, in his description of the form of Sappho's poetry, *Hermes* 71 (1936) 126–28, ventures a too elaborate and rigid scheme and thus undermines the credibility of his analysis, which is otherwise valid. The return to the start in Poem 1 is both

of theme and of language: ἔλθ' (5)—ἔλθε (24), θῦμον (4)— θῦμος (27). On the structure of this poem generally, see Bowra, *GLP*² 204–5, for excellent comments.

On structure in the poetry of Sappho there are comments and bibliography in Helmut Saake's *Zur Kunst Sapphos* (Munich 1971); see especially "Kunstwürdigung," pp. 205–19. Saake's book has extensive commentaries on the main fragments and exhaustive bibliographies.

26. Page, *SA* 42.

27. The last stanza is preserved by Athenaeus (11. 463e), but the text derives mainly from an inscribed sherd first published by Medea Norsa, *Annali della R. Scuola Normale Superiore di Pisa* 2. 6 (1937) 8–15. The text of the sherd is barely legible and presents acute problems of exegesis. I have adopted, mainly, the readings of Giulia Lanata, "L'Ostracon Fiorentino con Versi di Saffo," *SIFC* 32 (1960) 64–90. Her study is based on a fresh examination of the sherd, and contains extensive bibliography on the poem. For bibliography, see also Kjeld Matthiessen, "Das Gedicht Sapphos auf der Scherbe," *Gymnasium* 64 (1957) 554–64, and Voigt, *SetA* 34–35. See now also Thomas McEvilley, "Sappho, Fragment Two," *Phoenix* 26 (1972) 323–33.

Given the numerous and idiosyncratic errors that abound, much must remain quite uncertain. It seems to me unreasonable to believe, as some editors do, that the first word traces are not part of the poem. That they are wrong in dialect and do not fit the meter are inconclusive arguments against their inclusion, since the fragment is full of forms that fit no dialect and no meter. The most important guess that must be made concerns the form of the word that refers to Crete or the Cretans. Lobel and Page have ἐκ Κρήτας, but the original reading by Norsa, agreed to by R. Pfeiffer, "Vier Sappho-Strophen auf einem Ptolemäischen Ostrakon," *Philologus* 92 (1937) 117–25, is confirmed by Lanata: "Κρητες mi pare assolutamente preferibile a Κρητας." François Lasserre, *MH* 5 (1948) 15, and André Rivier, "Sur un vers-clé de Sappho (Ostr. 5)," *MH* 5 (1948) 227–39, argue cogently for this reading and evolve the text which I use for this line. Whether κατέρρει or κατάγρει is the right reading in line 10 is very dubious. As Lanata observes (op. cit., 82), Erinna 2. 2 (D) supports κατέρρει. The case for κατάγρει (to which κατέρρει

in the Erinna passage is sometimes changed) is well stated by
Ernst Risch, "Der göttliche Schlaf bei Sappho," *MH* 19 (1962)
197–201. But the meaning "seizes" is doubly wrong in the context,
not only in that it needs an object, as Page insists (*SA* 38), but,
more tellingly, in that it leaves the genitive unexplained. Κῶμα can
very well "flow down" from the leaves; it cannot very well "seize"
from them. In line 7, between the usual ἐσκίαστ᾽ αἰθυσσομένων and
ἐσκίασται θυσσομένων, which is argued for especially by V. Pisani,
Paideia 15 (1960) 245–46, there is almost nothing to choose. The
last strophe is thoroughly uncertain; Lanata's version seems to me
to combine the evidence of the sherd and Athenaeus's quotation
most plausibly.

Editors have been divided as to how much of the poem we have.
Lanata assumes that the end of the poem is given, because between
the word οἰνοχόεισα and the rough bottom edge of the sherd there
is, at one point, a space at least twice as wide as exists between any
two lines preserved; a following line ought to have been in the lower
part of this space. The reproduction given by Pfeiffer (op. cit.,
facing p. 117) shows this space clearly. Most editors think that
something must have followed because of the context in Athenaeus.
After the quoted lines (the last stanza of the sherd) Athenaeus
gives a sentence in prose that is difficult to interpret as other than
a paraphrase of a continuation of the poem. (The situation is nearly
analogous to the end of "Longinus's" quotation of Poem 31.) On
the analogy of other poems of this type the last preserved stanza
makes good sense as the end of the poem, and I agree with Lanata
in her assumption that not much is missing from the beginning.
There is no epigraphical evidence, but the word that opens the first
complete stanza, δεῦρυ, is invocatory, much like the ἔλθε in line 5
of Poem 1. Hence it is likely to be near the beginning of the poem.
It is a guess with some probability that the first words preserved
are at the end of Stanza 1.

28. I hesitate to ascribe any more precise point to the poem
on the basis of the description of the sanctuary, but two relevant suggestions are worth mentioning. Alexander Turyn, "The
Sapphic Ostracon," *TAPA* 73 (1942) 308–18, compares the description with various literary paradises and concludes that Sappho
"utilized the current pictures of paradisiac meadows of the Orphic

eschatology." In one of the most convincing parts of his pro-
vocative study, "Sappho und ihr Kreis," *Philologus* 101 (1957)
1–29, Reinhold Merkelbach compares the picture of the grove in
the poem with the "garden of the nymphs" in Ibycus and elsewhere, and declares that "der Nymphengarten ist das mythische
Urbild, dessen Widerspiegelung auf Erden der Kreis der Mädchen
um Sappho ist." Merkelbach's general purpose is to show how
closely myth and contemporary scene are related in Sappho's
poems. While his explanation of the Helen myth in 16 (see n. 17,
above) is dubious, this point is a good one and its elaboration in
connection with Poem 2 is impressive. The reading ἔναυλον, with
its echo of a Hesiodic "garden" ("glen," more literally) of the
nymphs, would suit Merkelbach's point well.

Robert Bagg, *Arion* 3 (1964) 52–54, emphasizes the sexuality of
the imagery of this poem. "Sappho grows a garden where sexual
responses are reached with the indirect power only available to
symbolic language." The aphrodisiac quality of the poem is both
sexual and reverent, and the reverence is at least as strongly felt as
the sexuality.

That Sappho intended the scene to have a trance-like, divinely
caused atmosphere of peace is strongly suggested by the word
κῶμα (line 8), which connotes not merely sleep but a divinely
induced and supernatural state. Cf. Page, *SA* 37, Ernst Risch,
"Der göttliche Schlaf bei Sappho," *MH* 19 (1962) 197–201, and
Peter Wiessman, "Was heisst κῶμα?", *MH* 29 (1972) 1–11.

Rivier, op. cit. (n. 27), has excellent comments on this poem.
My account is indebted to his.

29. In general, this is the text of LP. Berlin Papyrus 9722 is the
sole source. I do not hesitate, as LP do, to accept the emendation
σελάννα for the μήνα of the papyrus, on the assumption that μήνα is
a gloss. Page (*SA* 90), finds it hard to see why the common word
σελήνη should be glossed by the less common word μήνη. But it is
harder to see, when a word for "moon" is clearly demanded by the
context, how μήνα is *not* a gloss for σελάννα, as Bolling comments,
AJP 82 (1961) 151–63; cf. also Ernst Heitsch, *Hermes* 95 (1967) 96–98.
In the last stanza I follow, in part, Zuntz's reading and interpretation, *Mnemosyne* 3.7 (1938) 95–102; Bowra's compromise,
*GLP*² 193, would be attractive if it did not require arbitrary emen-

dation as well as restoration; Zuntz takes ζαφοίταισ’ as third singular, rather than a participle, marks line 17 off with dashes, and supposes that 18 (which he restores) continues the sentence. (Bowra punctuates after φρένα and adds a δ’ after κᾶρ.) But so close a syntactical link between stanzas is improbable, and therefore the lack of connective in line 17 is, as Page observes (SA 91), "disagreeable." How 17 can be restored remains obscure. The meaning "consumes" or "devours," excogitated by Zuntz, on the analogy of βόρα, δημοβόρος, etc., as being from an unattested verb βορέομαι, has had something like confirmation by its subsequent appearance in POxy 2221 (cf. Page, SA 92) with a middle meaning. The active sense is still in some doubt, but it is by no means as improbable as might previously have been thought.

The fragment goes on for another 19 lines, partly mere traces, partly groups of words yielding no sustained sense.

30. Reading τὸ μέσσον at the end of 20, Zuntz (109) insists that a substantive must follow for it to modify and that the poem therefore cannot end at this point. But, apart from the fact that restoration is so hazardous that it is unreasonable to insist that there is no room for a substantive before μέσσον, the first stanza of Alcaeus 326 provides an exact parallel for μέσσον used substantively.

31. Line 17 of this poem is much too uncertain to be used as an example. The one other place in Sappho is 94. 2, and there is some doubt as to the syntactical connection with the preceding line. See n. 56, below. Sentence asyndeton is common in Alcaeus.

32. Presumably we are to think of Sappho as singing this poem to console Atthis, who is mentioned in Fr. 49 as, apparently, a member of Sappho's group and in 131 as a deserter from it. This poem can accurately be called a "Trostgedicht" (Merkelbach, Philologus 101 [1957] 12–16); the designation is less appropriate for 16.

33. Page's comment (SA 95–96) is instructive: "The simile in this poem is not much more irrelevant and not at all less decorative, than the long description of Aphrodite's descent" in Poem 1. What Page finds irrelevant will be judged differently if we suppose that both parts of the poem are integral to its meaning.

"What does βροδοδάκτυλος mean, applied to the moon?" Page puts the question and answers (SA 90), that in the transfer of the

Homeric epithet for dawn Sappho changes the image "from the clear and brilliant to the dim and confused." It is undeniable that the evening moon (ἀελίω δύντος) does not shoot rosy rays into the sky as the rising sun does. But surely we can be satisfied with less of celestial accuracy than Page demands, provided there is a different point in the use of the epithet. Elsewhere Sappho calls dawn not only βροδόπαχυς (58. 19), a simple reminiscence of the Homeric phrase, altered for meter and perhaps for variety (with the thought that the traditional rosy fingers allow for the existence of rosy fore-arms), but also χρυσοπέδιλλος (103, 123). Eos does not have gold sandals any more than Selene has rosy fingers. In both cases Sappho has a naively pictorial expression: because the morning light changes from red to gold as the sun mounts, Sappho permits herself to think of the gold color as the sandals of the morning, as an extension from the Homeric imagery of rosy dawn. Here, the moon is called rosy-fingered to suggest the impression of the evening moon, which often has a reddish hue as it reaches upward into the sky. The Homeric imagery of the rising sun is again in the back-ground. Perhaps, too, the girl whose beauty starts the simile has gone away in the direction of the rising moon, and this brings us to an answer to another question asked by Page: "How is the definite article to be justified?" (90). It is not certain that we really have to justify the definite article; the rules of Lesbian grammar are only shakily established, and it is doubtful whether they should be given preference in the face of a textually clear exception. The setting of the poem, however, perhaps justifies the demonstrative use of the article. It is Mytilene, in the evening, as the moon rises over the just visible Asian coast where the girl has gone and over the intervening channel that separates her from Atthis and Sappho. (Perhaps, as Mr. Seamus MacMathūna has suggested to me, the "fingers" are the broken reflection of the moonlight in the water. Louise Weld and William Nethercut, "Sappho's Rose-fingered Moon: A Note," *Arion* 5 [1966] 28–31, justify the epithet on the rather forced grounds that the moon, in this scene of burgeoning vegetation, has the fostering role of the sun; they speak of a "fusion of contraries that has puzzled the unimaginative." Beattie, reviewing Page *SA* [*JHS* 1957, 321] proposes βροδοδακτύλλα, "with a rosy ring around it," a common phenomenon, Beattie says, of the full moon in summer in the Aegean islands.) See also Bowra, *GLP*² 195. On various literary occurrences of ῥοδοδάκτυλος and of the "rosy moon," see Folco Martinazzoli, *Sapphica e Vergiliana* (Rome 1958) 23.

34. Page, *SA* 27.

35. Bowra, *GLP*² 185.

36. The text and the interpretation, both of meaning in general and in many details, have given rise to a huge literature of criticism. The following comments touch on some of the *cruces*.

The reference of τό (5) is to what immediately precedes, and hence the meaning cannot be, as Page says it can (*SA* 21–22), "I am jealous when I see the man enjoying your favour; for when I look at you, sitting near him as you are and talking and laughing to him, I am overcome by emotion." The cause of excitement is specified at once by Sappho: "*for* (γάρ) when I see *you*" (not "him" or "you and him"). This is not to deny that Sappho's emotion is occasioned by the privileged place of the man; but it is essentially the beauty of the girl that Sappho reacts to. Cf. Garry Wills, "Sappho 31 and Catullus 51," *GRBS* 8 (1967) 167–97, and M. Marcovich, *CQ* 66 (1972) 19–32.

Bolling, *AJP* 82 (1961) 163, and A. J. Beattie, "Sappho Fr. 31," *Mnemosyne* 4. 9 (1956) 103–11, both propose ὡς γὰρ εἰσίδω (7). The MSS have ὡς γὰρ σίδω. Bolling argues on palaeographical grounds, Beattie apparently because he wants the poem to say that Sappho is in love with the man, not the girl. The reading is improbable, since the loss of part of a word that is required by sense is harder to account for than the loss of ἐς, which is not needed for sense; Beattie's interpretation is impossible in view of lines 3–6.

The difficulty of accepting εἴκει (8) as impersonal is overstated by Page (*SA* 23); *Iliad* 18. 520 is an acceptable parallel. Page holds that εἶκε there is a form of ἔοικα; but the Homeric forms are elsewhere always in the perfect system and εἶκε from εἴκω is therefore much more probable.

In line 9 I follow the traditional text. Bowra, *GLP*² 185, follows Cobet's conjecture πέπαγε, "is frozen," for which Catullus's corresponding *torpet* provides some evidence, but Catullus's imitation is not literal enough for this to mean any more than the evidence for ἔαγε provided by *infringi*, Lucretius 3. 155. (Malcovati, *Athenaeum* 1966, 9, on Lucretius's imitation: "L'audace traslato . . . che nessuno piu ha osato riprendere.") Beattie, op. cit., proposes ἀλλ' ἄκαν μὲν γλῶσσ' ἀπέαγε, "My speech is broken off, hushed (suddenly silenced)." This avoids the hiatus but leaves just as difficult a metaphorical use of ἄγνυμι and makes the clause repeat the one before it. That the assumption of Ϝ' before ἔαγε is reasonable is strongly and, I think, cogently argued by Ernst Heitsch, *RhM* 105 (1962) 285.

In line 13 I accept Ahrens's reconstitution of the text. The main decision is whether to omit ψῦχρος or part of κακχέεται (leaving ἔχει, to be taken with καδ), to fit the meter. Ψῦχρος seems a very likely gloss; to explain "sweat pours down me," the annotator comments, "i.e., cold sweat."

In "Longinus's" text, line 16 is incomplete. George Thomson, *CQ* 29 (1935) 37–38, restored αὔτα and maintained that the poem ends at that point. Papyrus evidence, consisting of eight lines of a commentary on the poem, and quoting from the middle of line 14 to the end of line 16 (Manfredo Manfredi, "Sull' Ode 31 L. P. de Saffo," *Dai Papiri della Società Italiana* [Florence 1965] 16–17), now completes line 16, with ἔμ' αὔτα but sheds no light on the problem of the following words in "Longinus." The final letter is missing and consequently so is whatever punctuation might have followed. With the completion of line 16, the ghost of "Agallis" is, presumably, finally laid. Ἄγαλλι, vocative case of a putative favorite girl, was the ingenious suggestion of W. R. Paton for completing line 16 using the letters of the next word, ἀλλά, which, though generally (and as we now know correctly) supposed to belong to a following line if to the poem at all, follows without a break in the text of "Longinus." It was a brilliant conjecture, and the persistence of its attractiveness can be measured by the fact that it was accepted in 1964 by Günther Jachmann in the valuable article referred to at the end of n. 37.

The papyrus discovery has encouraged Carlo Gallavotti to renew his suggestion that in line 1 we should read Ϝοι for μοι, in other words that Fr. 165 gives the right text for the phrase. Gallavotti, "Per il testo di Saffo," *RFIC* 94 (1966) 257–67, urges that the contrast with ἔμ' αὔτα is thus the more striking. But the weight of evidence remains decidedly for μοι, and Gallavotti's original argument for Ϝοι, *RFIC* 70 (1942) 103–14, based on Apollonius Dyscolus's habits in citing passages from Sappho, is inadequate against other evidence, particularly since the point he undertakes to establish—that Apollonius always quotes the first available example—depends on a single alleged parallel, hardly enough to demonstrate a habit.

No convincing interpretation of the words that follow, in "Longinus," ἀλλὰ πᾶν τολμητὸν ἐπεὶ καὶ πένητα, has been found. Milne, *SO* 13 (1934) 21, though virtually in accord with Thomson's reading—he proposed φαίνομ' ἔγωγε—was convinced that in the poems of Sappho, Book One, the final stanza recapitulates the poem; stanza 4 of this poem does not do so; therefore there must have been a fifth stanza. The words in "Longinus," Milne maintains in another article, "The Final Stanza of Φαίνεταί Μοι," *Hermes* 71 (1936) 126–28, are a transition to the recapitulation. Richmond Lattimore, "Sappho 2 and Catullus 51," *CP* 39 (1944) 184–87, seeks to establish an ancient poetic type on the basis of Sappho 16 (with lines 21 ff., as restored by Wilamowitz, assumed to be part of the same poem), Catullus 51, and this poem. In each case a personal experience is followed by a generalization growing out of it. There is little to support the thesis that a summarizing or generalizing passage is a typical feature of Sappho's poetry; our one certainly complete poem, Poem 1, does nothing to encourage such a thought. The extant fragments suggest that she is more likely to seek a broadening of her beginning theme by myth or descriptive passages. With the very striking ring form that is confirmed by the papyrus, it is more than ever tempting to believe that line 16 ends the poem. Bowra, *GLP*[2] 185–86, gives persuasive arguments for so believing. For interesting comments arguing for the continuation at v. 17, and discussing the nature of the continuation, especially in comparison with Catullus 51, see Wills, op. cit.

37. One of Page's main contributions to the elucidation of the poetry of Sappho is his demolition of the improbable but prevalent view that this poem is a marriage song, sung at the wedding in honor of the bride and groom, the girl and the man of the poem. No effective voice has been raised in rebuttal of Page's contention that "there was never such a wedding-song in the history of society; and there should never have been such a theory in the history of scholarship." Merkelbach in his article in *Philologus* 101 (1957) 1–29, is altogether unpersuasive when, maintaining that Page's dis-

satisfaction with this as a wedding song is only modern prejudice, he gives as a parallel—the only parallel he gives—Sappho Fr. 22, which seems indeed to be similarly worded (so far as the wording of this meager fragment can be determined) but which provides not a scrap of evidence to suggest that it is a wedding song. Nor is Merkelbach's argument helped by his notion that Sappho's expressions of emotions are simply exaggerations, uttered in the excitement of the occasion: "One must not take seriously everything that is said at a wedding." If a critic can suppose that the spirit of a poem that seems as heartfelt as any poem ever written is not to be taken to mean what it says, surely this is the negation of criticism: any poem can mean (or not mean) whatever we choose.

If other compelling evidence indicated that this was a wedding poem we should of course have to accept it as such, in spite of the intrinsic improbability. But there are no solid grounds whatsoever for so thinking. The best argument is the one principally urged by Merkelbach, who is essentially renewing and expanding Wilamowitz's position, *SuS* 56–61: all poems by Sappho *must* be connected with a specific, more or less formal occasion. If we grant this argument, which is not without force, it is hard to think of an occasion for this poem other than Sappho's loss of the girl to κῆνος ἄνηρ, and we may without any improbability guess that the girl is going to marry him. That does not make this a wedding poem. Sappho is much more likely to have sung her song at a meeting of the *Mädchenkreis*; a song need not be composed and sung at the moment of the emotional experience that gives rise to it. (Merkelbach is satisfied with a meeting of the *Kreis* as a sufficient occasion for Poems 16 and 96.) I shall return to Merkelbach's study below (n. 76), in a further examination of the question of "occasion."

Internal evidence for taking the poem as a wedding poem is, as Merkelbach recognizes, exceedingly slight; so slight that the readiness of scholars to accept the thesis is nothing short of bewildering. Among the accepters is Milne, who, in "Musings on Sappho's φαίνεταί μοι," *SO* 13 (1934) 19–21, declares, "It is only in recent times that a true construction has been put upon it, by Wilamowitz in the first place and latterly by Prof. Snell in a memorable essay." Milne's analysis: "Sappho's poems are all occasional and personal, all attached to definite events and people. . . ." The occasion of this poem is "the marriage of a favorite pupil. . . . And how does she (Sappho) behave? Nothing out of the way. She turns faint, like many another woman at such a time." Thus a poem that through the ages has stood as a model of passionate utterance is reduced to the ordinary and typical sentiment of a teacher at her favorite pupil's wedding. Others who accept the theory include Fränkel, *DuP* 237–39, Treu, *Sappho* 178–79, Bowra, *GLP*[1] 215–17 (contrast *GLP*[2] 185–89, after Page's criticism of the wedding poem theory).

In Wilamowitz's *SuS* there is little more than assertion that it is a wedding poem. The bulwark of the theory is Snell's "Sapphos Gedicht φαίνεταί μοι κῆνος," *Hermes* 66 (1931) 71–90, the opening pages of which are devoted to demonstrating the point. (Fränkel and Treu, as well as Milne, think it enough simply to refer to Snell's article, without further support.) "The formal unity of Sappho's poem depends . . . on the fact that it is based on the traditional form of the Hymenaios" (85). According to Snell, there is a *makarismos* (a likening to the gods) of the man at the beginning, and *makarismos* is a feature of wedding poems. Snell holds that we must take φαίνεται to mean "has the appearance of" rather than just "seems." Page has shown, *SA* 31–32, that this is an unjustified assumption. Snell maintains that ἴσος θέοισιν here is like ἴσος Ἄρευι in Fr. 111 (which is a wedding poem) and two passages in Fr. 44. But Fr. 44 is not demonstrably, only conjecturally, a marriage song; and the theme occurs elsewhere in Sappho (to say nothing of dozens of passages in Homer) where there is no evidence of a marriage hymn or where a marriage hymn is ruled out by the evidence. Snell himself gives two such passages (Frs. 23 and 68). For further rebuttal of this theory, the reader is referred to Page, *SA* 30–33. (In a reprint of the article in his *Gesammelte Schriften* [Göttingen 1966], Snell adds this note [p. 97]: "Obwohl dem besprochenen Gedicht Sapphos der Makarismos des Hochzeitsliedes zugrunde liegt, möchte ich heute doch nicht mehr annehmen, dass es bei der Hochzeit gesungen sein müsste.") For a judicious review of the history of the discussion, with ample bibliography, Günther Jachmann, "Sappho und Catull," *RhM* 107 (1964) 1–33, especially pp. 3–16, is recommended. On the insistence of Snell and others in taking φαίνεται as necessarily meaning "has the appearance of,"

Jachmann has words of general cogency (7): "Es zeigt sich nämlich erneut, wie gefährlich es ist, innerhalb des Bereiches der archaischen Literatur, die in so karger Menge und in so trümmerhaftem Zustande, auf uns gekommen ist, einem mehrdeutigen Worte die Möglichkeit der Verwendung in einem sonst üblichen Sinne vorschnell abzusprechen: ein Papyrusfetzen kann genügen, dieses— immer noch beliebte—verfahren zu richten."

38. The poem was probably short, with one or two more strophes, if any (see the preceding note). The length of Catullus's poem is some evidence for this, and so is the apparent length of other poems of Sappho. The ring-forming verbal echo, which the new papyrus evidence confirms and shows to be very pronounced, is a further indication. Page's rejection of the significance of ring form (*SA* 11) is far from convincing, and the new papyrus reading makes it less so than it was.

39. Perhaps it is old age that snatches Tithonus, but the passage in the *Homeric Hymn* to Aphrodite, the language of which Sappho is apparently imitating (ἔμαρψεν: ἥρπασεν 'Ηώς, ἔ]σχατα γᾶς: ἐπὶ πείρασι γαίης), would suggest that the snatcher ought to be Eos. (Note that Sappho replaces χρυσόθρονος 'Ηώς [*Hom. Hym.* 5. 218] with βροδόπαχυς Αὔως.)

40. The darkness is not complete. Some of the words of Athenaeus, who quotes these two lines (15. 687a, b), are clearly a paraphrase of the last line, which must therefore mean, roughly, "love of the sun (i.e. love of life) has in it for me both the bright and the good." In other words, what Sappho is talking about is a life of delight that is also a life of virtue.

41. Lobel, *Sapphous Mele* 26, suggests this as a possibility, without giving his grounds.

42. Cf. Eva-Maria Hamm, *Grammatik zu Sappho u. Alkaios* 159–60.

43. Cf. LP *ad loc.* Megara is mentioned in the *Suda* as one of Sappho's companions.

44. Cf. Treu, *Sappho* 187–88.

45. Cf. Page, *SA* 59–60.

46. The name occurs in Fr. 213 and probably in 22, and Gongyla is called in the *Suda* a μαθήτρια of Sappho.

47. Cf. Turyn, *TAPA* 73 (1942) 308–18, and n. 28, above.

48. See *SA* 128, note 4, and Gomme's argument against this judgment and against precise dialectal judgments in general, *JHS* 77 (1957) 265–66, with Page's rejoinder, 78 (1958) 85–86. Benedetto Marzullo, *Poesia Aeolica* (Florence 1958) examines the question at length and decides for the poem's authenticity. Treu, *Sappho* 148, suggests, rather regretfully, that it is probably "Eher ein Volkslied . . . als eine Dichtung Sapphos." Günther Jachmann, *RhM* 107 (1964) 25–33, examines particularly the question of the use of the article in relation to the problem, and concludes that its presence here is no argument against Sappho's authorship. Voigt, *SetA*, accepts it as genuine.

49. In Sappho's use of epithets for nature, there is little to suggest a strong, direct interest in the qualities of nature, such as is evident in some of Alcaeus's poetry. Sappho is content to call the earth "black," as a rule; when she becomes more venturesome, as in "rosy-armed dawn," "golden-sandalled dawn," and "rosy-fingered moon," the force of the epithets is more in their Homeric echoes than in their descriptive power.

50. Page, with unusual readiness to accept an uncertainty, say (*SA* 12) that it is "reasonably certain" that we have both first and last stanzas of this poem. The papyrological evidence is suggestive but inconclusive. There is an unusually wide margin both above and below the twenty partially preserved lines. Neither the plate in *Ox. Pap.* 1 nor the comments of any editor reveal whether the full height of the roll is preserved. The height of the papyrus is 19. 7 cm., a normal height for a complete papyrus. If it is complete, the long space following line 20 indicates little as to whether 20 is the end of the poem; if it is not, and we are to presume that more was written, lower in this column, then the wide space is strong evidence that 20 is the end of the poem. There is no other external evidence; since the left side is missing, there can be no *coronis*. Apart from papyrological evidence there is little to go on: there are no grounds, internal or external, indicating that the poem was longer, and twenty lines is a reasonable length for a poem by Sappho; but so is twenty-four lines. If the poem ends at 20, the likelihood of ring composition is good. It is clear, from POxy 2289, fr. 6, that there is an address in the final (?) strophe, and it seems to be Cypris who is addressed; the poem opens with an address to

the Nereids and someone else—Cypris, if the generally accepted supplement to line 1 is correct.

51. What light this story sheds on Sappho's own morality is not clear. Page's insistence on exaggerating evidence for Sappho's disagreeable behavior and character is no improvement on the more usual attribution of high character on inadequate evidence, which Page justifiably ridicules (*SA* 50–51). Gomme, *JHS* 77 (1957) 255–66, holds that since Herodotus speaks of only one poem in this connection (ἐν μέλεϊ), then Fr. 15, in which Doricha is mentioned, must be from the same poem as 5. But this takes Herodotus's casual reference too literally, just as Page's emphasis on the exact word of Herodotus (κατεκερτόμησε) stresses too much the choice of a word.

52. Carlo Gallavotti, in his comments on the poem accompanying a careful reproduction of the papyrus text, *Papiri della Università degli Studi di Milano* 2 (Milan 1961) 17–21, suggests that if both 98a and 98b belong to the same poem, if the column which they occupy was of normal length, and if only two lines of the poem are missing at the beginning of a, then there are two or three stanzas missing from the middle and the length of the poem was between ten and twelve three-line stanzas. This is all very speculative but not improbable.

The textual and metrical suggestions of G. M. Bolling, "Restorations of Sappho 98a 1–7," *AJP* 80 (1959) 276–87, are altogether unacceptable, partly because in reconstructing a metrical form Bolling completely disregards line 10.

53. The suggestive wisps of politics in 98b have inevitably led to ingenious speculation, much of which is catalogued and appraised by Page, *SA* 98–103. The suggestion of Gallavotti, "Rilievi storici sulla Nuova Ode di Saffo," *SIFC* 18 (1942) 161–66, that Alcaeus's name occurs in 98b. 8 is extremely improbable; for one thing, the double address (the form would have to be vocative) is impossible, and therefore 98b. 1–3 would have to be assumed to be from another poem. (Gallavotti does not renew this conjecture in his 1961 commentary referred to in n. 52.) To the references given by Page, add W. Schadewaldt, "Sappho: An die Tochter Kleis," *Studies Presented to D. M. Robinson* 2 (1953) 499–506, with the best set of restorations; P. Odo Bauer, "Sapphos Verbannung," *Gymnasium*

70 (1963) 1–10, who uses this poem and other material in some irresponsible historical and biographical speculations; and Treu's judicious note, *Sappho* 216–18. It may be, as Treu holds, that Sappho writes in exile, impoverished by the attendant confiscation of her property. But if Gallavotti is right in his reading of 98b. 6, there is also evidence that the poem was written in Mytilene. He believes that the poem was written after the exiling of the Cleanactids, during Pittacus's rule as *aisymnêtês*, and when Sappho was in distress as a result of Pittacus's sumptuary laws.

54. There is an important article on this poem by W. Schadewaldt, "Zu Sappho," *Hermes* 71 (1936) 363–73. Schadewaldt's analysis of it is especially valuable for its observations on form. A recent study of the poem by Thomas McEvilley, "Sappho, Fragment 94," *Phoenix* 25 (1971) 1–11, has interesting comments on what I have been calling the "myth" of a Sapphic poem: "(Sappho) seems to resolve the difficulty of life . . . by affirming that art and imagination are creators of stronger, healing realities." "This imagined life . . . is the central experience related in Sappho's poetry."

55. Schadewaldt (op. cit., n. 54) observes that there appears to be a rather precise arrangement of the material of this reminiscence: two strophes about flowers and garlands, two about the diversions and delights of the girls, and probably two on festivals and celebrations. The multiplicity of details, as he observes, is in keeping with usual archaic descriptive style.

56. It has been suggested (cf. Gomme, *JHS* 77 [1957] 255–66) that these opening words are spoken by the departing girl. This would provide a reason for the curious change of tone between these words and Sappho's following consolation of the girl. Also, it would explain the asyndeton of line 2; asyndeton is virtually non-existent in Sappho's poetry (see n. 31, above). But the style at the beginning is so unlike the style of what follows that the supposition seems improbable; the easy slide from a sentence spoken by the girl to a description of her tearful state and an introduction to her next sentence does not seem appropriate when what follows is in stiff and formal dialogue: "She spoke as follows," and "I answered her as follows." It is more natural to take the opening sentence as spoken by Sappho.

57. This information is purveyed by Stobaeus and by Plutarch, who says also that she was wealthy. There are minor problems of text; I have followed those emendations that keep closest to the traditional text. Antonino Luppino, "Una Formula Omerica in Saffo," *PP* 115 (1967) 286–91, argues that ἀφάνης κἀν 'Αΐδα δόμῳ is the equivalent of the Homeric τέθνηκε καὶ εἰν 'Αΐδαο δόμοισι (*Odyssey* 4. 834, 20. 208, 24. 264) and thus the καί is simply "and," not "even." The Homeric reminiscence is surely present, and Luppino is right in holding that there is no suggestion of a better after-life (apart from being remembered) for Sappho as a poet. But the suggestion of "even"—unseen there as here—is supported (as Luppino acknowledges that it may be) by the *Iliad* formula καὶ εἰν 'Αΐδαο δόμοισι (23. 19, 103, 179).

58. The exact text and meter of these two lines are uncertain. They seem to be Asclepiadic of some sort; it may be that neither line is complete. The sense is clear.

59. For discussion see ch. 3, n. 10.

60. On Sappho's wedding poems and on Greek and Roman wedding songs in general, see Erwin A. Mangelsdorff, *Das Lyrische Hochzeitsgedicht bei den Griechen und Römern*, Hamburg 1913. This is an orderly and judicious treatment of the subject, dealing with the principal surviving examples. It displays some tendency to assume as fragments of Sappho's marriage poetry more fragments than are certainly such. The six hexameter fragments, 104–9, are so taken, without proof but not without probability; the words ἀϊπάρθενος ἔσσομαι (Bergk 90) are so taken with neither proof nor probability. The fragment is now known to be a phrase from a poem about the birth of Artemis. The fragment is discussed later in this chapter.

61. As Page, *SA* 112, says, "Whatever can be, must be Epi-thalamian."

62. The fragment continues with three more lines, which either —the text is faulty—praise the bridegroom's charms or, perhaps, address the bride and praise her; cf. Treu, *Sappho* 90–91.

63. Text and meter of line 2 are most uncertain.

64. G. S. Kirk suggests (*CQ* 71 [1963] 51–52) that the point of the emphasis on the tallness of the groom is that he is "fantastically ithyphallic." This strikes a note not found elsewhere in what is left of Sappho's poems, but entirely in harmony with ancient Greek

marriage poetry, and comparable to the *fescennina iocatio* in Latin marriage poems. Cf. Mangelsdorff, op. cit., 7–9.

65. Servius's note on *Georgics* 1. 31 refers to a book of Sappho "qui inscribitur ἐπιθαλάμια." Fr. 103, a commentary on some poems of Sappho, in which the (apparently) first lines of ten short poems are quoted, may or may not identify these as ἐπιθαλάμια. Lobel, *Ox. Pap.* 21 (1951) 26, thinks so; Page, *SA* 116–19, thinks that the word ἐπιθαλάμια, which comes near the end of the fragment, refers to what followed. The matter is entirely uncertain; Page's argument seems too fragile and contrived to be convincing. If, then, these poems (or all but the first of them, which is being differentiated from the rest in some way, perhaps only in meter—wherein it is clearly different, all the rest being apparently identical—but perhaps also in category) are epithalamians, they give the following evidence about Sappho's wedding poetry: that she used a lyric meter not like that of any hitherto-known fragment of a marriage poem; that these marriage poems were very short, averaging under fourteen lines each; that the style and vocabulary are much like those of Sappho's other poetry. If these lines are epithalamians they give no support for believing that 104–9 are epithalamians.

Unless Page's very doubtful interpretation is correct, there is no reason to think that these ten short poems constituted any specific or complete book; and ten short poems would be a very strange book. They are much more likely to be a selection of some sort, as Treu, *Sappho* 168, suggests.

66. The presence of Attic correption in 16, which is not "abnormal," suggests that the significance of Attic correption is not as great as Lobel believes. His study of the "abnormal" poems constitutes pages x–xviii of *Alkaiou Mele*.

67. In a study of Himerius's imitation of Sappho, J. D. Meerwaldt, "Epithalamica II," *Mnemosyne* 4. 13 (1960) 97–110, reconstructs, not without some plausibility, nine lines of glyconic verse, which he finds paraphrased or quoted in Himerius, and ascribes them to Sappho.

68. The papyrus, POxy 1232, shows Fr. 43, the only other extant passage from Book 2, marked off in two–line stanzas. Possibly 44 (which has no *paragraphoi*) should be so marked too.

69. For a collection of the Homeric phrases of 44, see Page, *SA* 67–68, and Gallavotti (who calls line 11 "un centone omerico"), *Saffo e Alceo* (Naples 1956) 2. See also Treu, *Sappho* 198.

70. *SA* 70. Earlier, Page took a firm stand for the poem's authenticity, "The Authorship of Sappho B 2 (Lobel)," *CQ* 30 (1936) 10–15. He declared (15) that "the linguistic argument . . . is a gigantic irrelevance." It still is. Benedetto Marzullo, *Studi di Poesia Aeolica* (Florence 1958) 115–94, gives an exhaustive examination of the problem, and defends the poem's authenticity.

71. There is further confirmation: Athenaeus 11. 460d quotes most of line 10 as being from Book 2 of Sappho.

72. J. T. Kakridis, "Zu Sappho 44 LP," *WS* 79 (1966) 21–26, enlarging on a comment by Albin Lesky, *Geschichte der Griechischen Literatur*² 165, argues against the notion that the poem is an epithalamian, partially on the grounds that the story of Hector and Andromache, told, as Sappho here tells it, with powerful echoes of the *Iliad*, would constitute an extremely ill-omened nuptial hymn: "Wie könnte . . . ein Gedicht, das eine so tragische Szene heraufbeschwört, ein *carmen nuptiale* sein?" (26).

73. For discussion, see Lobel and Page, *CQ* 46 (1952) 3, Treu, *Sappho* 161–64, and Page, *SA* 261–64. The question of ascription cannot be firmly decided on present evidence. Lobel and Page assign the fragment to Alcaeus because of the use of *nu*-moveable for metrical length in col. ii, line 10, a practice not elsewhere attested for Sappho except in the particle κεν (but it is worth noting that there *is* an exception; cf. also Sappho 2. 11, which apparently breaks Lobel's rule that the third plural present indicative never has *nu*-moveable), but found several times in Alcaeus, and, further, because "there is no evidence that Sappho wrote poems of this general type, whereas it is known that Alcaeus did so," (Page, *SA* 261). Fr. 44, if it is not an epithalamian, contradicts this second point, especially since the very meter in which Page restores this poem is used by Sappho in 44 (and probably in all the poems of Book 2), but nowhere by Alcaeus. Treu's ascription to Sappho is partly on the basis of an interpretation of the very fragmentary lines of col. ii in which I am unable to place confidence; but I agree with him that the words of col. ii are more like Sappho's manner than Alcaeus's. To what he says can be added that

βράδινος, which occurs in col. ii, line 9, occurs nowhere in Alcaeus, twice in Sappho, and is in its meaning more likely to be used by Sappho than by Alcaeus.

74. Page says that "the Homeric Hymns provide no fit material for comparison" (*SA* 264). This opinion is hard to understand; perhaps it is based only on the fact that there is no comparable hymn to Artemis.

75. A fragment from Stesichorus's *Helen* (*PMG* 187), referring to the wedding of Helen and Menelaus, bears a considerable resemblance to Poem 44.

76. To regard 44 and P. Fuad 239 as simply lyric narrative poems flies in the face of a strong modern tradition about the poetry of Sappho. It suggests that Sappho wrote poetry that is essentially non-occasional, in that, regardless of when it was sung, it is not intrinsically concerned with a specific contemporary event. The question of "occasion" affects the appraisal not only of 44 but also of other poems, notably 31, and has important implications for the judgment of archaic Greek lyric generally and the poetry of Sappho particularly. The basic position underlying many judgments about Sappho's poetry is set forth by Merkelbach, *Philologus* 101 (1957) 1–29. According to this view, archaic Greek poetry was composed only for specific occasions—a festival, a wedding, a symposium, a war, a victory, a death, etc.—and since poetry was sung it was an outward and public product, not, as it can be in later periods, a private creation of the poet, composed only to express his personal thoughts and emotions. So far as choral poetry is concerned, the necessity of occasion is certain; but for monody the assumption requires some relaxation, and in the criticism of most poets the relaxation is tacitly accepted. Critics are much more inclined to posit a very specific occasion for the poems of Sappho than for those of Archilochus or Alcaeus or Anacreon. The question whether Sappho 31 is a wedding poem has been vigorously contested; but I am not conscious of any concern to determine the specific occasion of Alcaeus 130, the remarkable description of the poet in exile, for which it is difficult to think of any appropriate formal occasion, or the occasion of Archilochus's famous song of hatred for the friend who betrayed him (79a), or the specific occasion of any poem of Archilochus, Alcaeus, or Anacreon, except

where the subject of the poem readily suggests its occasion, as in some of Alcaeus's drinking songs.

Only for Sappho are the efforts of scholarship bent on providing occasions. Even Merkelbach, though he holds that all archaic poetry was composed for an occasion, is far from uniform in his application of the theory; there is a vast difference between the breadth and informality of some of the occasions that he posits— κῶμος ("celebration"), war, "wine," and the like—and the formal, ceremonial occasion of marriage that he and others insist on for Poems 31, 44, and others of Sappho.

Does it matter whether we think that these poems were written for wedding celebrations? I think that it does for the following reason. We know that Sappho had about her a circle of women, and we may reasonably suppose that poems that are not clearly for other occasions were composed for and performed at gatherings of the group. But there is a great difference between, on the one hand, assuming such a general and informal motive and outlet for her poetry and, on the other hand, positing a specific ceremonial occasion for a given poem and consequently interpreting the poem in accordance with that theoretical occasion. If we want to suppose that Poem 44, the subject of which is a mythological wedding, was composed for performance at a wedding on Lesbos, no harm is done and there is even some probability in the idea. But if we say that 44 is really *about* a wedding on Lesbos, this is a specific interpretation of the poem. If a critic wants to suppose that 31 was occasioned by the marriage of Sappho's beloved girl, we may allow that this is a reasonable and harmless guess. But if he goes on to say that the poem is in a formal sense a wedding poem and that it is about the *makarismos* of the bride and groom, he is distorting the poem to fit his theory. If an occasion is necessary, let us guess that the poem was sung not at a wedding but at a meeting of Sappho's group. This supposition does not compel us, as Merkelbach is compelled, to argue that this passionate song would not be out of place at a wedding and that objections to accepting it as a wedding poem are only modern prejudices. Above all, by allowing for informality of occasion, as everybody is willing to do with other poets, we avoid the disastrous tendency to interpret as epithalamian every fragment of Sappho's poetry that can be twisted into a semblance of having to do with marriage. Even Fr. 17, though there is not a scrap of evidence to associate it with a wedding, is called an epithalamian by Merkelbach, apparently because it cannot be proved not to be.

The consideration of occasion can be a useful check on interpretation. It can also be a prison. Occasion provided the ancient Greek lyric poet with a motive, an outlet, and a form for self-expression. But we must allow for the turning of traditional forms and occasions to new meanings that transcend the old associations. (We see this trend clearly, at a later date, in some of the poems that are formally classified as epinicians.) If 44 was sung at a wedding, it is nevertheless of greater importance that Sappho used that occasion to compose a narrative poem, not a traditional marriage song. If 31 is occasioned by a wedding, it is more important that Sappho turned that traditional public theme to a strikingly new and personal use.

For a reasonable view concerning the occasion of 31 and its possible connection with marriage, see Lars Rydbeck, "Sappho's Φαίνεταί μοι κῆνος," *Hermes* 97 (1969) 161–66.

77. POxy 2291 is assigned doubtfully to Sappho by Lobel, *Ox. Pap.* 21. 10–11, on the sole grounds that the meter is Aeolic three-line stanzas. Page, *SA* 144–45, seems more certain of ascription to Sappho: "(It is) not outside the bounds of possibility that the author is Alcaeus, not Sappho. But the evidence tells against the supposition (see *Ox. Pap.* 21. 10) and I do not reckon with it seriously." The evidence is only the meter. It is hard to see why Page feels such confidence in the ascription to Sappho. Both Snell, "Der Anfang eines Äolischen Gedichts," *Hermes* 81 (1953) 118–19, and Gomme, *JHS* (1957) 255–66, think Alcaeus more probable; Treu omits it from his edition of Sappho; Voigt, *SetA*, ascribes it to Alcaeus. There seem to be two mentions of a Polyanactid (apparently a man, judging from 23–24), and, though Sappho once refers to a female Polyanactid (155), a reference to a male, especially an unfriendly reference, as this seems to be, is more likely for Alcaeus. The matter is of some general importance because the coarse word ὄλισβος or perhaps ὀλισβόδοκος (as Gomme plausibly suggests) occurs. If Sappho wrote it, we must, as Page says, "admit that entirely new light is shed" on the topic of Sappho's references

to lesbian practices. Furthermore, it introduces a degree of coarseness of topic that is not found elsewhere in Sappho, though frequently in Alcaeus, who was famous for his use of abusive language. The evidence favors assignment of the fragment to Alcaeus. We know that Sappho was capable of sharpness, but it runs counter to everything else that we know about her poetry to suppose that she composed in coarsely abusive language. The use of σύνδυγος (213), of one woman in relation to another, may suggest a lesbian relationship but is not much of a parallel because it is not coarse. It is more like the sharpness of tone in such a reference as 133: "Andromeda has got a fine bargain," probably a sarcastic reference to a desertion to Andromeda by a girl who had been in Sappho's group.

78. Page, *SA* 110.

Chapter Five: *Anacreon*

1. A brief, judicious analysis of Anacreon's art and a superb edition of the fragments, with translation, notes, and bibliography, are to be found in Bruno Gentili's *Anacreon*, Rome 1958. Bowra's chapter, *GLP*[2] 268–307, is the best account in English. Also to be consulted is the *RE* article by Crusius, brought up to date by Treu in Suppl. Vol. XI. A pleasant and competent recent appreciation is that of M. H. da Rocha Pereira, "Anakreon," *Das Altertum* 12 (1966) 84–96.

2. On the *Anacreontics* see *RE* 2045–50 (Crusius), and Edmonds, *The Anacreontea*, in *Elegy and Iambus* 2.

3. There are some grounds for believing that Anacreon wrote one kind of choral poem, the Partheneion. Cf. Fr. 155 (*PMG*). It has been thought (cf. ch. 1, n. 19) that the two fragments of Ibycus's which I have referred to are monodic. But the relative elaborateness of the strophic design tells against this view, which has, so far as I know, no specific, objective evidence to support it. For an analysis of these fragments see Hermann Fränkel, *Wege und Formen Frühgriechischen Denkens*, 43–47.

4. The *Suda* says that it was διὰ τὴν Ἱστιαίου ἐπανάστασιν that Anacreon went into exile from Teos, in the time, that is, of the

Ionian revolt, at the beginning of the fifth century. While this is the only specific mention of exactly when Anacreon left Teos, all other evidence about his life suggests that the exile must have come earlier, at the time when Persia conquered Lydia (cf. Crusius, *RE* 2035–36).

5. It is generally assumed that his life can be divided into successive periods in Teos, Abdera, Samos, and Athens (with a late interlude in Thessaly, evidence for which is extremely slight) and such a scheme, though quite uncertain, does no violence to probability. (The evidence for a visit to Thessaly consists of two dedicatory epigrams, 107 D and 108 D, attributed—by no means certainly—to Anacreon and mentioning Thessalian persons.) Bowra's chapter, *GLP*² 268–307, assumes this scheme, including the Thessalian period. Geographical references are not always reliable. When Anacreon writes a poem calling a girl "Thracian filly," it is tempting to suppose, as Bowra does, that the poem was written during Anacreon's Abdera period. (*GLP*² 271: "It must too have been here," i. e. in Thrace, "that he fell in love with a Thracian girl and wrote some enchanting lines to her.") But equally Thracian Smerdies (*Anth. Pal.* 7. 25. 8, 7. 27. 6) belongs to the Samos period (Fr. 69).

6. The number is specifically given in an epigram of Crinagoras, *Anth. Pal.* 9. 239. Gentili (xxvii–xxviii) contests this evidence on the grounds that lines 3–4 of the epigram, where Anacreon's name is given, are spurious. There is indeed room for doubt. The epigram has six lines, the first two and the last two being elegiac couplets, with two iambic trimeters intervening, a most unusual mixture. Paton, in the Loeb edition of the Anthology, omits lines 3 and 4 without mention. Stadtmüller's Teubner text marks the lines as spurious; line 3 is in fact unmetrical, though emendation is not difficult. But spuriousness would not altogether invalidate the evidence; somebody thought that "five lyric books, the work of the Graces," referred to Anacreon's work, even if it was not Crinagoras. The evidence from elsewhere, such as it is, supports the total of five: in the quotations by later writers, only Books 1, 2, and 3 are mentioned, but there is specific mention also of the *Iambics* and the *Elegies* of Anacreon. There is fairly good evidence that the arrangement was—as in the Alexandrian edition of

Sappho's poetry—by meters. Gentili (*Anacreon* xxvii–xxviii) believes that there were nine or ten books, metrically disposed, with some metrical types subdivided. The evidence is not in my opinion strong enough to outweigh that for five books.

7. Strabo (14. 638) asserts that the poetry of Anacreon "is filled with references" to Polycrates of Samos, which might suggest political poetry, presumably in support of the tyrant. But there is virtually no other evidence for this; a few fragments seem to be linked to war and patriotism, such as 74, an epigram for a friend who died on behalf of his country, and 46 and 48, which mention war, but none of these has any perceptible link with Samos. Strabo's remark probably means no more than that the poetry of Anacreon contains much evidence of his presence at the court of Polycrates.

8. 'Εκ λεπάδνων can be taken as meaning either "freed from their yokes" (Gentili: "dal giogo / liberate," Lobel, *Ox. Pap.* 22. 58) or "fastened *by* their yoke-straps" (Merkelbach, *Archiv für Papyrusforschung* 16 [1956] 97). It seems to me that both normal Greek idiom and the poet's image are better served by the latter. The point of mentioning the λέπαδνα, I should suppose, is to suggest the control of Aphrodite over her creatures; she has them harnessed to obey her will. (Gentili, *Anacreon* 187–89, argues that the meaning is "legare le cavalle al pascolo, cio è lasciarle libere all'amore.")

9. The principal discussions and editions of the fragments are: the *editio princeps*, *Ox. Pap.* 22. 54–59, Gentili, *Anacreon* 179–94, Page, *PMG*, Bowra, *GLP*[2] 286–89, R. Merkelbach, *Archiv für Papyrusforschung* 16 (1956) 97, and A. Barigazzi, "Sul Nuovo Anacreonte," *Athenaeum* 34 (1956) 139–51.

10. Παῖς meaning girl is common enough in Sappho, as in the poem to her daughter (132: ἔστι μοι κάλα πάις); if Sappho is too special a case, the use in Sophocles' *Antigone* (948, 987)—the chorus addresses Antigone—is evidence enough that παῖς = "girl" is normal Greek.

11. The text is as in Page *PMG*, except that I adopt the very probable restorations ἐν δόμοισι (4) and μήτηρ (6) as do Gentili and Bowra. These were first proposed by Carlo Gallavotti, "Un restauro d'Anacreonte," *PP* 10 (1955) 47–50. Gentili's ὁμάδῳ (11), with its echo of Homeric battle din, seems quite wrong in this landscape of hyacinthine fields. To change κατῆξας to κατῆξας, "you rushed" (as

Gentili and Bowra both do), is tempting (κατῆξας is harder to imagine a context for) but it seems to me presumptuous. For a substantially different and, I think, much less probable set of restorations cf. Merkelbach, op. cit. (n. 9).

12. I have followed Gentili's text for this fragment. Since the word ἀνορέω is not found elsewhere and since there is an apparent breathing over -ο- in the papyrus, perhaps the ἀν- should be separate. With the following ἀνακύπτω, the meaning is clear. See Lobel, Ox. Pap. 22. 59.

The relationships of the words in lines 3–5 are uncertain. I follow Gentili (Anacreon 203) in taking δεσμῶν as well as ἔρωτα with ἐκφυγών. As Gentili observes, there is Homeric precedent for a combination of accusative and genitive with ἐκφεύγειν.

Πάφλαζον (8) is probable. The papyrus has ὕδω[]. λαφλ]. Lobel (Ox. Pap. 22. 60) considers πλάφαζον a possibility, but since λ is agreed upon as the apparent reading, since the metathesis πλαφ- for παφλ- does not occur elsewhere, and since πάφλαζον is thoroughly suitable in meaning, it should be read. Both Lobel and Page (who also suggests, in PMG, πλάφαζον) appear to be influenced by their reluctance, wrong in my opinion, to accept the scattered instances of Attic correption that occur in archaic poetry. The meaning is probably not "boiling," as Lobel supposes, but akin to καχλάζειν in line 2 of Pindar's O. 7. Παφλάζειν clearly need not literally mean "to boil," for it is used of κύματα, Iliad 13. 798. Both words suggest by sound the splash of liquid, here as in Pindar the pleasant splash of wine in the mixing bowl, serving pitcher, or cup.

13. Page, PMG 173, says that line 7 is "fort. novi carminis initium." Since there is no visible connective, it could be the beginning of a poem. But there is no evidence of this from the papyrus and the meaning very well suits the supposition that the previous poem continues. There are no adequate grounds for supposing otherwise. The meter is too uncertain throughout to give any guidance.

14. Anacreon 202.

15. The echo of Archilochus 25. 2, ἡ δέ οἱ κόμη / ὤμους κατεσκίαζε is striking.

16. The presence of a paragraphos below line 10 is evidence neither for nor against the ending of a poem.

17. See *PMG* 69.

18. Κόνις is associated with death at *Iliad* 15. 118 and other places; σίδηρος is often "weapon" in the *Iliad*. Περιπίπτειν is often associated with misfortune, as, e.g., in Herodotus 6. 16.

19. Gentili (*Anacreon* 210) supposes that the boy cut his own hair as is the case in the line quoted by Stobaeus (Fr. 69). The description of the hands that did the cutting as αὐχμηραί makes this unlikely. The tone of the poem is much the same in either case.

20. The mock-serious language of lines 4–8 may be intended to suggest a sacrificial scene. Cf. *Iliad* 23. 24–34.

21. *Ox. Pap.* 22. 63.

22. J. A. Evans, "A Fragment of Anacreon (POxy 2322)," *SO* 38 (1963) 22–24, undertakes an imaginative but unconvincing explanation in which Thrace, i.e. Smerdies's mother country, is pictured as having cut the youth's hair and now regretting the act.

23. As in Fr. 1. 1, there are no positive grounds, papyrologically, for this assumption. But there the content of the two parts has a clear and reasonable connection; here it has none, and to interpret the two as belonging together raises enormous difficulties. M. L. B. Emley, "A Note on Anacreon, *PMG* 347," *CR* 21 (1971) 169, points out verbal similarities in the last two stanzas to Helen's unhappy words about herself, *Iliad* 6. 342–48, and suggests that Anacreon is in fact talking about Helen. There would then be no doubt about the separateness of these stanzas. The echo is clearly present, but the identification of the "preeminent woman" with Helen is unsupported by anything else in Anacreon's style.

24. *Anacreon* 217. That such a term as ἀρίγνωτος could be used of a *hetaira* is probable in the light of the statement, in the *Suda*, that Anacreon called a *hetaira*, among other things, πολύυμνος. (Cf. Fr. 101.) Moreover, the irony of so decorous an epithet is just what we might expect from Anacreon.

25. The context of the fragment, in the *Etymologicum Generale*, states that the word occurs ἐν ἰάμβῳ. ῎Ιαμβος in late Greek is regularly used for "satire," rather than specifically for "iambic meter."

26. *Odes* 3. 11. 9–12 seem modeled on this poem; 1. 23 is reminiscent, but gentler in tone and closer in imagery to another short fragment (63) of Anacreon.

The reading of the MSS at line 11, ἱπποσείρην, offers no acceptable meaning, and both Page and Gentili adopt Wilamowitz's ἱπποπείρην, supported in *Sappho und Simonides* 118–19.

27. The σοφία of love is a thought traditionally associated with Anacreon, as in Fr. 155, a quotation from Athenaeus in which Anacreon is ὁ σοφός in a context that features Eros and erotic poetry.

28. On the concept here cf. M. H. de Rocha Pereira, *Das Altertum* 12 (1966) 88–89. M. L. West, *CQ* 20 (1970) 209–10, maintains that the picture of the poet's "search" and the boy's failure to "heed" is a literal one: "The fuddled Anacreon, on the way home from a party, has been 'given the slip' by his handsome boy guide." The analogy he gives from Heraclitus (117 D-K) is cogent, especially in view of the similarity of phraseology (ὑγρὴν τὴν ψυχὴν ἔχων); but he is wrong, surely, in supposing that δίζομαι *must* mean literal search. The phrase at *Odyssey* 23. 253, νόστον διζήμενος, is not quite literal search, and introduces the idea of desire that is appropriate here. Cf. also Theognis 183, which implies choice as much as literal search. In any case, the metaphorical and epigrammatic force of the final word is undiminished.

Κοεῖς in line 2 is preferable to κλύεις, which Page gives in *PMG*. Both are emendations for the MSS οὐ καίεις.

29. The connection was made by Bergk. Cf. *PLG* 3. 255.

30. Archilochus Fr. 70.

31. Cf. J. Labarbe, "Anacréon contemplateur de Cléobule?" *RBPh* 38 (1960) 45–58.

32. Cf. Gentili, *Anacreon* 13.

33. Among recent discussions of the poem the most important are those of J. A. Davison, *TAPA* 90 (1959) 40–47 (reprinted as pp. 247–55 of *From Archilochus to Pindar*, London 1968) and Bowra, *GLP* 285–86; Gentili, *Anacreon* 12, gives other bibliography.

34. There is some question whether Lesbos had yet at this period acquired any special reputation for female homosexualism. The question is discussed, though inconclusively, by Davison (who thinks it had not) and Bowra (who thinks it had); for further discussion see Wilamowitz, *SuS* 68–78, Page, *SA* 140–46, and Kroll, *RE* 12. 2100–2, s.v. "Lesbische Liebe."

35. It is possible that χάσκει has an obscene implication; the use

of ἐγχάσκειν, Aristophanes, *Wasps* 1349, and the fact that λεσβιάζειν could be identified with *fellatio* (Wilamowitz, *SuS* 72–73) suggest it. For discussion, see Michael Wigodsky, "Anacreon and the Girl from Lesbos," *CP* 57 (1962) 109, Giuseppe Giangrande, "Sympotic Literature and Epigram," *L'Epigramme Grecque* ("Entretiens sur l'Antiquité Classique" 14 [Geneva 1967] 112, 176–77), Davison (44), and M. L. West, *CQ* 20 n.s. (1970) 209.

36. Cf. Demosthenes, *De Corona* 18. 296.

37. The meter is problematical; Page daggers μηροῖσι. Possibly there is a gap between πλέξαντες and the rest.

38. Fr. 72 of Archilochus is quoted and discussed in ch. 1.

39. Gentili *Anacreon* Fr. 56 (not in Page *PMG* because not lyric).

40. Fr. 28, a three-line fragment on a convivial scene, gives a similar picture and adds the element of music.

41. *Anacreon* xxi, xxiv.

42. For a presentation of the evidence on this point see Page, "Anacreon fr. 1," *Studi in onore di Luigi Castiglione* 2 (Florence 1960) 659–67, and T. Kehrhahn, "Anacreontea," *Hermes* 49 (1914) 481–94.

43. Cf. Page, op. cit. (n. 42) and Bowra, *GLP* 273–74.

44. The attribution of this poem to Anacreon has been questioned, in a long study by M. H. da Rocha Pereira, *Sobre a autenticidade do fragmento 44 Diehl de Anacreonte*, Coimbra 1961. I have not seen this monograph, but the author briefly returns to the topic in her general study in *Das Altertum* (cf. n. 1, above), where (87) she argues that the differentiation between Hades and Tartarus, the comedy-like "Realismus" of γηράλεοι ὀδόντες, the use of κάθοδος for descent, and the style of διὰ ταῦτα are symptomatic of Hellenistic or later writing. The points are not conclusive, but it is true that the poem is unique in Anacreon, and in a way that verges on the style and spirit of the *Anacreontics*. I should not want to use this poem extensively as a basis for judging Anacreon. M. L. West, *CQ* n.s. 20 (1970) 210, proposes κεῖ for καί (line 11); καὶ γάρ is not attested earlier than Sophocles; the emendation is worth considering if we are to ascribe the poem to Anacreon. The ingenious interpretation of Giangrande, op. cit. (n. 35, above) 109–11, finding a *double entendre* with a sexual meaning in ἀναβῆναι, is not persuasive to me. It involves finding in the first stanza evidence that the poet

is asserting that he is still *puellis idoneus* (the poet was gray-haired from youth; he still regards himself as in a state when life is sweet, etc.), which the tone and emphasis plainly contradict. And without more preparation than this poem gives, the possible *double entendre* would surely fail to register, since ἀναβῆναι is a common word.

45. Fr. 27 mentions Artemon in a similar setting: "περιφόρητος Ἀρτέμων is a concern to blond Eurypyle."

46. Page, "Anacreon and Megistes," *WS* 79 (1966) 27–32, argues that several fragments featuring Megistes (7, 8, 71), who was, as is known from references in Hellenistic epigrams, a favorite of Anacreon, suggest political troubles and the exile of Megistes. The case is speculative but attractive; Fr. 8 clearly involves politics, though the place of Megistes in the political references is unclear. If Page is right, we find irony and satire, politically connected or inspired, overriding the erotic element.

47. Adelmo Barigazzi, "Sul Nuovo Anacreonte," *Athenaeum* 34 (1956) 141: ". . . poeta cortigiano, che non è scosso da nessuna idealità . . . dedito unicamente al piacere: amore e vino, ma fin che non procurare dolori, fin che rendono la vita più allegra e più facile."

Chapter Six: *Minor Voices*

1. Biographical information is assembled by Bergk, *PLG*⁴ 3, and Edmonds, *Lyra Graeca* 3.

2. Plutarch, *Quaestiones Graecae* 40.

3. A brief reference to her by Maximus of Tyre, 37. 5, likens the effect of her poetry on the Argives to that of Alcaeus's on the Lesbians and of Tyrtaeus's on the Spartans. This suggests at least a semipublic performance, if not a formal occasion.

4. Paul Maas, *Epidaurische Hymnen* (Halle 1933) 140–41, ascribes to her a poem on the Magna Mater composed in Telesilleans and inscribed on a stone. The evidence is not convincing: the meter, the provenience of the stone (near a sanctuary that Telesilla is said to have written about), and the naïveté of style. Page, *PMG* 503, supports a later dating on grounds of meter and diction. What Maas calls naïveté might better be called bareness of style; whatever

merits the poem has are merits of sophistication, and the combination of bareness and sophistication suggests lateness. The cult lyric poetry of the fourth century and the Hellenistic age has similar features. W. J. W. Koster, "De Epidaurische hymne op de Magna Mater," *Mededelingen der Koninklijke Nederlandse Akademie van Wetenschappen*, Afd. Letterkunde Nieuwe Reeks, Deel 25, No. 4 (1962), assigns it to the age of Hadrian on grounds of diction, meter, and content. (I am indebted to Professor Douglas Gerber for providing me with an English translation of this monograph.) M. L. West, *CQ* n.s. 20 (1970) 214–15, argues for the third century B.C.

5. This is suggested by W. Aly in his *RE* article "Praxilla."

6. Page, *PMG* 375, describes it as being "non sine colore Rhodio." Perhaps the εν of Λευτυχίδαν is Rhodian.

7. Two epigrams of Timocreon are preserved, one of them (*AP* 13. 31) a *jeu d'esprit* using the same words in two successive lines in different meters, modelled on a similar effort by Simonides, and at the same time replying to an abusive mock epitaph composed by Simonides for Timocreon, celebrating Timocreon's prowess in tippling and in abusive poetry.

8. See ch. 1.

9. The evidence for the addition of Corinna is all very late, probably not earlier than the second century A.D. Cf. Färber, II, 7–22.

10. Page's monograph, *Corinna*, is the most thorough study of the text of the poetry and the problems of dating. Although he concludes that (84) "there is not sufficient evidence . . . to establish" Corinna's date, Page leans toward the later dating, about 200 B.C., on grounds of meter and dialect. One of his principal grounds is that some of the lines of the first column of the largest papyrus (the Berlin papyrus) project much farther to the right than any of the rest of the poem; this, Page believes, suggests a change of meter within the poem, since a change of poem at the necessary point seems ruled out by the sense of what immediately follows. A change of meter would be much less improbable in a poem of 200 B.C. than in one of 500–450 B.C. But the argument is not strong, because, as A. E. Harvie, "A Note on the Berlin Papyrus of Corinna," *CQ* 49 (1955) 176–80, shows, the notion of a single change of meter

does not account for the peculiarities of the line lengths. Harvie plausibly supposes instead (following a suggestion of Lobel) that the colometry of the opening lines is faulty. Kurt Latte, "Die Lebenszeit der Korinna," *Eranos* 54 (1956) 57–67, questions the validity of some of Page's arguments, based on dialect, for late date.

George M. Bolling, "Notes on Corinna," *AJP* 77 (1956) 282–87, finds support for the late date from the similarity of the voting (in P. Berol. 284) to that of democratic Athens; Page, on the same point (*Corinna* 76–78), finds the evidence inconclusive. Bolling's view depends on taking the "smooth stone" of line 31 in the first poem of the Berlin papyrus as a voting pebble, the one vote for Helicon. There is too much conjecture involved in this argument for it to be taken very seriously.

M. L. West, "Corinna," *CQ* n.s. 20 (1970) 277–87, argues for the third century B.C. on various grounds of language, meter, and content. The case remains inconclusive; much of the evidence is susceptible of extremely varied interpretation. Cf. Gerber, *Euterpe* 394–95, for further bibliography and discussion; Gerber inclines to the early dating.

11. A very slight piece of ancient evidence may seem to suggest a later rather than a contemporary date, though its weight is not enough to tip the balance. In the fragment of a biography of Pindar that constitutes POxy 2438, published by Lobel in Vol. 26 (1961) of *Ox. Pap.*, the first sentence is: "Pindar, the lyric poet, a Theban by birth, was the son of Skopelinos, according to Corinna and other poetesses but of Daïphantos according to most poets." That Corinna is cited as a source for biographical information about Pindar suggests that she is later than he rather than an elder contemporary. Lobel (note *ad loc.*) argues that if Corinna were a contemporary her evidence would be more authoritative than it appears to be; on the other hand, if the "other poetesses" are Boeotian and include Myrtis, the same argument ought to prevail for her, but does not, since we have no reason to doubt that she was a contemporary. Why poetesses and poets should be cited as categories of witnesses is unclear.

12. Cf. Bolling, op. cit. (n. 10) 283; he points out that "in a literary report of an ἀγών the last contestant will be the victor," as

in three plays of Aristophanes. I follow the text of *PMG* for this and other fragments of Corinna.

13. *Ibid.* (n. 10) 283.

14. Pierre Guillon, "Corinna et les Oracles Béotiens," *BCH* 83 (1958) 47–60, argues that the name of no prophet occurs in the fragment (he would, as Lobel has proposed in "Corinna," *Hermes* 65 [1930] 356–65, read Ἀκρηφνείν in line 31 instead of Ἀκρηφείν), that no reference is made to Ptoon, and that the context gives historical evidence confirming a late date for Corinna. The proper name seems to me the most probable reading. The rest of Guillon's argument is more speculative than the one it undertakes to supplant.

15. There is much doubt as to the meaning of Ϝεροῖ' in the papyrus, here translated "deeds of heroes." The word appears in Hephaestion, who quotes some of what has now turned up in POxy 2370; the MSS of Hephaestion give both καλὰ γέροια and καλαγέρεια. Antoninus Liberalis refers to a story as being told by Corinna, "in Book One ἐτεραίων" or "ἐγεραίων." The usual editorial choice has been γεροίων interpreted as meaning "stories of old." But it now seems certain that Antoninus Liberalis is referring to Ϝεροῖα, and that καλὰ Ϝεροῖα are some species of poetry. The fragmentary remainder of POxy 2370 gives some reason to suppose that they are poems telling "heroic" stories.

Jose S. Lass de la Vega, *Emerita* 28 (1960) 135–42, argues for καλὰ Ϝερεῖ, with Terpsichore as subject ("Terpsichore will speak to me"). I am not persuaded, in spite of this critic's careful presentation, that the evidence from Antoninus Liberalis and Hephaestion can be so readily dismissed.

16. M. L. West, "Corinna," *CQ* n.s. 20 (1970) 277–87, assumes (280) that when Corinna says that she sings "for the women (or girls) of Tanagra" she means that she is composing choral poetry for them to sing at a festival. This view has little to support it. Sappho makes a very similar reference to singing for her friends (ἐταίραις ταῖς ἔμαις . . . ἀείσω, LP 160), but it would be rash to assume that she is referring only to choral poems, of which she composed apparently relatively very few.

Chapter Seven: *Monody and Epigram*

1. As we have observed (ch. 1, n. 19), Richmond Lattimore maintains that these poems were in fact monody. But we know that Ibycus, who wrote them, wrote choral poetry.

2. James Hutton, *The Greek Anthology in France* (Ithaca 1946) 1: "From the Hellenistic period onwards, the epigram may be said to have been . . . the chief medium in which poetical ideas found expression—the vehicle of love-poetry, of grief for the departed, of the pleasures and the pathos of simple life, of wit, of satire. The epigram *is* Greek poetry throughout a long period when the realities of life could sustain little other poetry of genuine meaning . . . the influence of the Anthology has fallen less on the modern epigram so-called than on those types of verse usually classed as lyrical." Cf. also Hoyt H. Hudson, *The Epigram in the English Renaissance* (Princeton 1947) 8: "The quality in the Greek Anthology which commentators love to emphasize, the element of sincere, passionate, yet restrained statement, is a lyrical rather than an epigrammatical quality," and Lesky, *Geschichte der Griechischen Literatur*[2] (Bern 1963) 790.

3. Cf. Paul Friedländer and Herbert B. Hoffleit, *Epigrammata* (Berkeley and Los Angeles 1948) 3: "Inscriptions in verse, at least those of the archaic period, are not poetry in the full meaning of the word, but stand as documents of its forensic influence."

4. Cf. Friedländer-Hoffleit 66–67. A. F. Raubitschek, "Das Denkmal-Epigram," *L'Épigramme Grecque* (Geneva 1967: Fondation Hardt Entretiens 14) 3–36, gives good grounds for supposing that many actual inscriptions of a dedicatory or memorial nature are likely to have been in existence as poems before the monuments to which they were attached.

The first three essays in this volume, Raubitschek's, Bruno Gentili's "Epigramma ed Elegia" (39–90), and Giuseppe Giangrande's "Sympotic Literature and Epigram" (93–177), are all valuable on this topic.

5. Friedländer-Hoffleit 66.

6. Friedländer-Hoffleit 66. Cf. Gentili, op. cit. (n. 5) 64–65.

7. Ascription to Archilochus is questionable. Cf. Friedländer-

Hoffleit 67. Gentili, op. cit., p. 62, among others, regards the lines as "certainly spurious."

8. Cf. Wilamowitz, *Sappho und Simonides* 204.

9. Cf. Friedländer-Hoffleit 69–70, and Wilamowitz, *Sappho und Simonides* 211–12.

10. Treu, *Archilochos* 10.

11. Gentili, in an Appendix to his article (op. cit. n. 5), lists a number of striking similarities between inscriptions and elegy. More examples, both epigraphical and lyrical, of phrases about the loss of youth could be adduced. Several are cited in *Ox. Pap.* 22 (1954) 8. A conspicuous early example is Solon 3 (D) 20.

12. *Sappho und Simonides* 211.

13. Cf. Friedländer-Hoffleit 141–42.

14. Fr. 2 (Diehl) = 5 in Powell's *Collectanea Alexandrina* is perhaps the best example of Cercidas's lyric quality.

Appendix on Meters

I. A Glossary of Metrical Terms Used in the Text (See also II: A List of Meters)

acephalous: lit. "headless," a colon without the initial syllable. E.g., a Telesillean is an acephalous glyconic.

Aeolic base: × × (× = anceps, q.v.).

Aeolic meters: a number of common cola beginning with the Aeolic base and built around the Aeolic unit –∪∪–∪– or –∪∪– –.

anaclasis: lit. a "bending back," an exchange of place between a long and a short syllable. E.g., the Anacreontic, ∪∪–∪–∪– –, may be regarded as an Ionic dimeter with anaclasis of fourth and fifth syllables.

anceps (pl. ancipitia): a metrical position that can be occupied by either a long or a short syllable. E.g., both elements of the Aeolic base are ancipitia (though both are almost never short at once). Anceps is indicated by ×.

asynarteton: an epode-like combination of meters. See ch. 2, pp. 43–44.

Attic correption: a syllable ending in a mute plus a liquid which, contrary to usual practice in archaic poetry, is short.

caesura: a division between two words within a foot or metron, metrically significant when it occurs frequently at the same point in the verse, as it does in the third or fourth foot of a dactylic hexameter and after the second anceps of an iambic trimeter.

catalectic: a colon or verse without the final syllable.

clausula: a metrical unit that closes a series of units; the clausula is usually shorter than the preceding units.

colon: a lyric verse.

coronis: a papyrus marking, indicating the end of a poem, placed in the left margin and centered under the final verse.

diaeresis: a division between words at the end of a metron, metrically significant when it occurs regularly at the same point in the verse, as it does after the second metron of a trochaic tetrameter.

dimeter: consisting of two metra.

dithyramb: a type of choral poem in honor of Dionysus.

epinician: a type of choral poem composed in honor of an athletic victory.

epithalamian (-ium): a poem for choral performance at a wedding.

epode: see ch. 2, pp. 43–45.

length: Greek rhythms depend on the time occupied by a syllable. A long syllable (–) takes roughly twice the time of a short (∪). Generally, long syllables are those containing a long vowel, a diphthong, or two or more consonants following a short vowel. But a mute plus a liquid does not always make a long syllable. In classical and later poetry it usually does not, in archaic poetry it regularly does but not always.

long: see under "length."

metron: a minimal metrical component in stichic poetry, such as the dactyl, –∪∪, or the iambic metron, ×–∪–.

paean: a type of choral poetry in honor of Apollo.

paragraphos: a papyrus marking, usually a short horizontal line, placed under the beginning of a verse to indicate the end of a stanza.

partheneion: "maiden song," a choral poem composed for performance by a chorus of girls.

period: a metrical unit in lyric poetry at the end of which there is a distinct pause; it may be a single colon or a group of cola.

propemptikon (-con): a send-off poem.

scolium (skolion): a drinking song. Lit. "crooked," a name supposed to have arisen from the custom, at symposia, of calling upon the company in irregular order to sing a song.

short: see under "length."

stichic: poetry composed by line, such as dactylic hexameter and iambic trimeter, rather than by couplet or stanza.

strophe: in monody simply a stanza. In choral poetry the strophe or

stanza is also a dance unit, followed by a metrically identical
stanza called an antistrophe, during which a corresponding dance
movement was performed. In tragedy, there are "systems" of
strophe and antistrophe, each pair differing from the others in
the song. In some choral poetry, notably Pindar's epinicians,
there are series, called triads, of strophe, antistrophe, and epode.
An epode is a stanza metrically similar but not identical to the
strophe and antistrophe of its triad.

tetrameter: consisting of four metra; but a trochaic tetrameter is
   normally catalectic.

trimeter: consisting of three metra.

II. *A List of Meters*

adonic: $-\cup\cup--$.

Aeolic unit: $-\cup\cup-\cup-$ or $-\cup\cup--$, the nucleus of most Aeolic cola.

Alcaic strophe: lines 1 and 2, $\text{x}-\cup-\text{x}-\cup\cup-\cup-$.

             line 3, $\text{x}-\cup-\text{x}-\cup--$.

             line 4, $-\cup\cup-\cup\cup-\cup--$.

Anacreontic (anaclastic Ionic): $\cup\cup-\cup-\cup--$ (often combined by
   Anacreon with Ionic dimeters).

anapaest: $\cup\cup-$.

Asclepiadean, greater: glyconic with two choriambs added after the
   Aeolic base.

Asclepiadean, lesser: glyconic with a choriamb added after the
   Aeolic base.

choriamb: $-\cup\cup-$.

cretic: $-\cup-$.

dactyl: $-\cup\cup$. In most dactylic meters, the spondee is allowed as a
   substitute for the dactyl in most positions.

dactylo-epitritic: a colon much used in choral lyric, consisting of
   units of "D" ($-\cup\cup-\cup\cup-$) or parts thereof, and cretics, linked by
   anceps, usually long. A cretic (or "e") plus an anceps is called an
   epitrite. In monody the unit "D" is sometimes used, as in Archilochus 81 (an epode) and 118 (asynartetic).

dactylic hexameter: $-\overline{\cup\cup}-\overline{\cup\cup}-/\overline{\cup\cup}-\overline{\cup\cup}-\cup\cup--$. / marks caesura,
   which is commonest in the third or fourth foot.

elegiac couplet: dactylic hexameter followed by pentameter.

enoplion: × – ‾υυ‾ – υυ – –.

glyconic: × × – υυ – υ –.

Hipponactean: × × – υυ – υ – –.

iamb: υ – is an iambic foot, but iambic verses are always measured by the metron, × – υ –. The long syllables can be replaced by two shorts in most positions.

Ionic: υυ – –. This is sometimes called Ionic a minore, but the corresponding Ionic a major, – – υυ is rarely found.

ithyphallic: – υ – υ – –.

lecythion: – υ – × – υ –.

pentameter: in elegiac couplet, the second line is called a pentameter, but is really two short dactylic units, – ‾υυ‾ – ‾υυ‾ –, – υυ – υυ –.

Phalaecian: × × – υυ – υ – υ – –.

Pherecratean: × × – υυ – –.

polyschematist (literally "of many forms"): a dimeter the first metron of which is variable, × × – ×, the second a choriamb.

Praxillean: – υυ – υυ – υυ – υ – –.

Sapphic strophe: lines 1-3, – υ – × – υυ – υ – –.
 line 4, adonic.

spondee: – –.

Telesillean: × – υυ – υ –.

tribrach: υυυ.

trochee: – υ is a trochaic foot, but trochaic verses are measured by the metron, – υ – ×. The long syllables can be replaced by two shorts in most positions.

III. Index of Meters of Passages Quoted in the Text

A. Alcaeus

6: Alcaic strophe.

10: Ionic a minore.

34: Sapphic strophe.

38: glyconic lengthened by two dactyls after the Aeolic base.

42: Sapphic strophe.

69: Sapphic strophe.

70: lines 1 and 3, iambic metron, glyconic; lines 2 and 4, lesser Asclepiadean.

72: Alcaic strophe.

73: Alcaic strophe.

129: Alcaic strophe.

130: lines 1 and 2, lesser Asclepiadean, line 3, Hipponactean, line 4, acephalous lesser Asclepiadean.

283: Sapphic strophe.

298: (included in *LGS* 138).

319: acephalous glyconic (Telesillean) plus an iambic metron.

326: Alcaic strophe.

332: Alcaic strophe.

335: Alcaic strophe.

346: greater Asclepiadean.

347: greater Asclepiadean.

LGS 138: Alcaic strophe.

B. *Anacreon*

1 fr. 1: three-line stanzas, variations of anaclastic cola; line 1, Anacreontic plus opening long; line 2, Anacreontic; line 3, Anacreontic with – × inset.

1 fr. 4: undeterminable; some lines seem to be Anacreontic preceded by an unknown number of syllables, some cannot be Anacreontic.

2 fr. 1: three trochaic dimeters, followed by a clausula of the same colon catalectic.

3: glyconic with Pherecratean clausulae (lines 3 and 8).

11: Anacreontic, but fifth line of each stanza Ionic dimeter.

12: glyconic, with Pherecratean clausulae (lines 8 and 11).

13: glyconic, with Pherecratean clausulae (lines 4 and 8).

14: glyconic, with Pherecratean clausula (line 3).

15: glyconic, with Pherecratean clausula (line 4).

43: combinations of choriambics and iambics, with clausulae of iambic dimeter (lines 3, 6, 9, and 12).

44: iambic dimeter plus choriambic dimeter.

50: Anacreontic, with Ionic dimeters in lines 5 and 11.

51: Anacreontic.

53: line 1, Anacreontic plus initial long; line 2, Anacreontic.

56 (Gentili): elegiac couplet.

62: Ionic.

65: Anacreontic plus an Ionic metron.

68: uncertain; perhaps an initial Ionic metron followed by an expanded Anacreontic.

72: trochaic dimeters with catalectic clausulae (lines 4, 8, and 12).

83: iambic dimeter.

87: line 1, iambic trimeter; line 2, Aeolic unit $-\cup\cup-\cup-$.

94: unidentifiable; part can be emended to make a Pherecratean.

C. Archilochus

1: elegiac couplet.

2: elegiac couplet.

6: elegiac couplet.

7: elegiac couplet.

12: elegiac couplet.

15: elegiac couplet.

18: iambic trimeter.

25: iambic trimeter.

41: iambic trimeter.

56: trochaic tetrameter catalectic.

56a: trochaic tetrameter catalectic.

58: trochaic tetrameter catalectic.

60: trochaic tetrameter catalectic.

66: trochaic tetrameter catalectic.

67a: trochaic tetrameter catalectic.

68: trochaic tetrameter catalectic.

71: trochaic tetrameter catalectic.

72: trochaic tetrameter catalectic.

79a: couplets of iambic trimeter and dactylic dimeter ($-\cup\cup-\cup\cup-$).

81: couplets of iambic trimeter and dactylic dimeter ($-\cup\cup-\cup\cup-$).

88: couplets of iambic trimeter and iambic dimeter.

88a: iambic dimeter.

89: couplets of iambic trimeter and iambic dimeter.

103: iambic trimeter.

104: couplets of dactylic hexameter and iambic dimeter.

112: line 1, four dactyls plus an ithyphallic; line 2, iambic dimeter catalectic.

118: dactylic dimeter ($-\cup\cup-\cup\cup-$) plus iambic dimeter catalectic. POxy 2310: iambic trimeter.

D. Carmina Convivialia

7D (*PMG* 890): lines 1 and 2, glyconic plus $\cup--$ (initial $\cup\cup$ for $-$ in line 1).

line 3, $-\cup-\cup--\cup\cup-$.

line 4, choriambic plus glyconic.

13D (*PMG* 896): as 7D.

E. Carmina Popularia

PMG 869: various Aeolic cola. Line 2, if -α- in ἄλει is long, is Pherecratean.

F. Corinna

P. Berol. 284, Col. 1 (*PMG* 654), Ionic dimeter with clausula $\cup\cup--\cup\cup-\cup--$ (lines 4 and 11). Col. 3, polyschematist choriambic dimeter, with some glyconics; Pherecratean clausula.

G. Praxilla

747 (*PMG*): dactylic hexameter.

749 (*PMG*): greater Asclepiadean.

754 (*PMG*): Praxillean.

H. Sappho

1: Sapphic strophe.

2: Sapphic strophe.

5: Sapphic strophe.

15: Sapphic strophe.

15b: Sapphic strophe.

16: Sapphic strophe.

17: Sapphic strophe.

31: Sapphic strophe.

44: glyconic with two inset dactyls.

55: greater Asclepiadean.

57: only one of the three lines is complete, line 1, a greater Asclepiadean.

94: three-line stanzas; lines 1 and 2, glyconic; line 3, glyconic with
 inset dactyl.
96: three-line stanzas; line 1, cretic plus glyconic; line 2, glyconic;
 line 3, glyconic plus one iamb and an anceps.
98: three-line stanzas; lines 1 and 2, glyconic; line 3, cretic plus
 glyconic.
98b: same as 98.
105a: dactylic hexameter.
110: Pherecratean with one inset dactyl.
111: uncertain; line 1 may be Pherecratean; lines 2 and 4 are anceps
 plus cretic; lines 3, 5, and 6 are largely dactylic.
112: Aeolic unit twice, linked by anceps.
114: line 1, three choriambs plus ∪– –; line 2, corrupt.
115: Pherecratean with two inset dactyls.
121: line 1, Pherecratean; line 2, glyconic (?); lines 3 and 4, glyconic.
132: doubtful; largely trochaic, close to two lecythia.
150: line 1, acephalous lesser Asclepiadean; line 2, iambic metron
 plus Aeolic unit.
ALG 94: acephalous Hipponactean.

I. Telesilla
717 *PMG*: acephalous glyconic (called a Telesillean).

J. Theognis
667–82: elegiac couplet.

K. Timocreon
727 *PMG*: dactylo-epitritic.
729 *PMG*: iambic dimeter.
731 *PMG*: trochaic dimeter with clausula of trochaic dimeter
 catalectic.

Index

EARLY GREEK MONODY

Designed by R. E. Rosenbaum.
Composed by The St. Catherine Press, Ltd.
in 11 point Baskerville monotype, 2 points leaded,
with display lines in Baskerville monotype.
Printed offset by Vail-Ballou Press, Inc.
Bound by Vail-Ballou Press, Inc.
in Joanna Linen Finish book cloth
and stamped in All Purpose gold foil.